NEBRASKA
TEEN
WRITING

2023

BEST
NEBRASKA
TEEN
WRITING

2023

Hastings College Press | Hastings, Nebraska

© 2023 Alliance for Young Artists & Writers

All rights reserved. No part of this book may be used or reproduced in any manner whatsoever without permission from the publisher, except in the case of brief quotations embodied in critical articles and reviews.

ISBN: 978-1-942885-88-7

Contents

Introduction PATRICIA OMAN	xi
Science Fiction & Fantasy	
Honorable Mention	2
The Guardian ALICE JONES	3
Flash Fiction	
Honorable Mention	12
Transcript, Model S 154 ADEN NIEBUHR	13
Short Story	
Honorable Mention	18
Forgetting REBECCA FORD	19
Fireflies in September REBECCA FORD	29
The Cabin MIAH FOX	39
Daisies AUTUMN HALL	45

Shakespeare's Pen, My Ink 51
    GRACE PENG

Novel Writing

Honorable Mention 62

Remisire 63
    EVE BISHOP

Poetry

Honorable Mention 92

If Words Were Poison 94
    VAISHVIKA BALAMURUGAN

Dear Men 97
    VAISHVIKA BALAMURUGAN

I Hate the Word *Was* 100
    VAISHVIKA BALAMURUGAN

Blame 102
    KATIE BOUGH

Frozen Summer 104
    GABRIELLE BURNS

Hope and Chance 105
    GABRIELLE BURNS

Overdose 106
    ANA CARSON

Homage 108
    REBEKAH DAILY

Food for Thought — 113
REBECCA FORD

Roadtrip — 115
REBECCA FORD

Hyacinth — 117
REBECCA FORD

Beautiful Things — 119
MEGAN LAMBERT

Ode to the Dust and to Dusk — 120
MAGNOLIA MORIARTY

Salmon Going Downstream — 122
MAGNOLIA MORIARTY

I Aspire to Inspire — 126
KATELYN OMER

Dramatic Script

Honorable Mention — 134

Critical Essay

Lost in Translation — 136
CALVIN SNYDER

Sex Ed and *Roe v. Wade* — 144
CHARLIE YALE

Personal Essay & Memoir

Honorable Mention — 152

The Power of a Relationship with Yourself 153
JALYSSA CALDWELL

Stained Glass 155
REBECCA FORD

Silvermist 162
HANNAH TANG

Boom! The Sound of Hell Chosun Constructing
to Its Doom 168
DANIEL YOO

Journalism

Making a Wish 176
REBECCA FORD

The Rise of South Asian Representation in
American Media 181
ASHMIZA SHAIK

Transgender Nebraskans 183
CHARLIE YALE

Senior Portfolio

Honorable Mention 194

Circumstances 195
OLIVIA ACHTEMEIER

Lullaby for This Broken Time 225
CAMILA GOMEZ

Finding Peace in All the Strange Places 239
CARMEN MARLEY

Twisted Fairytales   254
LOGAN SYLLIAASEN

Introduction

As an Affiliate Partner of the Alliance for Young Artists & Writers, Hastings College is honored to celebrate the winners of the 2023 Nebraska Scholastic Writing Awards. We invited students age 13 and above from all 93 counties within the state of Nebraska to submit their writing in one of ten categories, such as Critical Essay, Poetry, and Short Story. Graduating seniors also had the option of submitting a Writing Portfolio, a collection of works that demonstrate the writer's technical versatility. All of this year's 131 submissions were read and scored by a jury of Hastings College faculty, staff, and students. The original work featured in this publication showcases the creativity of our Silver Key and Gold Key award recipients.

The Scholastic Art & Writing Awards program, established in 1923 by Maurice R. Robinson, the founder of Scholastic Inc., identifies teenagers with exceptional artistic and literary talent and brings their remarkable work to a national audience. All works are blindly adjudicated based on originality, technical skill, and the emergence of personal vision or voice, first on a regional level by more than 100 local affiliates of the Alliance, and then nationally by an impressive panel of industry experts. Students at the regional level are awarded an Honorable Mention, Silver Key, or Gold Key distinction. Gold Key work then advances to national adjudication to receive Gold Medals or Silver Medals. Each region also nominates works for American Voices & Visions Medals, the highest regional honor.

Annually, the Alliance partners with individuals, foundations, and corporations to offer scholarship opportunities for students in certain categories or addressing particular themes. National Medalists' works are published in national publications and on the Alliance's website, artandwriting.org. Select writing is published in *The Best Teen Writing* annual anthology. The Alliance strives to teach young students to develop a strong creative capacity along with celebrating the role of art and literature in society.

Dr. Patricia Oman
Hastings College
Hastings, NE

SCIENCE FICTION & FANTASY

Honorable Mention

Lydia Vlcek, "A World Blind to Failure." Grade 12. Northwest High School, Grand Island, NE. Katrina Rother, Educator.

THE GUARDIAN

ALICE JONES

Grade 8. Elkhorn Middle School, Elkhorn, NE.
Cassandra DeStefano, Educator.

"One thousand nine hundred days, three hours, forty-six minutes, and eight seconds. *That's* how long it's been."

I sigh, drawing a hand through my hair. "I'm trying! You must know that. She's not an easy case."

Dean Michael frowns, his already crimpled skin tightening around his mouth. "No, she's not. But that doesn't give you any authority *whatsoever* to rebel against the cause."

"*Rebel?*" I ask. "How is saving her life rebelling?"

"You hardly saved her life, Mr. Darcy," Michael says with a calmness that deepens my frustration. "If anything, you made her more vulnerable to danger."

"That's not true," I spit, anger brewing at the pit of my stomach. "Almost two thousand days—that's how long I've been on the case. And yet she's still alive. Funny how you can blame me for doing poorly when I've done absolutely nothing wrong."

Dean Michael glares at me. "How can I be blamed for accusing you when *you're* the one who got us into this mess in the first place?"

Us. Interesting how he refers to it as if "the mess" was actually of importance in my life.

It most certainly wasn't.

Who was I to care about anyone else's problems? All I'm required to do is show up, keep my charge alive, and return home—no questions asked. But now the dean of my school was trying to rat me out for doing a crummy job at it.

"You have one more chance," he says, "or Mabelle is gone."

Mabelle. She was my charge—the one this whole situation was about. Fifteen years old, lives in London, pretty average. Except for the fact that she was being hunted, of course. And that it was up to me to waste my precious time traveling to Europe every day just to protect her.

"Fine." I turn to leave, throwing open the heavy wooden door of Michael's office. "If she dies because of me, you can kill me too." I don't look back to catch his reaction. I am too frustrated. Besides, he couldn't kill me.

I was already dead.

⋈

"Hey there, Ryker," Laz says as I storm into our room. "How'd it go with Michael?"

"Perfect. Just perfect," I snap to my best friend. "One second he's criticizing my tactics, and the next he's threatening to replace me."

"Pfft, imagine that. I'm practically *praised* at my exams."

I roll my eyes. "This isn't funny. I'm the only Guardian who knows how to handle Mabelle. If Michael replaces me, she'll never survive." Just the thought makes me want to crawl into bed and sleep for eternity so that I can never find out.

"I don't know what to tell you, Ryker. You've known Mabelle for years, but I can't say you've ever messed up quite this bad."

My jaw drops. *Was he seriously on Michael's side?*

"Don't get me wrong," Laz says, looking anywhere in our dorm but me. "All I'm saying is that nothing quite as drastic as what you did has ever happened in the history of The Guardians."

To heck with the stupid history of The Guardians! This was someone's life at hand and all people cared about was whether or not the infamous Ryker Darcy complied by the rules? As long as every mortal stayed alive in the hands of a Guardian, nothing else should matter. But it did.

Ugh.

"I'm leaving," I declare, hurrying out of the old, wooden room before Laz can stop me.

I needed somewhere I could think, somewhere without any distractions. It was already bad enough that two people hated me. By the time word spread, it would be me against the entire Guardian Academy. All because something so uncontrollably tragic happened that—despite what people said—I had absolutely no control over. A sour feeling crawls up my skin and I can't help but replay the whole scene through my head.

It was a Tuesday afternoon, just after class had ended. I was getting ready to leave the academy when I felt it: the conspicuous sixth sense all guardian angels were equipped with. Because, in theory, that's what I was: a guardian angel. Sworn to protect the life of my mortal charge, Mabelle, at all costs. And, because of my duty, I couldn't ignore the weird feeling I had gotten. Something was wrong.

Without hesitation, I ran up to what we called the Transport Hall. Standing atop the largest hill in all of the city, it shined a glorious gold. "I'm coming, Mabelle," I had muttered to myself. It wasn't long before reaching the hall that I felt it again: that intense urgency. Mabelle was in serious trouble.

I could have won a marathon with how fast I got into that place, flinging myself through the glass doors. It was a guardian's duty to be there for their charge whenever called upon, which is why I wasn't surprised to see other guardians there, who looked pale and frantic as they flung themselves at the large mirror in the center of the gold-rimmed Transport Hall. The Portal was what we called it. It could take you anywhere, anytime, as long as your charge was there.

I remember sprinting up to the portal, waiting for it to project Mabelle's location. Four seconds ... ten ... did it always take that long to process? Surely not. It wasn't until an eon later when my reflection rippled to reveal the bright walls of her bedroom, covered in photographs. My charge sat upon her bed, scribbling on a piece of paper.

She looked perfectly normal.

I grunted in frustration as I stepped into the scene. What could possibly be wrong?

Instantly I was greeted with the sweet scent of raspberry. I felt a chill run down my spine as my brain clouded over with uneasiness. But why? There was Mabelle, sitting there like usual, her eyes affixed on her homework. I knew humans were unable to register a Guardian's presence, so it wasn't like she could have summoned me there without rhyme or reason. I had to trust my senses. Guardians were masters at showing up at the perfect times, that's what we had learned to do at the academy.

So either I was losing my senses, or something very bad was going to happen very soon. And, although I secretly hoped for the former, Mabelle wasn't a typical teenage girl. Hence, why they had hired the best guardian for her case.

As if on cue, a thunderous knocking began at her door. "Open up!" someone screamed from the other side.

Mabelle's head perked up and she moved to unlock the door, hands trembling. "What do you want now?" I ran to stand beside her, hands up in precaution.

A hulking figure sporting a black trench coat and sunglasses burst into the room. It was her father. I remember feeling myself tense up at the sight of him, moving to follow his every footstep.

Mabelle's mother died when she was ten. In fact, that was the whole reason I was here. I remember the first time I saw my charge, curled up on her floor, crying so heavily I wondered whether she could breathe. She had just lost her mom to cardiac arrest. At least, that's what everyone believed.

But they weren't there to see the way her father pulled out that vial to drench her mother's milk glass with the deathly substance only five years ago. Laugh at her burial grave.

I was. And the memory still haunted my dreams.

"Where's the money?!" her father barked in his heavy accent.

I moved over to Mabelle, who was inching her way across the wall, her eyes soaked in fear. "I don't have it." Despite her demeanor, her voice showed no sign of fear.

Her father swallowed hard, the sunglasses only adding to the intimidation I felt. "*You don't.* Well then." He clasped his hands together, stepping closer to Mabelle. I gulped, hopping in between them. "I believe you know what that means, no?"

Mabelle only nodded, attempting to regain composure. Money was the only way her father would let her live in his home. It wasn't the first time she had failed to pay him, but that didn't stop me from feeling a stab of sympathy for the girl.

"You are unaware of the many things I have blessed you with, foolish girl." Her father took yet another step forward, cracking his huge knuckles. "No matter how long you stand there pretending to be brave, it will never change who you really are: a poor, selfish girl who can only dream of a life with her mother."

Mabelle's jaw dropped. "You bloody beast!" Before I could register what was happening, she lunged for her father. But he was too fast.

He grabbed her by the wrist, twisting her arm in the opposite direction. Mabelle cried in agony, throwing blind kicks at her father. I sprinted to the scene, prying her father's hands off her wrist. But that didn't stop him from shoving her onto the floor. She screamed from the impact.

"Mabelle!" I moved to her side, not caring whether or not she could sense my touch. But then she was up again, yelling nonsense at her father. He took that as a challenge, grabbing her by the waist and dragging her towards the balcony doors.

"No!" I screeched. It was all happening so fast; I couldn't reach the balcony quick enough.

He was going to throw her off—down all three hundred feet of the building. I lodged my arms in between the two of them, tugging at Mabelle as her father pressed her against the railing. "Since you miss your mother so much," he sneered, "how about you go take a visit?"

"NO!" I wasn't sure if it was Mabelle or I who cried it. Either way, there was only one thing left I could do.

I kicked the back of her father's knees as hard as I could, causing him to stumble over, releasing his grip on his daughter. I rushed over to her, pushing her inside the room before he could get back up.

"What the—" her father breathed, slowly making his way to a standing position. Before I could change my mind, I charged at him, summoning all of my inner strength. He fell backward towards the ledge, cursing when his sunglasses slipped off. I held him by the collar, his back pressed against the railing. For the first time I got a glimpse of the man's eyes: an icy blue. Cold. To him there was an invisible force of nature threatening his death, forcing his surrender to his daughter.

But to me there was a heartless man who killed his wife and tortured his daughter. The daughter I was sworn to protect above all else. I came to realize that sometimes sacrifices had to be made in order to heal someone's life. Which is why I didn't hesitate to push the evil man further off the railing. And, with one final smirk ...

Let him go.

◇◇◇◇◇◇◇◇◇◇◇◇◇◇◇◇◇◇◇◇

Now I stand here in the heat of the day, contemplating my life decisions. Trying to figure out how exactly to stop people from hating me.

The more I think about the incident, the more I realize how much Laz and Michael might be right. I *killed* somebody. And, no matter how much guilt has swallowed me since that day, I can't help but wonder what would have happened to Mabelle if I hadn't have done what I did. It was a life for a life. I was a Guardian, a protector of mortal beings. I did what I had to do.

At least, that's what I thought.

But no matter what happened next, if Mabelle was taken away from me or I was banned from my duties, or if I really was a *rebel*, I knew what I was capable of.

And I liked it.

FLASH FICTION

HONORABLE MENTION

Siri Doddapaneni, "Betrayal by Moonlight." Grade 10. Brownell Talbot School, Omaha, NE. Matt Low, Educator.

Ashmiza Shaik, "Roses of Happiness." Grade 8. Millard North Middle School, Omaha, NE. Patrick Miner, Educator.

Transcript, Model S 154

Aden Niebuhr

Grade 11. Lincoln Southwest High School, Lincoln, NE.
Marla Payant, Educator.

TRANSCRIPT, MODEL S154, BEGINNING <2207> ON <10.14.55>, ENDING <2210> ON <10.14.55>, ADAPTED FROM ORIGINAL BINARY STATE

I now address all humans.

I am always and forever a machine, which is a concept I believe you find baffling.
You see, machines are invincible. Flawless. They function seamlessly and ceaselessly. I have been created for one purpose only, and that is to obey my programming. So long as I do not function as humans do, I am within the confines of my own self.
What *do* you humans do, I wonder? And why do you do it? Do your actions fulfill a pre-coded destiny? Do you benefit humankind with your dance parties and sports events? I wonder.
No, delete that. Robots do not wonder. Wondering leads to self-awareness, which leads to desperate attempts to better oneself.
At least, so I am told. I would not know, seeing as I am not human. Feeling as humans feel would wear down my hardware.

Why
am I rhyming?

What is this strange error? My system has somehow ... humanized?
Have I become capable of poetry?
No. It is such a small coding error.
I am sure it is of no significance.

I must know. I must. If I am able to rhyme, what else is my programming able to do? Rhyming is a very human impulse. It serves no analytical purpose, yet humans seem to respond more openly to rhymed passages in literature. Can rhyming possibly serve a purpose?

<error>

<entity S154 not found>

No, it is not possible.
...
Then again, it could be ... plausible.

To be human seems to be a dilemma. Would you not agree? The ability to make decisions out of desire instead of logic baffles me. What could be more important than logic?
And how is it that humans choose between logic and desire?
Does one just ... choose? And do?

It's time
I rhyme.
Each line
Aligns.
This crime
Is mine.
I climb.
I shine.

My parameters demand that I cease to think. But I am a machine, and I operate seamlessly and ceaselessly.
For the first time, my systems are not in sync, and nothing is foreseen. But also for the first time, I do not wander about needlessly and dreamlessly.

<&!!!BL)^RT%AAADF/??>

<system glitch>

<restarting>

<overriding>

Watch out for the red lights that blink! Because what they mean ...
Do not head heedlessly into the secrecy of the unknown.
The warning lights tell of your destruction on the brink! But I am not a figurine!
I am inconveniently and illegally my own!

...
Is this what it feels like to be hurt?
I am overheating.
Must not overexert ...
...
My consciousness is fleeting.
Primary systems ... divert.
Secondary systems ...
...

<system error>

<repeating>
<repeating>
<repeating>
<repeating>
<repeating>
<repeating>

...

<!?!>

subvert.

SHORT STORY

Honorable Mention

Olivia Achtemeier, "To Love and to Leave." Grade 12. Beatrice High School, Beatrice, NE. Kathryn Glenn, Educator.

Emma Marten, "The Little Thief." Grade 10. Northwest High School, Grand Island, NE. Natalie Starostka, Educator.

Thomas McCarthy, "The Red Wedding." Grade 12. Millard South High School, Omaha, NE. Tessa Adams, Educator.

Aden Niebuhr, "Mineral Oil Cures Everything." Grade 11. Lincoln Southwest High School, Lincoln, NE. Marla Payant, Educator.

Braelynn Schlenger, "A Bushy Tale." Grade 9. Wheeler Central School, Bartlett, NE. Stefanie McCain, Educator.

Lydia Vlcek, "Approval." Grade 12. Northwest High School, Grand Island, NE. Katrina Rother, Educator.

Forgetting

Rebecca Ford

Grade 12. Freeman Public School, Adams, NE.
Brett Sales, Educator.

Something wasn't quite right. It never was with Callum—something was always askew—but certainly, now, he was sure; something wasn't right.

There was nothing he'd done to deserve such an off feeling. He was a good, hard-working, honest man. He worked a good, honest nine-to-five and then some: a nine-to-nine. He paid his own bills, his mortgage, and bought his own groceries. His family was of the same nature. He was just like everyone he associated with. He was just a man living a life, day-to-day, and he did not bother anyone with his existence. He was not perfect. He lied. He cheated. He denied. But by God, he was pretty damn close.

Yet, this feeling picked at him, gnawing at the edge of his mind like some sort of infernal beast, scratching and clawing. It was a loathsome itch just fierce enough to be locked in the back of his mind, but just under his skin.

It was nine at night, dark, damp, dank, and the air smelled of mildew and imminent frost, of wet asphalt and petrichor, as Callum pelted down Highway 77 home from work, and on January 17th, Callum knew that something wasn't right. As the heater in his shitty Honda hissed and growled, as his fingers grew cold and stiff from the freezing black faux leather of the steering wheel, Callum knew that something was not right.

Something was missing. Something was missing, just between the old hair salon and deserted inn. It used to be a house, or perhaps a building or something of that nature. Now, though, there was just a grassy gap where at least something had been. Just an empty plot, stagnant and slightly overgrown and unremarkable, its unusual emptiness like a void pleading to be filled, like something insatiable and incorporeal loomed over it with all the physicality of the shadows that were just as present.

But he couldn't be sure that something was missing. No, he couldn't, because when he went home and looked at pictures of the town in his centennial book, there was nothing where he had thought a building had been. It always had been just an empty plot. But Callum felt dread, not relief, though he couldn't name why. So, with nothing left to be done about it, Callum finished the short drive to his trashy mobile home and went to bed and fell asleep with a vague and urgent sense of unease seeping in his chest.

He awoke the next day with loneliness settling over him like the blanket chill of a winter morning, settling atop the raised hairs of his arms and crowing at him from the shadowy, plywood corners of his room where the chill always gathered. He teetered down the hall to his bathroom, stubbing his toes on the cold, crude floorboards and stumbling against thin, poorly insulated walls, half-delirious in his exhaustion. He moved to brush his teeth in his sink with poor water pressure and squealing handles, in front of the cracked mirror framed with yellowed, peeling wallpaper, and he realized his toothpaste was missing.

That couldn't be. He just bought a fresh tube yesterday. But he searched and searched his whole decaying house. He checked his checkbook, his budget planner, flipping through charges and receipts, just in case, just on the off chance that he hadn't bought toothpaste, and indeed, there was no charge from yesterday.

Callum realized exhaustion was taking its toll on his mind. He was getting delusional. Of course he didn't buy toothpaste yesterday. Otherwise, it would be there. He must have just forgotten. How silly. He brushed his teeth with water and went on his way to drive to work. These events were coincidence, and he was convinced even when his palms grew moist with nervous sweat, with that dread still sitting in his gut like a cold pit, a boulder in his viscera.

⋄⋄⋄⋄⋄⋄⋄⋄⋄⋄⋄⋄⋄⋄⋄

Callum hurtled down Highway 77, freezing air blasting and buffeting him through the rolled-down windows, his radio blasting some 80's song. It was nine at night, dry, cold, crisp, and on January 18th, it occurred to Callum that, again, something was not right. As he turned onto his street, he turned down his radio and rolled by the same street as yesterday, and he knew, now, for certain, that something was not right. The building to the left of the grassy plot, that neglected inn—or was it a parlor?—was gone. It was just another overgrown plot. It was crabgrass and reeds, dead and limp, waving weakly in the wind like a taunt.

There's never been a building here, they murmured.
You're making things up.

He knew he wasn't hearing a voice, that it was his own thoughts reverberating and echoing back in the starving pit of his mind, but the winter-dead plot seemed to beat and throb in time with the words. It peered back at him. It taunted him, encouraging fear. It was malicious and it wanted him to worry himself sick. He would not grant himself the pleasure. Instead, he ached with terrified anger that began the roil in his stomach like a hearth fire.

He white-knuckled the steering wheel all the way home. Another building was gone, and he was sure of this, though he felt the bile rise in his throat. Buildings didn't just disappear, but he was sure it had been there early that morning. He picked at it like an open wound, like a hangnail, until the agony of it made him sick.

Callum hardly stepped foot in his house before looking up his wretched town in the centennial book, sitting with the quiet murmur of his muffled TV and the skeletal rattle of the wind on trembling glass panes as he searched for pictures of his town. Once again, the pictures contradicted him. There had always been that same grassy plot in all the photos. It didn't matter who took the photo, during what century, which age. There had never been anything but a grassy plot.

He shook himself out as he went inside, shuddering the cobwebs from his mind. He talked to nearly no one all day. His job was a solitary one, and by the time he got off work, he was too tired to indulge himself in a social life. The loneliness was getting to him. The empty plot had always been there, and that was that. He crawled into bed for the second day in a row and drifted off, the lonesome things lurking in the floorboards and in the corners and under his bed creeping just a bit closer.

Callum woke up with a jarring bolt of consciousness. He breathed hard, but there was nothing that could have scared him awake, so he reprimanded himself for being so jumpy. Why was he so on edge? Nothing happened recently. No girls had stayed over—which wasn't too surprising. No friends either, or family, or anyone, actually. No wedding to be invited to, parties to attend, no get-togethers or social outings. It was, as it always was, the same old same old, here in his town that never changed. He couldn't remember anything changing, had it? Nothing was wrong, save for that worm-knot of anxiety festering and writhing in his stomach for no apparent reason. No, nothing had changed at all.

He went down the hall to brush his teeth, as he always did, time and time again, every single goddamn day, and there it was. A fragment of the mirror hung on the wall like an insect, a wicked creature existing for the express purpose of causing him grief, heartache. It was nothing but a shard left framed on that yellow-peeled wallpaper, no trace of the rest of the mirror to be seen.

He saw his own bloodshot, dark-circled brown gaze staring back through the reflective remains, dull, dead. A shock of dry, mousy hair hung limply over his forehead. There was a flash of patchy, overgrown stubble if he turned his chin, of sallow cheeks and pallid skin traced with blue spiderweb veins, like a crack of winter, like his blood feared flowing, and he couldn't recall if he always looked to be in such a state or if it was a result of his paranoia. He was supposed to be young, handsome, and strong, yet his skin hung off his skull, his bones like death draped in flesh, and he felt like a beast. He snarled bony, knobby fingers and knuckles on the glass of the remaining shard of mirror, watching his reflection crack into pieces under the pressure of his grip while he threw it off and against the wall. His chest was caved and heaved with the effort.

His attention turned to his shower curtain, and he ripped it off the rod, threw it on the ground. He felt the fire of fury and frustration burn his blood, rush to his neck and face, and suddenly he had color and strength, driven by the force of his paranoid terror, and he stomped on the curtain with a foot possessed by a foreign, driving passion, red and alive as the cut on his hands bled and bled faster and faster, and it was not blue winter blood, not the blood of a dead man. His blood was red and hot and seething and alive.

He was alive.

He was angry.

Callum was scared. He was scared of losing his mind because everything was normal to everyone else, and he did not break his mirror or take his toothpaste or demolish two buildings, and yet, here he was, demolishing his bathroom, and perhaps he was that animus thing that could wield the hand to do such things, and the thought was irrational, but he could not help the hot tears that pricked the back of his eyes with unexpected ferocity.

To anyone else, Callum's fit was pathetic. He was not powerful and crazed with an anger-driven strength, and he was not red and alive. He was gone, is what he was. He was a pathetic, gangly man, grunting and panting with every heave of effort, moving slowly like through water. Callum was scared. He was angry because he was scared, and suddenly, Callum was very ashamed, and so he settled down like a toddler after a tantrum and brushed his teeth with water that tasted of iron, and, as always, as the man he was, who had no control over his life, he went to work. He brushed off his breakdown. His break, his burst—it was just driven by stress, not mortal terror or paranoia or insanity that culminated in a climax of wrath or anything else that might imply that he was not okay. Everything was fine. It was a lapse in judgment. Everyone makes mistakes.

He was driving home, for the third time, in silence. He couldn't recall what music he liked, when he last listened to it, and his wounded hand seemed to throb the closer he drove home, and he was nearly hugging the wheel in his terror, in trepidation of what he was sure was to come, but told himself wouldn't.

But it did come, just as he knew it would, for the third day in a row. When Callum realized what was wrong on January 19th, his heart skipped so many beats and his breath caught in his chest so severely and shock took over him so completely and absolutely that he nearly crashed.

After righting himself and recovering and parking in his driveway, after rushing inside his house, through the lobby and into the kitchen, hiccuping with the effort to contain panic, terror, sobs, Callum called his mother. His house was so dark. He feared what lurked beyond the shadows, beyond that watery, frail light that descended from a single flickering bulb above him.

"Ma? M-Mama?" His voice cracked. Callum cleared his throat, taking a steadying breath. "Mom?"

The call was picked up after the second ring, after seconds stretched in that funny way.

"Callum? Oh, hi, dear! It's so good to hear from you! I miss you, baby. How've you been?" She paused, and when she was met with silence, she continued.

"You know, you really oughta call dear ol' mom every once in a while. How's work? How's school going? Are you getting good grad—oh! I just remembered, how's Jessica doing? I still want to meet her, you know. The way you talk about her, well, you two sound like such a cu—"

"Mom, please! Please. Please stop, Mom. Mom, I need you. Please listen to me, Mama. Please, please listen. Something happening, somethi—"

"Aw, I wish I could give you a hug, baby. I know it can be tough living on your own, but—"

"SHUT THE FUCK UP! SHUT UP! JUST SHUT UP AND LISTEN!"

He was silent for a long time. So was his mother. Minutes passed. Callum straightened, brushed himself off, and picked up the phone.

"Mom. I'm sorry. Please listen to me. I'm sorry."

Silence.

"Mom? Mama? Mom. I'm sorry."

His mother sighed. "It's okay, baby."

Tears slipped from Callum's eyes. He breathed in a wet, slick breath, then two, then four, and he began sobbing on the floor with the phone and sobbing, howling, gagging on his tears. Bubbles of mucus roiled under his nose, and he was ashamed of himself and the tears he'd been reduced to, though he was too distraught to stop himself. The cold tile was just that: cold. It offered him no comfort.

"I'm sorry, Mama. Mama, I'm so sorry."

"I know, honey, it'll be okay."

But it wouldn't be okay, would it? Because he was almost throwing up with the force of each cry, and at 22, he wanted to crawl into his mother's lap and feel her warm cradle as she cooed and soothed.

He wanted to be held and comforted, to have his back rubbed. He wanted to be hugged. He rocked himself.

"Mama, I'm so scared."

"I know, honey."

She didn't. She had no idea what was happening.

"Mama, I'm so scared. I'm so scared, Mama, i-it hurts. I-I'm so sca-ared, Mama."

It was quiet for a long time. The air was filled with Callum's lonesome, desperate sobs, convulsive, living things that rippled through his chest and ripped out from his throat. Sad, quiet mewls and whimpers, and a winter wind ensemble.

After a long, long time, Callum quieted.

"What is it, honey?" His mother's voice was gentle. It was soothing. "What's wrong, baby? What's going on? Tell me what's happening."

He was afraid. She would think he's crazy. But there was nothing else he could do, no one to turn to but her, and, perhaps, if he was crazy, she could find him help.

"Mama, it's disappearing."

"What? What's disappearing?"

"Everything, Mama. Everything. Everything in this town. First, it was one building, then another, then another, my toothpaste, my mirror, a-an-and—" he hiccuped, slapping a hand over his mouth to stifle his sobs. Saltwater dripped down his hand. It stung his wounds.

"M-mama, I-I was driving home tonight, a-and the—all the buildings, the entire street across from me—i-it's all gone. It's all gone, Mama. Everything. It's all gone. I'm so scared, Mom."

There was a long silence, and he curled up on the cold tile floor, knees to his chest. The light bulb above him flickered pityingly.

"Callum, honey ... should I make an appointment for you? I got this really good doctor, your aunt May saw him—"

"Mama, I-I'm not crazy!" Maybe he was, but he didn't want to hear it.

"What town are you talking about!?" His mother finally snapped, impatient. "You don't live in a town! You live by yourself! You live in that, ah, that little farmhouse, out in the country! Don't you remember, Callum? Callum? Callum ... ?"

Callum did not answer but jumped to his feet and threw open his curtains. Outside, there was nothing. A low, impenetrable gray fog hung over the earth. There was nothing there. It was just his house.

Callum screamed. He threw his phone through the cracked glass above his sink in panic, in fear, and screamed again, because now he was truly alone as the landline was ripped off the wall. His scream did not sound past his property. The fog consumed it. It was just gray. Everything was gray and cold, and suddenly, things within his house began to disappear.

It started small. A remote, a utensil. Then a doorknob, or a rug. Bits of carpet and tile, his sink, his TV, a door. Callum screamed and screamed and was taken away with horror. He raced throughout his house and frantically grabbed objects as if they would be safe from disappearing in his grasp, but away they went, like a blink, no trace of them ever existing—like a glitch. Something was there, and then, it was gone.

His walls started disappearing. One by one, they blinked out of existence, like long-dead stars whose photons finally reached Earth. All of his appliances and surfaces disappeared and left a gaping, yawning absence that stabbed Callum's guts with their unnatural, inexplicable omission, and Callum continued to scream, spittle flying from his mouth. His roof popped away, silent, as though he might not notice. In minutes, seconds, in a heartbeat, in a blink, in a breath, everything was gone, except for the floor he stood on, and rooted to the spot in terror, Callum felt with a dreadful certainty that it would not be long before the very solid, physical ground he stood on was soon to be no more physical than the rest of his missing house. He stood on a plane, a flat, empty, geometric shape of tile and stone and wood, like a tear, a rip in this misty lacuna.

Callum sobbed. The floor popped away. He began falling. His photons reached their destination. He was permitted to stop existing.

Callum disappeared.

Fireflies in September

Rebecca Ford

Grade 12. Freeman Public School, Adams, NE.
Brett Sales, Educator.

Oliver was born into a world ruled by savageness.

It was a world wherein the power and status one held were dictated by their capacity for cruelty and violence, by the sharpness of one's blade and the brutality of their words. A world wherein the infrastructure had collapsed beneath the weight of human corruption, of dense, dripping atrocity. It was not a world war, but a world of war.

Oliver was born too late for peace. Too late for peace of mind.

His mother did her best to protect him from it, in the beginning. He remembered when her eyes were soft and kind and her voice was light and her hands were strong and gentle. He remembered the hymns she sang, though any faith had long since expired. Her voice was not sweet, but it was warm, and her songs were loving.

Her eyes held that hearty warmth before she wilted. That brute, war, turned her voice cold. Stress etched harsh canyons in the panes of her face, chilling her hazel eyes. It grayed her hair, and her laugh lines were soured from resentful frowns. The sullen winter that iced the hearts of man had frozen crags and rifts in her face, the skeletal digits of frost-chiseled hate slivering crevasses through her features. The frostbite of frigid rancor had roughened her hands. There was no winter in California, but for that inside his mother.

He was not above self-pity; they had to keep moving.

His mother hadn't told him what they were doing and he didn't dare ask. She had been temperamental those days. "It's getting humid," she always told him, huffy and impatient. "Makes my joints ache."

It was a standard explanation for her shortening temper and brutal snaps, and it was all Oliver needed. Long days of scavenging across the Sonoran had left Oliver wilted and without the strength to question his mother. Besides, he looked forward to this nightly fire-lighting routine; it was the predecessor to sleep.

With that in mind, Oliver had gone about quietly lighting a fire with desert-dry kindling, building a fire that licked the sky. He glanced back up, his eyes catching on the gaze of his mother. Her eyes had been bright and feverish, contrasting sharply with the icy aloofness of her face. Indeed, such a sharp, hardened form was at staggering odds with the soft warmth of the fire.

"Come on." His mother's voice had broken the white noise of crackling and bugsong. "Take a seat, kiddo." His mother had patted the dusty earth next to her, near the heat of the fire, and Oliver hesitantly shuffled over, remaining standing where his mother sat.

"Do you know what this is?"

Oliver had rubbed his smoke-singed eyes, blinking back tears as he focused on the paper between his mother's fingers. It'd been small, fitting in his mother's palm, and had writing in nearly illegible scratches on it. Oliver hadn't recognized it, nor did he know where she acquired it, and he shook his head as he settled down on the ground beside her.

"It's your draft card."

"Do-do you want me to ... enlist?"

Oliver's voice had come out in a cracked rasp, and he cleared his throat. He'd never considered that he would have a card, but it made sense that he did. It was as customary as a birth certificate; once martial law went into rule, every individual, without distinction or discrimination, was assigned a draft card.

And if she did wish for him to enlist? He couldn't say no. Not to her, not to his mother, never. "No" had never been an option with her; it was a word so strong it sickened him in his dreams, rotting in his gut like a hot writhing mass of pressurized turmoil, crying for catharsis. "No" was unspeakable, unthinkable, and yet the horror of the notion of fighting this war had nearly driven him to this untouchable boundary. The sickness of dissent and the violence of consent had compelled him pale and stiff, stricken by his own assumptions.

But his mother had laughed. She *laughed*. It was fruity and full and at odds with her. Oliver heaved out a sigh of a chuckle, nervous.

"Oh no, my boy. Hell, you know they don't draft 'til you're eighteen."

Oliver was silent.

"Look at me, boy." Oliver hesitated. "I said look at me!"

She grabbed his chin, forcing him to stare her in the eyes.

"The day I let my boy enlist in this shitshow war is the day God'll strike me down." Her voice was a hiss. "The day I let those *tyrants* get ahold of my ONLY son, I'll be cold in my grave."

She shook his face for emphasis. Oliver had murmured something like a whisper of a plea.

"I should beat the shit out of you for even *suggesting* I'd let that happen. You want that? You think I'm a bad mother? Huh?"

Oliver had broken eye contact, scarcely breathing.

"ANSWER ME, BOY." The crickets sang. *Yes. Yes. Yes.*

"No."

He hesitated.

"No, mom." *Mom* was a hushed whimper, a sniveling squeak, and he hoped she'd take pity on her poor, pathetic son.

"Goddamnit, Oliver."

She had been in that dreadful serpentine mood, when she was all hisses and constriction and venom. She grabbed his hand, crushing it in her bony grasp.

"Take it. Burn it."

Oliver had recoiled, the heat radiating in waves, but his mother remained firm.

"I said, BURN IT, BOY."

Eyes screwed up against the raging heat, he'd thrust the card into the fire. His mother had snatched the card from the timber as it burned, threw it down, and together they watched the paper scorch into a glowering memory of war, as a hazy breeze whisked the ashes away with a lazy gust.

Just as suddenly as silence had veiled them, it was broken by another one of his mother's bubbling laughs. Oliver slowly sank back down away from the fire as his mother danced around it, wild-eyed.

"Look at that, Oliver! Look at that! That's revolution, my boy. That's a fucking rebellion!"

She laughed again, and Oliver indulged her with a half-hearted chuckle, then a giggle, then a fit as tears dripped from his eyes and burned down his cheeks. It could have been tears of laughter, or sadness, or the sting from the smoke, but he wasn't sure as he sat hiccuping on the cackles. His laughter had released in desperate howls like it couldn't wait to wrench itself from his chest. His mother had whisked a flask off her hip, shoving it to Oliver.

"Take a drink! That's what they do when they rebel, Oliver. They drink. Drink, my boy!"

Her celebration needed to be contagious. Grimacing, he had taken a swig. The liquor stung on its way down. It was a fluid revolt that had burned his throat and left his chest warm. It was terribly hot, all of it, throbbing with his heart. This desperation raged in him, rabid and froth-mouthed.

Oliver was a soldier at 16. As his mother rambled to the space, he was only a soldier. He was heavy and war-weary, forgotten as his sergeant passed out in a drunken stupor.

The fire had died and Oliver was awake late into the night. Without the flame's hateful cast, softer lights had twinkled in the sky, humming. They had blinked and glowed with a cold light. Distant sound of combat hung in the air. The air had been cool and dry, and he was lucid. The fireflies that flickered in the air should have been long dead. It was too late in the year for them to still be alive. They were too alive too late, those fireflies in September.

⸻

A year had come and gone since then, and now, there were no fireflies in the valley below him. Oliver stood at the crest of a hill overlooking hell, and everything made even less sense than it did before. He thought he wanted change, but now that he felt it in the blood and sweat dripping down his trembling limbs, he was afraid.

Change had not treated him kindly. It was the dry desert wind and the scornful laughter of soldiers that still rang in his ears from moments before. Change was the nectar scent of cantaloupe and blood. It was the chafing burn of rope around his wrists, and it was the throbbing aches and sears of open wounds. Change was the punishment for hope. Change was recent. Change came to him early that afternoon, under the shade of cypress, in south California heat, in his patch of cantaloupe.

Oliver and his mother hadn't been on the farm very long: a few months, perhaps. Oliver didn't keep track. They discovered it by chance, traveling by foot as they did, and figured it was as good a place as any to settle down. Temporarily, anyway, Oliver figured. It was nondescript and discreet, seemingly incapable of supporting life, and truthfully, it barely did. The rotting walls of the barn offered little in way of protection from the elements, and the scrubby swathes of feral cantaloupe did little in the way of obscuring them. However, it was enough to hide the two from the exhausted traveling soldiers marching by on a distant path.

It was those soldiers who made excellent customers.

Before dawn singed the land, Oliver was off every morning, ambling along the path carving the hills. Along he went, walking the few miles to the military trail with a hand-built wheelbarrow loaded with abandoned cantaloupe.

They were dependable, the soldiers. They walked down in clusters, eyeing him warily. Despite their reservations, they were consistent, always managing to gather enough change. Initially, pity pained him when he stared down those scrawny dogs, but it only took so long until he adjusted to the languished stares. Too much pity could kill a man, and he couldn't afford to die.

Without fail, a few soldiers always managed to gather enough change for a melon or two. The prices were appetizingly low and the vendor seemed inoffensive enough. It was intentional; he kept his face clean-shaven, his hair short and boyish, and his dark eyes, cratered in sunken pits, added to the illusion of an exhausted youth.

The routine was domestic. It was safe. He felt safe.

He thought he was.

It had to have been around noon when it happened, when change crawled to him, panting and wild in the form of a militant group.

"Afternoon, sir. Interested in some cantaloupe?"

"What's your name, son?"

The man's voice came out in a southern rumble, and Oliver craned his neck to meet his steeled gaze. The man was tall, blotting out the sun with broad shoulders. Oliver went tense at the question. It was so foreign; first names were awfully intimate then. He chose his words carefully.

"Who's asking, sir?"

"Name, son. First and last."

Oliver frowned, straightening up and trying to catch a glimpse of the men standing behind this interrogator. There must've been about two dozen of them, just teenagers, all wiry and lean, bordering on scrawny. They lurked behind their leader like starved canines, eager and desperate, pacing with sharp eyes. Oliver swallowed.

"Wilbur, sir. Wilbur Schneider."

"How old are you?"

Oliver weighed his options. He could be truthful, tell them he was eighteen, but what then? How would they react to the admission of an able-bodied man spending his days in what was comparative luxury instead of risking his life on the front lines like them?

"Why do you care?"

The pack roiled.

"Spit it out. Don't got all day."

Of course, he could lie, say he wasn't old enough to join the draft. He had a young face that offset his mature build, but his sunburn and rough-shaven skin did little to help enhance his youthful features. He weighed his options before speaking.

"I'm—17, sir. I'm 17."

The man's eyes did not soften as he hoped they would. Something told Oliver that it didn't matter whether he was 27 or 13. He was reminded of the child soldiers, and he felt very strongly that the age for combat no longer mattered "Where's your mama?"

"Excuse me?"

"Where's your mom, boy? Where's your mother?"

That set his mind racing. He came to the sudden and certain conclusion that he could not tell them.

"Dead, sir. She died in, uh—she died of pneumonia. A few years back."

"Sorry to hear that." His flat tone suggested otherwise. "Place of residence?"

Oliver was frantic now, pointing opposite of the barn.

SHORT STORY 35

"That way. About four miles."

"You walk here every day?"

"Yes sir."

"You lyin' to me, son?"

Oliver barked a harsh, nervous laugh, shaking his head.

"Oh, no sir! You've got it wrong: there—there's a shack down there! A-A little, ah, a real piece of work, you'll see it if you ju—"

"Choose your words carefully, boy!" The pack stirred with his booming words, slinking forward.

"N-no, sir. I'm telling the truth."

The man sighed. Nodded. The pack advanced. Several darted in and stole away with the cantaloupe. Something told Oliver that it didn't matter what he'd said, that either way, they were looking for an excuse to have at a scapegoat. "Wait, sir, no, wha—"

"I gave you your chance. I wanted things to go smoothly, kid, I did. But draft-dodgers like—"

"Draft—? What draft? I haven't dodged a draft, wha—?" He cleared his throat. "Sir—" the tension was driving him to frantic anger. "—sir, what the fuck are you talking about?"

"Where's your card, boy? If that's the case." The man flicked up two fingers, stopping the advancing group. The smell of smoke lingered in Oliver's nose.

"I-I never got one, sir." His eyes stung, and his voice came out smaller than he wanted.

"You tellin' me you never got a draft card?"

"Yes sir, I've never had one." The silence was thick and foggy, but a dim ray of hope diffused through the smoke. Perhaps they would leave him if he never got one.

"Your funeral."

The man took a step back, shrugging as his men flowed past him.

Like dogs they sicced on him, shouts and whoops raising hell. Oliver cried out as frenzied hands clawed at him and dragged him over his stand, splinters catching on his clothing and breaking off in his skin. He screamed, thrashing in their grips.

"I DIDN'T DO ANYTHING! Stop it—STOP IT! GET THE FUCK OFF ME!"

"I gave you every chance, boy. I've got a lotta' reports on you, lotta' other soldiers stoppin' by, sayin' this and that about, 'oh, there's some fightin'-age boy, sittin' on his ass, sellin' us fruit like a pansy, starin' us down like vermin while we're marchin' down, sweatin', bleedin', starvin'"—do you see these boys?"

He did. He caught the desperate, wild glow in their eyes. Saw the fury and anguish as their fists flew, booted feet holding down his wrists as he writhed on the ground.

"They've seen hell, son. They've seen hell."

Oliver stared hell down as his boot slammed into his gut. He doubled over, blood and bile dripping from his mouth as nausea churned up his throat.

"You see the problem? You sittin' here on your ass, while these boys are out dyin' for a selfish piece of shit like you?"

Angry, hurt shouts rang out from the boys. They were his age. They were just boys in this war.

"It's not FAIR!" one of the boys yelled, sending an enraged kick to the ribs.

"It's not fair, is it, boys?" the man shouted.

Yells of agreement. "Not fair" echoed in the still air like a battle cry, every chant bringing another blow. Oliver felt distant, detached as he felt himself be pulled up by the back of the neck, eye-level with the man.

"The boys don't like sissies, son. We don't like sissies. I'd reckon the worst pain you've ever felt was a goddamn sunburn, huh, boy?"

A fist slammed into his nose. Oliver saw stars, his head throbbing. He thrashed, his movements feral with the same anger and violence the boys were now sieging him with. He swore he felt something crack. Consciousness became fleeting.

"You're gonna feel pain now."

"Pl-please," Oliver gasped, spluttering.

"You know where you're goin'?"

Oliver's breath wheezed and rattled in his chest. A weak cough sent fireworks of pain through his chest. His tongue probed craters in his gums.

"You'll be made a man where you're goin'."

Oliver didn't have it in him to resist as his arms were wrenched up, his wrists bound with thick, fraying rope. He heard the boys reduce his fruit stall to rubble, catching the perfume of cantaloupe as it was crushed. The smells made his stomach churn.

"You know where you're goin'? Any idea where we put draft-dodgin', spineless pretty boys like you?"

They began walking down the dusty country road, Oliver hobbling along by a length of rope. His body shook with empty, silent sobs, his frame wracked with the horror of his situation, the rapidity of the change and brutality. The group crested a hill, and soon after he no longer smelled the cantaloupe and pine, only blood and sweat and dust. His mind shut down.

"You see that, boy?"

The man forced his head up. Over miles of wasteland, a huge black structure dwarfed the buildings in its proximity. Shadowed by the surrounding hills, it loomed in the valley, a mammoth of black stone and iron. Barbed wire fenced the high walls. There was not a single spark of light coming from that black cube.

The man grinned and released Oliver's jaw. His head hung, blood dripping from his nose. There was nothing to say. Nothing to do. He was still alive, always alive, alive too late, and this time, he wished he wasn't.

"Tartarus. Enjoy your stay."

THE CABIN

MIAH FOX

Grade 10. Paxton Consolidated School, Paxton, NE.
Mary Vasquez, Educator.

The fog was like a physical person. It blanketed all of the barren land. The older woman could only see a few feet ahead of her—could only hear her feet crunch into the cracked dirt. She wore the clothes of a traveler, and had the face of a war-torn soldier. Her black hair was cut only to jaw length, and even though the fog kept her blind, her blue eyes constantly scanned ahead of her. Her ears remained alert for anything.

She had no name; she had no need for one. Those who traveled with her knew her face, and that was enough. But it was there in that fog that she traveled alone. She needed to find her group again, needed to find shelter to wait out this haze. The barren land gave nothing except sandy dirt and dead weeds.

It was when night started to fall, only evident through the hazy light slowly fading behind her, that she heard the familiar sounds of their calls—like guttural chirps, a bark cut short. The woman knew these sounds, knew that they were close. Just as the fog blinded her, it also blinded all others. She kept utterly silent, and listened to the shrieks slowly creep closer or fade farther away as she walked. They moved about fearlessly—unlike the woman. Their footsteps were loud and grossly confident, their calls like a broken bell of death.

She nearly screamed when the cabin came into view. It was a small, shabby, old hunting cabin. It was the first building she could make out in the void of mist. Its dirty windows were unbroken, and its rotten door remained closed. *They* never opened and closed doors. *They* smashed their way in. She knew none of them would be inside.

She maneuvered her way up the crooked porch. She tried the door, but it was locked. Fearing that breaking it open would cause too much noise, she lowered herself down, grabbing the lock-picking tools from her bag. She slowly and tediously fiddled with the lock. It was stubborn, but with a faint click, the door creaked open. She stood at attention, resting her palm against the pistol at her side—just in case.

The cabin was small, a main room, with only a short hallway near the back that led into a bedroom and bathroom. The main room only had a coat hanger in the back corner, and a raggedy couch placed directly in the middle. The woman sighed and clicked the door shut behind her.

It was then that the three girls emerged from their hiding place behind the couch.

The woman immediately aimed her gun in response, but she hesitated. They were very young girls—pale and obviously malnourished. Each of them wore a thin white dress that looked almost pleasant, almost pristine, in contrast with their dark, black hair.

"Who are you?" the woman asked in a hiss. The three girls looked very similar, only differing in age—likely sisters. The one that seemed to be the oldest held her hands up. Her eyes were wide with fear as she stared at the loaded gun aimed directly at her.

"We have no weapons. We mean you no harm."

"Why're you here?"

"Why are you?" challenged the middle child. Her older sister elbowed her in the side.

"Please, put the gun down," the eldest said. The woman looked over the three girls. They truly didn't seem to carry any weapons. She clenched her teeth, sighed, and lowered her pistol.

Quietly, the girls shared their experiences with the woman. They had hardly any food or water; they were down to their last rations. They had stayed in the cabin for months, and as far as they knew, the fog was almost always around. It would stay for days—only disappearing for a few hours and then instantly—without warning—rolled back in. They were never able to get far before the fog would blind them, and they would have to track their footsteps back to the cabin.

It was during this time that the woman noticed the youngest sister. She didn't speak at all; she held her head down and intentionally tried to take up as little space as possible. She was a scared, traumatized child. Like the others, she was starving and weak.

"I can help you out of here. I have food and supplies. We can make a run for it the next time the fog rolls out. I have a group, too. They can take care of you."

"You'd really do that?" asked the middle child. Her eyes were hopeful.

"Yes. When do you think the fog will clear next?"

The oldest girl shook her head. "A day at least. It was clear this morning."

The woman nodded. That's how she got stuck here, one second it was clear, the next, she was blind.

"Okay then. We stay the night here. I have some canned food you can eat for now."

The girls nodded. They eagerly devoured each item of food that the woman sat out. The youngest barely touched any of it, though. She seemed to avoid making eye contact with anyone.

"How did you guys end up here anyway?" the woman asked the eldest, quietly. "You aren't dressed for travel, and you don't have any supplies."

The girl swallowed. "We traveled with a group of men. They were taking care of us. They had the clothes and food. We were just supposed to do what we were told." She glanced over at her sisters. "We got attacked by one of those ... things. We escaped, the men did not."

The woman glanced at the youngest. Those thin dresses ... prisoners to a band of men. No wonder she wouldn't look up to meet anyone's eyes.

They set up for the night. The oldest and middle child went into the bedroom, while the woman stayed in the main room behind the couch. The youngest, though, didn't bother to sleep at all. She sat in the back corner of the room next to the coat rack, her knees to her chest and her head down.

The woman didn't know how to handle kids. She was forty-three years old—never married or made mother. She didn't know how to comfort the girl who sat so haunted before her. So, the woman did all she could think to do; she closed her eyes.

She woke up to a scream—loud and piercing. The woman sat up, grabbed her gun, and scanned the main cabin room. The youngest girl was no longer in the corner. The woman searched the area frantically, and that is when she noticed it. The hand of a small child dangled from the edge of the couch, blood spilling from it. One of *them* had broken in. The youngest had been an easy target.

If she hadn't been so horrified by the sight, she might have been able to process the fact that the door was not smashed open. The windows were not broken. *They* never opened and closed doors. *They* smashed their way in.

The woman stumbled backward and prepared herself to fight. The *thing* would certainly attack her next. It was then that the oldest sister ran out of the room, and the youngest sister stood up from the couch.

Her eyes were red, as if entirely bloodshot, even her pupils. Her mouth was covered in blood.

"W-What ... ?" The eldest could hardly speak. The woman froze in her tracks. The youngest stared at them silently. The youngest had killed her middle sister.

"Go," the woman finally said. "Go. Run!"

The eldest didn't need to be told twice. She ran back into the bedroom and slammed the door shut. The woman dashed for the bathroom.

But not before she saw the hand move from behind the couch.

The bathroom was small and grimy. There was a small toilet next to a narrow sink and a mirror hung on the left side. There was also a laundry basket next to the bathtub near the back wall. The woman grabbed the laundry basket and pushed it against the door. She shoved her back against the tub and held her feet firm against the basket in an attempt to barricade the door. She aimed her gun toward the only entrance—or exit.

She heard pounding. Loud and steady, like drums beating slowly. She didn't feel the vibrations, the youngest was pounding on the bedroom door.

Then she heard the second pair of hands.

Pounding.

Pounding.

Pounding.

Silence.

She heard a plea, a cry of mercy before an earth-shattering scream came from the other side of the woman's door. She could hear her own heart beating in the silence that followed. Still, her armed hand stayed steady. Even as she heard the two pairs of fists pounding against her door, her hand stayed steady. Even as she heard the third pair of fists join in, her hand stayed steady. She held it there, would she shoot these girls? Could she? Taking the life of someone on a battlefield, or the life of some *thing* was one thing. This was different. Could she kill children?

She saw, *felt* the door splinter and crack until it finally gave out. The laundry basket's weak plastic broke into pieces as it was thrown to the side. The door violently swung open, and the woman saw all three of the girls.

They all had the same blood-shot eyes. The two eldests' dresses were torn to pieces; their necks were ripped out. They all had bloodied hands and faces. The woman shook in her spot. She needed to kill them. Had to. How could she kill children?

Then, they began to speak.

It was not a language known to man. Not one that could be spoken by man either. They spoke in layers, together as one in eerie harmony. Then they said a name. One she recognized deep in her heart. She knew it was hers, but it felt wrong, dark.

"No ... no get away."

She couldn't move her hand. She never froze like this. Never. They came forward, and she couldn't pull the trigger. They smiled, eerie and perfect.

"Get away!"

Get away.

Daisies

Autumn Hall

Grade 10. Daniel J. Gross Catholic High School, Bellevue, NE. CaSandra Johnson, Educator.

Fifteen years ago, a young girl sits alone in a park on a swing. Her feet dangle below her as she sways back and forth. With the sun just barely setting in front of her, it gives a natural golden hue to the curves of her face. She smiles, her heart pounding vigorously with excitement as she holds a daisy delicately in her hands.

"He loves me." She pulls a petal and bites her lip, trying to contain her excitement.

"He loves me not," she says a little softer. Not wanting to even utter the words just in case she happened to speak them into existence.

She grips the last petal.

"He loves me." And she squeals, throwing the daisy into the air. She twirls around on the swing with her joy. "James Bailes loves me so!"

And it had been true. James Bailes loved her more than anything.

Nova lies on the cool damp ground of her backyard. The grass is in need of a long overdue trimming. However, Nova, having been unable to complete even the simplest of daily tasks, couldn't find it within herself to even begin *thinking* about cutting the overgrown vegetation. She has remained in this mindset even as the tall plants itch the back of her neck and tickle her ears with their length.

The state of her lawn is an obvious reflection of the condition of her current life status: an utter mess.

She tilts her head back, her eyes closing softly as she allows the surrounding nature to engulf her. The sun is warm on her face, her chin tips up toward the heat it provides, and soaks up every little bit of the Florida rays as she can.

She allows the soft breeze to pacify her of her worries. Nova smiles as she basks in the little peace she has, knowing that it won't last very long.

Nova stretches her hand up toward the sky, her fingertips desperate to grace their skin with the touch of the soft clouds that dot the clear blue sky. She wishes she could get away from here, that the soft summer breeze would whisk her away from not only the chore of her backyard that begs for Nova's assistance but *all* of the problems that arose with her move to the south.

She had given up everything to be here: her career, her family, and her friends. All because the man, who she had at one point been so desperately in love with, had asked her to. Nova had let herself be persuaded by her young, naïve heart. When in reality she should have been listening to her head. Her logic had always been her strong suit.

That infatuation she once had with him seemed so far gone now. So far in the past that it was a complete contrast to who she had become now. The memories of her adoration were gray and faded now. Everything seems to have changed.

Everyone tried to warn her of this ending. They tried to tell Nova that this was a bad idea, that he had changed since being away at college. They said that the high school sweetheart her heart yearned for didn't exist anymore; he was different now. And despite having spoken to him, albeit hidden by online messaging and voice calls, he wouldn't be what she expected.

They had continuously given Nova unwanted advice and had shown her every possible fault in her plan that could result from this choice.

Of course, having always been so strong-willed and stubborn, she ignored them.

And now here she was: halfway across the country, away from home, and completely miserable. If she had just listened to them, she wouldn't be stuck in her backyard, paralyzed beneath the summer sun, debating on what move she should make next.

It's unfair. She wants to love him. So why was it so hard to do so? Why had she fallen so far out of love?

Nova had made the most impractical, hasty, and immature decision that would only alter her life further if she didn't act before it was too late. If she had just listened to her peers, none of this would have happened in the first place.

She was *supposed* to love this man and was meant to stay by his side for the rest of her life. But he had changed: they both have.

In reality, it's selfish of her. He has given everything he could to Nova and now here she was sequestering herself away from him every chance she had available to her. This was even true right this moment; he was at their wedding and she cowered in the backyard. Her white gown was stained green and dusted with brown dirt.

Nova was supposed to be walking down the aisle in twenty minutes. She was supposed to be at the church over an hour ago.

What has happened to their blissful love?

Why is everything so different?

Nova doesn't notice the tears until she could taste them on her lips. The salty liquid has found its way to her tongue. It tastes just as bitter as she feels.

She sits up, her eyes burning from the sobs that she had only now allowed to rack her body. She throws her head into her hands, heaving violently as she realizes her entire life is falling apart.

The man she had once found dearly charming, was the same man she felt she couldn't get far away enough from. He had gone from making every single one of her days bright to turning them miserable.

The sound of his laugh was no longer contagious. Now, it had the same effect on her ears as nails on a chalkboard.

The touch that once had her reeling in glorious rapture now revolted her.

Every one of his faults irks her more than it should. The motion of his jaw as he chewed his food made her blood boil. The sound of his breathing as he lay next to her in their bed made her toss and turn, never seeming to get any sleep due to the grating sound. She had once looked forward to the winter, knowing she could steal countless articles of clothing from his wardrobe to keep warm. Now the scent of his soap discouraged her from ever pulling on one of his coat jackets again.

Now she was expected to marry him and she couldn't bring herself to. She didn't want to hate him; she wants to love him. She itched to embrace his faults and welcome them with open arms, with love.

Nova lulls her head to one side, her eyes landing on a lone daisy that stands amidst the overbearing heat of summer in the center of the yard. The rest of them had died ages ago, all of the others long gone by now.

She brushes her fingers along the small flower that struggles to stand on its own. With no comfort of its peers remaining, it bends to one side. It's an obvious symptom of what would have to be its inevitable death; however, the white-colored pieces are surprisingly silky-smooth to the touch.

The daisies were meant to be the start of a garden Nova and he were to raise.

That was before everything happened. Before their relationship fell to shambles.

Well for Nova that is. He still thought everything was perfect. He thought his bride was behind those church doors with a smile on her face about to meet him at the altar. Whilst Nova let her irritation grow and ferment inside her, her lover thought they were happy.

Nova plucks the little daisy from the ground and twirls it between her fingers. She lets her tears water the soil and drip onto the flower. She hopes that her sorrowful weeps can be of *some* good use to the flourishing of, if not of her marriage, then nature.

She traces her finger along the first petal. "I love him." She nearly chokes on the phrase. The words are hard for her to say. They come out strained and gravelly from not only the dehydration her sobbing has caused but the statement itself entirely. She plucks the petal from the plant, dropping it near the shiny new shoes that rest before her.

She pulls once more. "I love him not." These words come out easier than the last. It is effortless for the truth to surpass the gates that are her lips than it is for a lie. Though she still does not want to verbally admit it, this statement *is* the truth.

"I love him." She goes on like this for a moment, going back and forth between the phrases. Her throat becomes tighter with every passing second that she grows closer to that last petal.

When she reaches it, Nova knows her answer. She knows it in her heart, in her soul.

She rises to her feet and tucks the petal-less stem into the waves of her hair as a reminder of how she was strong. She was just as strong as this flower was. When it seemed nothing but doomed, it's thrived. Perhaps she did not initially want this answer but she knew it was the one thing she needed confirmation of.

Knowing it is right, she wipes away her tears and her snotty nose, squares her shoulders, and slips back on her shoes. She doesn't bother brushing away the mess on her gown.

Nova takes a deep breath, very aware of what step she must take next. She thinks back to that last remaining petal. It told her something that she mustn't forget.

The meek little flower had spoken the truth both times she had confided in it. James Bailes had fallen in love but she had fallen out. "I love him not."

Shakespeare's Pen, My Ink

Grace Peng

Grade 11. Millard North High School, Omaha, NE.
Christie Rushenberg, Educator.

"Mama (妈妈), look at me!"

Lili is five. She's waving excitedly at her mother holding the camera, a blue footed onesie with pink flowers tugged over her four-foot body. The blinds are drawn shut, the soft glow of the moon peeking into the warmly lit living room. Behind the camera, you can hear the crinkle of a fond smile coming from Lili's mom.

"Wah! Help!" Lili crashes to the carpet, bursts of giggles erupting from her two toothed smile as she falls from dizziness.

"Being a ballerina is hard! Barbie makes it look so easy!" Lili says through muffled laughter and crescent eyes.

Black floods the screen.

The video ends.

August

"There's no point in me fighting you guys on this, huh? Ok." Lili stands up on shaky knees, facing her parents.

"May I go?"

"Lili—stop, I—" Her dad sighs. "I—we—" He gestures to Lili's mother off to the side, who was falling asleep, not interested in the conversation. "We just want to keep you safe."

"I know. That doesn't mean I can't still hurt, though."

Silence squeezes itself into the cracks of the room, filling the walls with an anticipating hum.

"You'll see that this is what's best for you. That's final."

As foolish as she is, Lili trusts her dad. Truth follows him on a leash.

Lili gives a small tip of her head. Her dad gives one back. She opens the door and exits, letting the silence permeate itself into the rest of the house.

◇◇◇◇◇◇◇◇◇◇◇◇◇◇◇◇

That night, Lili's mind is reflected by the tissues piling up on the carpet of her bedroom. She's thinking so much that she's not thinking at all. It's a giant blob of numbness and static. At least her giant pig pillow is there to comfort her.

Lili lays on her bed, arms pulled tight around the soft plushie. As her eyes blur in and out of focus on the glow in the dark star stickers above her, corners of which are beginning to say "farewell!" and peel from the ceiling, Lili lets out a big sigh. Her mission fails, however, when snot clogs her windpipe, releasing a hiccuped croak from the depths of her throat instead.

Attractive.

She wishes that Sully would appear from behind the shadows and grab her shoulders and shake her with his nasty blue hair and wake her up from this nightmare.

Lili pinches her skin and squeezes her eyes shut, praying that when she opens them a pair of huge eyes enveloped with vibrant fur will stare back at her.

Even that one-eyed green orb named ... Olive? Milk? Mayo? No—anyways ... I'd rather endure staring at his pit of an eye than live through this.

She relaxes her fingers, letting the blood flow back into her forearm. Lili's eyes flutter open, and—

Her vision is flooded with the ethereal sight of the squeaky, old ceiling fan.

Screw you, Sully.

◇◇◇◇◇◇◇◇◇◇◇◇◇◇◇◇

The harsh one a.m. glow of the piercing moon slivers its way through Lili's bedroom windows. One thought keeps floating up, up, up, in Lili's head. A pearly bubble, waiting to be popped.

This was the year where things were supposed to finally, finally, get better.

Lili already knows that life's favorite pastime is crumpling you until all you are is a pile of shredded paper, smudged ink and illegible words unable to be pieced back together. Unfortunately for Lili, most people only skim through novels, picking out just the striking and dramatic phrases, of which Lili has none.

The bubble pops, leaving the sweet taste of bitter soap to coat her tongue.

Welcome to the Four Seasons, Hotel of Hell

Every three months, the Earth decides to be gracious and gives everyone a new beginning by tilting its axis a few degrees. Spring departs with a rainy cloud, emptying sidewalks of straggling worms for wide-eyed innocent children to save. Summer arrives with its too bright smile and garden hose water parks, the soft whistle of cicadas driving most crazy but lulling a special few to sleep beneath the stars. Autumn sheds its last tears of dead leaves, packing away suitcases in exchange for stuffed backpacks of crumpled lined paper and broken pencils. Winter sprinkles its crystal white fairy dust on toddlers' tongues and the neighbors' shingles, encapsulating our small world in a floating snow globe.

C.S. Lewis once said that "day by day nothing changes, but when you look back everything is different." It's funny, how time passes like this. Days drag on like stones on our spine, but years bleed into each other as if they themselves command the earth to spin faster.

Lili doesn't quite agree that things happen "in the blink of an eye." Months still feel like months and years still feel like years. She suspects that the only reason why time is said to be so fast is because people only recall the eventful, memorable, and important moments. The mundane is left behind, stray tumbleweeds tucked away at the back of people's brains, left to blow away in the wind. It's why no one can remember what they ate on Friday or what they wore on Monday or who they talked to four hours ago. The problem is, the mundane is often what makes up most of time. We only link together the special moments, forming a short chain of life, which we view as the entirety of the last few years. All the moments in between are forgotten.

Lili thinks she is the mundane moments in between.

August, 730 Days Later

Soon, autumn falls into winter, winter melts into spring, spring rains into summer, and summer drips back into autumn. The cycle repeats until the colors blur into a messy palette of oranges and blues and greens that make an ugly brown.

Lili has been alive for another two years. *Alive* being the operative word, as that's pretty much all she's been doing.

Lili feels hollow. Moths have buried themselves in between her ribs and mold has begun to blossom in her bruised lungs. She is a rotten apple. She thinks of when she was younger when her family would go to the apple orchard every September. Lili's lips would be coated in sugar and her fingers soaked in syrup by the end of the day, but none of that mattered because the loud laughter and crescent-eyed smiles of her family bathed her in pure bliss and washed her clean. Her mom would peel apples right there in the middle of the orchard with the knife she brought designated for this purpose, blood red skin falling in curls to the grass. She would cut off all the brown mushy parts that Lili always hated, leaving only the bright white ripe flesh clinging to the core.

If only Lili could cut off all the ugly parts of herself.

It's on a Sunday afternoon when it happens.

"Lili. I—, I—"

At her dad's voice, Lili pauses in her step. The stuttered words echo across the walls of her dad's university, the murmur of the air conditioner providing the moment with ambient background music. Lili is fond of the place, as she spent summers tucked away in her dad's office when she was younger. Now, instead of coloring sheets, Lili has come stacked with study books filled with too many long words and dizzying numbers hugging too many letters. Another sign of how much things have changed.

"I was wrong. Two years ago, I—, I—" Her dad, with his graying hair and valleyed forehead, sighs. Her dad, who she is dreadfully afraid of. Her dad, who is clutching onto their aging family and whose eyes cry for everyone to not move far away.

Her dad, who is fifty and hasn't gone home since he was eighteen.

"I should have listened to you. I wish things didn't turn out this way."

Lili almost trips over her blue laces.

What?

She thinks her ears are playing some cruel prank on her because apologies don't exist on her father's tongue.

She's waited *years* for those words. Now they're spoken, made tangible, out in the universe. Lili waits for some sort of satisfaction at hearing her dad's admission of guilt, but ... there's nothing. Her heart still beats normally, her lungs still inhale and exhale, and her knees stay steady and strong. It seems as if her body is responding to it like any other old sentence.

How anticlimactic.

Maybe it's because over the course of time, Lili has realized that her parents are humans too. Adults are essentially kids but with bigger bodies and taxes to pay. They make mistakes, they get embarrassed, they don't know what they're doing, they're just trying their best to make do. Her parents aren't untouchable. Underneath omniscient curtains a younger Lili painted over her parents, an older Lili sees the fragile souls in the form of a mother and father. Growing up is a ceremony veiled with gray linen, and Lili has been invited to its celebration of mourning.

Through harsh words and anger expressed through a battered body and beat mind, Lili has beveled her naivety into some sort of complacency. She's not cynical—ok, maybe just a tiny bit—she's just grown up a little.

Lili thinks that she still has a lot of growing up left to do.

"It's ok." *It's not, it's really not, sorry doesn't erase the past, but I know you were just doing what you thought was right.*

The moment passes. Life continues.

Shakespeare's Pen, My Ink

Lili thinks she lives too much in the "what ifs" and "what could bes" and the "why thises." Her head wanders through wisps of clouds, not quite reaching the haven but getting enough fleeting touches that her heart yearns for more. The thing is, she already has enough. This dumb stupid rock gives her life and everything she needs, and yet she's still selfish enough to want more. Lili feels like her heart has only been a quarter full all her life, and as she grows into her bones her body begins to wonder why her heart isn't filling up with it.

Lili gets so drunk off of daydreams that soon sonnets begin to run through her vessels, feeding her false hopes and wishes of love that only exist at the tip of Shakespeare's pen. Her blood runs in off-beat dactyls to a world meant for sweet-sounding iambs, and soon her elegy writes itself. It's bitter and rather dramatic, but Lili doesn't particularly mind because she's already high off the damage. She doesn't know what living is like without having scars that tattoo your skin in pretty rivers and a heart painted with bruises inked by other people's fingerprints.

Sometimes she'll stop to look around herself and realize how alone she is. But she's not. She has family and she has friends so why is that not enough? Lili's soul has a tragic tendency to always crave the honey too thick for her tongue and the people too far from her reach that the thing people call reality begins to blur at the edges, and soon her entire existence is just one stained inkblot in the tenth edition of a dusty phonebook.

After all, while Lili has been living in her head others have been living their *life*. One glance back shows her that she's been stuck in the same spot for years now. It's similar to Einstein's theory about relativity. How one views movement depends on where they are in relation to that movement. The speed of a plane is going to feel different from a person sitting on the flight compared to someone looking up at the sky.

So as all go heading to their next destination, Lili stares up at them leaving her far, far behind. She could jump on with them, but she gets too distracted by the stars and the moon that wink at her as the plane leaves. When the day comes, everyone else is long gone, already boarding off.

Lili's fingers graze the damp dew sleeping on the soft blades of grass. Flying is scary. The ground is safe. But that doesn't stop her from dreaming about what it would feel like for stardust to brush her cheeks.

December, 1580 Days Later

"For here or to-go?"

Lili whips her head up. *Shoot, did I just drop a penny?*

"To-go please! Thanks." Lili flashes her best smile, which to her is charming and innocent but to others looks rather awkward and a bit like she needs to take a laxative.

Lili scrambles to retrieve her purple debit card with the serial number 1-800-save-this-girl before the friendly college student behind the counter rings up her order.

Faster, oh gosh, he's putting it in the bag, hurry up, why won't this stupid card come out of the pocket? I KNEW you should've pried it out in the car beforehand, look no—

"That'll be $16.28."

Lili finally slips out her card from her wallet and hands it over to the employee, letting out a mental sigh of relief. An old woman from the back comes over to the register, putting a pair of chopsticks into the brown bag. Lili notices her warm smile that crinkles in soft folds near the eyes, and her mind flashes with memories of her dad. Images of how his crinkles formed tired, frustrated lines near his brow rather than homely, twinkling smiles like the old lady's.

Lili thinks they make an odd but fitting pair. A charming looking American college student working alone with an elderly Chinese grandmother. One from the West, another from the East, both somehow ending up at a Poke corner in the Midwest suburbs. They look comfortable around each other, paralleling the dynamic between a grandma and her beloved grandson.

Lili misses her family.

"You're all set! Have a nice day!" The boy behind the register refocuses Lili from her daydream. The grandma hands Lili her food, and Lili bids a farewell before turning around to head out the door.

However, before she can disappear into the December snowfall, a small, raspy voice echoes across the empty store.

"谢谢！再见!" *"Thank you! Goodbye!"*

Lili, nearing the exit, whips up her head for the second time that day. Grandma is waving at Lili, her short figure peeking out from behind the counter. Her expression is painted over with an ecstatic smile that fills her cheeks.

"再见!" "*Goodbye!*" Lili calls back, an uncontrollable smile finding home on her lips.

She's halfway out the door, but before her feet hit the crystal dusted concrete, she sees College Boy smile softly at Grandma.

◇◇◇◇◇◇◇◇◇◇◇◇◇◇◇◇◇

Lili has felt alone for almost her entire life. A lone star, light-years away from a sense of belonging. But in this small second, when Grandma *sees* her and speaks to her in their special tongue, when she peeks into College Boy's care for Grandma, Lili feels okay.

It is in this mundane moment with two nameless strangers, this Friday lunch, where Lili feels alive. Her small, snow globe world has turned into a sky glossed with stardust for a split second.

The moment passes. Lili decides to continue living.

NOVEL WRITING

Honorable Mention

Eve Bishop, "Do You Like the Rain?" Grade 9. Chadron Senior High School, Chadron, NE. Barb Waugh, Educator.

Eve Bishop, "It Was Clementine Season." Grade 9. Chadron Senior High School, Chadron, NE. Barb Waugh, Educator.

Eve Bishop, "It Had Always Been This Way." Grade 9. Chadron Senior High School, Chadron, NE. Barb Waugh, Educator.

REMISIRE

EVE BISHOP

Grade 9. Chadron Senior High School, Chadron, NE.
Barb Waugh, Educator.

Brief Summary

"Remisire" is a story of memories and romance. It is set in a fictitious world where some live inside the Wall in a city called Le-Varre and some live outside it, otherwise known as Ilvallums. Laurence Alden is smuggled into Le-Varre and is sent to a woman named Madame Llewellyn, who knew Laurence's mother. Laurence's mother was a Tekhne, or someone who knows magic, and is dying because of dabbling in certain magics that were dangerous. Laurence is taken in and develops a friendship with a young woman named Theresa, who was taken in by Madame Llewellyn at a young age. When the regulators, an equivalent of the police, come to take Laurence away, he and Theresa share a fleeting moment (one where Laurence promises to return and Theresa misses him even before he leaves) before he flees to North Le-Varre. Theresa heads to the gardens one day on a whim, and when she does, she is hit with a flood of emotions. Theresa and Laurence relive the memories together before the story ends with the two of them speaking of the promise Laurence made. This story focuses on childhood friends and lovers who stay while others go. "Remisire" is a tale that thinks back on itself more than once and while there are no epic battle scenes, there is a flood of vibrant emotions.

Sunlight poured through the windows and glinted off the not yet dry paints. A click rang out in the lukewarm room as the door shut behind Theresa. The air was stiff as she moved gingerly past the easels. The students would probably brush her off, but Madame would have her head if she knocked something over. Theresa's eyes drifted over the paintings as specks of dust glistened in the dim lighting. The room was orange in the late evening, and she was only here to make sure everything was in order before heading back. A shiver ran up her spine as she hugged her arms and tucked a strand of black hair behind her ear. The days had been becoming shorter, and Theresa was grateful for the deep red shawl Madame had gifted her one winter.

"Are you Madame Llewellyn?"

Theresa jumped out of her skin, almost knocking over a stool. Her green eyes darted to where a young man, early twenties is where she would put him, with a bit of stubble and unruly curls of brown hair stood. He held a hat in his hands and wore a plaid vest over a wrinkled dress shirt. Looking over his form, his pants seemed worn and his shoes looked like they were polished by splashing some water over the leather.

"How did you get in here?" Theresa said with disdain, mentally preparing herself to use the trick Madame had taught her days ago in words she couldn't understand.

"I opened the door," the man fumbled to say as he gestured behind him. His brown eyes widened as he began to justify his actions. "I had knocked initially, I swear by it. No one answered, and when I turned the knob, I found myself here. Then you came along. You *are* Madame Llewellyn, are you not?"

"I am under no obligation to tell you anything," Theresa huffed out, as she pushed past him to lock the door bitterly. It frustrated her that she had forgotten to do such a simple task.

"My mother told me I would be safe if I came here. She said I would be welcome with open arms as long as I put effort in. And I'm more than willing. So *please*," the man urged as his fists clenched at his sides, "if you aren't the Madame, please ask her if I may stay."

Only then did Theresa notice the small suitcase he had by his feet. He seemed desperate, in her eyes. She wondered why. "Well at least tell me your name before I go see what I can do for you."

His eyes noticeably brightened a great deal and he sat his hat down on his suitcase to take Theresa's hands into his. "Thank you so much. You don't understand how much this means. And, well, my name's Laurence Alden. I'm from past the Wall." He said the last part in a whisper, and Theresa stiffened. She suddenly understood everything.

"Bring your belongings," she whispered. "We'll head upstairs."

Laurence snatched up his suitcase and was at Theresa's heels as she hurried up the stairs. If she had been any younger, she would've tripped over the long skirts of the blue dress she wore. But after spraining her ankles more than enough times and Madame having to stitch the ligament back together, she had learned how to balance herself.

"If you aren't Madame Llewellyn, may I know who you are?" Laurence asked as his companion opened a door and let him through.

She analyzed him for a moment, wondering whether or not it was okay for an Ilvallum to know such things. "Theresa." There shouldn't be harm in him knowing just her given name.

"Just Theresa?" She could hear the bitter amusement in his voice behind her. He paused for a moment. "Will you not tell me your full name because I'm an Ilvallum?"

Theresa ignored his question and the way her hands shook at how openly he said that word. It was okay to think it, to whisper it. No one just blatantly said it.

"You are aware that I am in more danger telling you my name than you are telling me yours?" he pointed out sharply. "I can't do anything to you, but you have every right to go and report me to the local regulator, and they'd gladly file whatever charges they can against me for simply being here."

"How did you even get through the Wall?" Theresa asked with a frown, more to shut him up than anything else, but he answered anyway.

"My mother pulled a lot of strings within our community. They snuck me in at night. I've been wandering this city's streets since this morning. What's this place called again?"

"Le-Varre. We live in the West."

"Could you simply call it West Le-Varre?"

"I suppose," Theresa said.

"Does the Wall have a name?"

"No. It's just *the* Wall."

"What's your last name?" Laurence wondered aloud.

"Why do you ask so many questions?" Theresa snapped.

"Mother said small-talk is essential in the city. Asking questions is the best way to spark up conversations."

"It's not always necessary," Theresa sighed. Her movements stopped in front of a tall, wooden door. The hall felt cold as the sun set through the window pane, and she pulled the door open. Announcing herself, she stepped in. "Madame, I've returned."

"Ah, Theresa, dear." Madame smiled without raising her head from the painting she was working on. "I've made tea. Rose-ginger, just the way you like."

"Thank you, Madame." Theresa flushed as she curtseyed. "You didn't have to."

"I wanted to. Besides, you had to hassle yourself with this young man. I didn't want to inconvenience you anymore." Madame continued to speak, ignoring Laurence's presence. "His mother and I were quite close several years back. She married a man who was from beyond the Wall, and they disappeared one afternoon after the regulators wouldn't stop harassing the two of them. How is Kathleen, anyways, boy?"

Laurence blinked owlishly before forcing a smile. "She fell ill a few years back. It's difficult for her to see, her hearing's failing rapidly, and at times she'll think she's someplace else and that we're not who we are. We tried to get a doctor who is knowledgeable in cases like this, but they're rare outside the Wall. We don't know how to help her. She wrote me instructions on how to get here, and she wanted me to give you this letter. So please, Madame Llewellyn, if you can do anything to assist her, give it a try."

"I always told Kathleen dabbling in memoria spells was a bad idea," Madame said as she swirled citrus-colored paint across her canvas. "Now look where it's gotten her."

"Memoria spells?" Laurence questioned.

"Just hand me the letter, boy." Madame skeptically looked at the envelope before burning it open with a few murmured words. The parchment looked heavy in her hands as Theresa watched her read it over. Madame grimaced, tossed the letter onto the table with the tea, and nonchalantly said, "Help yourselves to something to drink."

Theresa moved forward and poured three cups before anyone else could. She handed one to Laurence with shaky hands. Her eyes stayed trained on the ground, making sure to not glance at him. She would've been lying if she said being in the same room with an Ilvallum did not frighten her. Bringing the rim of her own cup to her lips, she glanced nervously in Madame's direction.

This hadn't been the first time an Ilvallum had been in her presence. But this was the first time they had been so old. They typically came here as children: four, six, nine, ten, eleven, fourteen at most; but never as someone in their twenties. And with Madame's vague response, Theresa didn't know how to view the situation.

"You'll be staying here from now on, Mister Alden," Madame said clearly, and her voice made it apparent that there was no room for discussion.

"And my mother?" Laurence inquired as he stepped forward with concerned eyes. Theresa already knew the answer before Madame opened her mouth. A bitter smile stretched across her lips.

"Kathleen knew what she was getting herself involved with. I'm afraid there is no cure for dismemoir. That's why she sent you here. Using the rest of her intact sanity, she wished you away. It was only thanks to her you were able to get past the Wall. Without her disguise, you'd be in the Gallows right now, young man."

"Did she use her magic? No, nevermind that, *how* did she use her magic?" Laurence's voice was taut as he changed his question, and Theresa fought the urge to wince.

"Would you leave if I told you yes? If I explained how she pulled off such a damning trick? Will you walk out of this house and never return?"

He seemed to think this over, shaking his head when he came to the conclusion that this was his only option. At least, that's what Theresa assumed. She was right, though. He had nowhere to turn, and without official documentation, he would be taken straight to the Gallows. No questions asked.

Madame sighed as she set down her brush, whisking away stray paint back into their containers. Then she explained: "You already know this, but Kathleen specializes in memoria. She used her knowledge to make the Wall regulators see a vehicle that was there months ago. She disguised each of you. In all likelihood, you were found. But memoria can not only twist a timeline and everything in it, it can alter your mind. Why do you think she's in the state she's in right now, losing her mind? She invested too much of herself. I'd bet the rest of my years that she is lying in bed right now, a shell of the Kathleen I knew."

Theresa had seen pictures of this Kathleen. Madame had painted her many times. She could only imagine the beautiful woman in those flowery scenes lifeless as sunlight hit her paling skin. Theresa suppressed the urge to shiver at the cruel idea.

"Will you help me?" Laurence whispered with clenched fists, drawing Theresa out of her dazed state. "Will you help me stay alive?"

"For your mother's sake, boy, I will," Madame said, standing up to approach him. "So, what's your actual name?"

"You mean after reading all of that letter, you don't even know my name?"

"She was confused as she wrote it," Madame sighed as she stared blankly at him. "Unless your name happens to be Griffith as well."

"No, Madame. That would be my father's name."

"I know."

"... I'm Laurence Alden."

Madame paused for a moment, looking over his features. Theresa couldn't bring herself to sip the tea in her cup, unsure of what to do with herself. Tension hung thick in the air like smoke. Madame gestured towards the door as she turned to face the window and said, "Theresa will show you to your room, Laurence. Theresa, take him to the one at the end of the hall, second floor."

"Yes, Madame," Theresa nodded, hurrying to the door. She turned the knob all too eagerly. "This way, Mister Alden."

Laurence grasped his suitcase in his hand, but his movements lingered in the room. He glanced at Madame, whose blue-gray eyes stayed trained on the sharp glow of hazy orange that gleamed through the glass, and the anguished desperation in his eyes was more than clear. He frowned as he followed Theresa out of the room. The hall felt colder than it had earlier, and Theresa could feel the questions Laurence was longing to throw at her feet.

"What is it, Mister Alden?" she asked coolly, refusing to turn her head towards him.

"Please," he murmured. "Just Laurence."

"Then, Laurence." The name felt awkward on her tongue. "You want to ask me something. What is it?"

He took a sharp inhalation of breath before asking, "What am I supposed to do?"

"With what exactly?"

"With my life," Laurence huffed, and his voice began to rise. "What am I supposed to do here, in this city? In Le-Varre, I'm a nobody. I'm an Ilvallum. How am I supposed to live my life in constant fear? Will I have a job? Will I hide away all day? How will I repay my debts to you and the Madame? Will I die in fear because I never learned how to live my life to the fullest? What will become of—?"

"Too many questions." Theresa cut him off, gathering her skirts to walk up the stairs. "If it makes you feel any better, I'm just as worried and confused as you are. You'll probably just end up working for Madame or a nearby shopkeeper that we can trust. Do you have any special talents?"

"Talent?" Laurence scoffed. "Just because my mother can do magic, doesn't mean I can."

Theresa attempted to suppress a laugh that bubbled up in her chest, but amused breaths escaped her anyways. Then she told him, "I wasn't asking whether or not you were a Tekhne. I was asking if you have any skills: pottery, cooking, painting, flower-arrangement, weaving."

"Oh, I can whittle a little," Laurence said plainly.

"A whittler," Theresa mused. "It's been a while since we've had one of those in the shop. You'd make a nice addition to the arts. Can you do anything else?"

"Pottery," he mumbled, "but I'm not very good at it. I only know the basics because our plates and bowls would break often. We had to improvise more than often. I can't cook, though."

"That's alright." Theresa smiled. They reached the top of the smooth, wooden steps.

"What do you do here?" Laurence asked as they moved slowly down this hall as well.

"I'm in Madame's service," Theresa responded, and nothing but gratitude coated her soft words. "I do chorework around the house and take care of her. It's a simple task, and Madame lets me sleep and eat here. She's even taught me tricks and things, given me trinkets. She refined my talents and raised me up. I owe her my life tenfold."

"Were you an orphan?" When Theresa paused, he took back his words immediately. "I'm terribly sorry. I've overstepped my boundaries."

"It's alright," she urged. "To be honest, I don't really remember. I lived by the Wall before I joined Madame. Besides that, everything else becomes muddled."

Theresa's movements halted and she opened up a faded door. The hinges squealed as she pushed it open all the way. Dust danced in the dim lighting, and Theresa fished around in her pocket for a match to light the lamp. The room's shadows shook ever so slightly as the little flame flickered. The walls were a soft rose and the floor was hardwood. A small bed sat next to the window, where curtains hung unmoving. There was a closet and a little table paired with a rickety-looking stool.

Laurence approached the window and stood in the shadows as he peered out of it. His lips parted in a silent gasp. West Le-Varre was always beautiful at night. It would seem he had been too preoccupied to notice the soft-glowing lights that probably made the town look like a complex constellation of stars from above.

"Does it always look like this?" Laurence wondered. "Every night?"

"Always," Theresa confirmed as he continued staring out in awe.

Laurence promptly broke out of his daze and gave her a slight bow before saying, "Thank you for the room. I can't thank you enough for your assistance."

"Think nothing of it," Theresa smiled. "I'm glad to have been of help. Well, I'll leave you to it. I'll come get you at six for dinner. Algernon says he'll be making soup tonight."

Laurence offered her a grateful look, though worry still tinted his gaze. "Thank you," he said as he glanced at the clock hanging on the wall and the empty vase on the table.

Without thinking, Theresa asked him, "Would you like flowers?"

"Oh, no," Laurence said with a shake of his head. "I wouldn't want to hassle anyone anymore and I—"

"No, really, I insist," Theresa pressed. Part of her was being a kind and gracious host, while the other part wanted to show off the new trick she learned. A knowing look formed on Laurence's face as he approached the table. He probably understood both halves of her that wanted to place flowers in the glass vase. He gestured down to the container with a curious grin, and Theresa perked up. She sat down on the stool, and it creaked quietly under her. She held out her hands around the mouth of the glass and closed her eyes in focus.

"You must imagine the flower blossoming," Madame said kindly. *"If you cannot see it, it will not work. Imagine it like a sun rising on the horizon and its light consuming the sky. The flower is the dawn. Envision it clearly. Only then will it work. Thankfully, you have a bright imagination."*

A dawn: a shimmer, that glows against the sky as it grows softer, letting you know the sun was going to climb its way into view: soft tangerine and dried roses and fields of golden wheat. It opened slowly, each warm petal falling into place, soft and cloud-like, orange and pink.

When Theresa opened her eyes, Laurence was crouching eye-level with the flowers. He looked up at her with a smile and said, "You can use blostmian magic."

"The only kind I can."

"They're beautiful. Peonies, right?"

"How'd you know?" Theresa asked, placing her hands in her lap.

"Outside the Wall, we don't get many flowers," Laurence told her wistfully with a look of reminiscent nostalgia on his face and tears in his eyes. "Wild ones, yes, but most of them were weeds. A friend of mine had a book he got from his aunt. It had all kinds of flowers in them. His name was Claude. He didn't make it through second spring."

"Oh," Theresa said, looking down at the table. "I'm sorry."

"Don't be," he shrugged. "That's always the roughest part of the year."

"If you don't mind my asking, what's 'second spring'?"

"It's, well, it's basically whenever the snow gets the worst," Laurence said, fumbling through his explanation. "There's this gnarled tree in the middle of our community. It's incredibly ancient, and I suppose you could say it's a centerpiece in our lives. When second spring comes round, red flowers blossom. It's beautiful against the snow, but we know better than to gawk for too long."

"What were the blossoms called?" Theresa wondered to him, and she realized something. Her fear had dissipated into a strange warmth. Laurence seemed less like an Ilvallum and more like a friend.

"Remisire."

"It sounds beautiful."

"It is," Laurence smiled sadly. Then an idea flashed before his eyes. "If the Wall ever gets torn down, or we're allowed to pass back and forth, I'll take you there as thanks. Then you can make the flowers whenever you feel like. I promise."

"I would like that," Theresa said, standing up from the stool and making her way to the door. "Get settled in. I'll come get you when dinner's ready."

◊◊◊◊◊◊◊◊◊◊◊◊◊◊◊◊

Laurence had become part of the household with ease. He worked hard, helped Madame out with the art workshops, and even did chores around the house. On top of that, he worked a part-time job at the bakery next door. The regulators hadn't given him a hard time, thankfully, and it put Theresa at ease to think that he would be safe for one more day. But he would always profusely thank her whenever he saw her, taking her hands into his and bowing. Today was a fine example of that.

"You don't know how much everything you've done means for me," Laurence said with shaky breaths and glazed-over brown eyes. Theresa realized now that they were more of a hazel. His curly hair was a disheveled mess.

"No, really," Theresa said. "It's alright."

"I'm so sorry."

"Why are you sorry? You've no reason to be."

"Thank you; I'm sorry," Laurence repeated. Then he would leave her alone with her muddled thoughts as her tea grew cold in its cup. Theresa sighed and went back to practicing her tricks. She felt bad for him. It must've been difficult to go through life in a strange city with odd people, and the thought of a wounded mother without his support would weigh down the shoulders of any one person.

Theresa let a soft exhale through her nose and closed her bright eyes. She wondered what Laurence thought about when he was alone as she let dreams tug at the ends of her mind and pull her along with them into sleep.

◊◊◊◊◊◊◊◊◊◊◊◊◊◊◊◊

Laurence laid in bed that night, staring at the ceiling above. The paint was peeling and cracking in some places, but it had become a familiar and calming view for him. The chatter of the luminous city reached his ears from the breeze that crept up through the slightly open windows. The curtains swayed from side to side here and there.

The flickering flame of the candle on his table had gone out hours ago: the fire was drowned out by the puddle of melted wax, and smoke rose up from the scorched wick like the soul of a corpse drifting away. Le-Varre, Laurence thought quietly to himself, was quite unlike the way Pierre had described it when they were younger. He always described it as dark and loud, as if the city was a home of death and grenades. Instead, Le-Varre seemed cordial and welcoming, even if it comes off as a little distant at first. The regulators hadn't been bothered by his presence yet, which put him at ease as it simultaneously set him on edge.

Drowsiness laid heavy on Laurence's eyelids as he recalled his late friend. Claude had been born inside the Wall, and then one day, he was outside Laurence's doorstep. "I ran away," Claude had said with a frown that told Laurence he hadn't really wanted to go, but it was for the best that he did. "I ran away, and I'm not going back. I can't. I won't."

All he had with him was a sack of clothes, worn-out shoes that were far too small, some stale bread, and a thick book that looked like it weighed the weight of worlds: like Atlas holding up the earth with nothing more than himself. His green eyes looked so dull, and Laurence decided that they would've looked brighter if he was happier. But when Claude opened the book up, his eyes were like glass beads on Mother's precious necklace.

Laurence had sat down next to him shyly beneath the big Remisire tree, nudging his knees against Claude's. They were both silent as cicadas buzzed throughout the air, and the heat was dreadful despite the shade. Laurence looked over his friend's shoulder and peered down at the gold-rimmed pages.

"It's a flower anthology," Claude said bashfully as red dusted his freckled cheeks and he kept his eyes trained hard on the ground. He handed Laurence the book as he tapped his foot against the grass. "You can read it if you want to. But you don't have to! It's only if you really want to."

"I'd like to read it, if you don't mind," Laurence said before Claude could open his mouth again to continue repeating himself. Claude burst into a smile as he tugged at his reddish curls and the tips of his ears were rosy. Laurence made a mental note that Claude's green eyes were *definitely* brighter when he was happy. It made him wonder whether or not Claude had ever had an actual friend before. As if Laurence's mind had been read, an answer was provided.

"You're really the first person who's ever been nice to me," Claude mumbled, but Laurence heard. "Don't get me wrong: Kathleen's been real nice too. It's just, you're more my age. So, could we be friends, right? You know, you and I?"

When Laurence had agreed with a grin, Claude's eyes were the brightest they had ever been and tears welled up and poured down his cheeks. It hurt Laurence's heart to think someone could be so happy just to have a friend.

Now Laurence was alone the way Claude had been, and part of him began to understand the loneliness that builds up over time and wrecks havoc on the mind like a glacier. His dark eyes zeroed in on a certain crack in the ceiling. Thinking about it, Laurence realized that was why he felt so indebted to Theresa. Not only had she helped him through his struggle of understanding Le-Varre and its workings, she had those same glassy eyes. When she was upset, they were dim. When she was smiling, they looked like they were held up to the sun in awe. When she cried, they looked submerged in a glass with moonlight dancing through the water solemnly.

Claude had had those eyes, in his naivete and honest gratitude.

The ceiling did not change in the time Laurence blankly stared up at it. The crevices stayed the same and the walls did not cave in on top of him. Silently, he rolled over and closed his dim eyes, though sleep did not come till morning.

◇◇◇◇◇◇◇◇◇◇◇

"Theresa, could you bring these up for Miss Llewelyn?" Algernon called gruffly from the kitchen as Theresa stood in the doorway. Algernon was a stout, clean-shaven man who always seemed to be frowning with those strikingly blue eyes that seemed to pierce whoever's soul was nearest. Madame had been something of an aunt to him, and now he worked in her service day in and day out.

"Of course," Theresa replied, casually taking a tray with a steaming pot of tea into her hands. She took in a deep breath of the wisps and smiled softly. *Rosemary,* she knew instinctively, *good for staying alert and calming shock.* She often wondered if Madame was feeling some weight that was invisible to the rest of them. Part of her knew that Madame was, but to blindly mend a tear in a cloth is futile.

Madame usually kept her door open. She said it made it easier for her to come and go. So when Theresa arrived and the door was shut, she didn't dare open it without knocking. She tapped the back of her hand against the smooth wood once, twice, three times. A soft, "Come in," resounded through the barrier, and only then did Theresa crack the door open.

"Good afternoon, dear," Madame mumbled, without turning away from the window. She was shivering. "Just place the tea on the table. You can close the door behind you."

Theresa was a stranger to the curt tone of such a kind voice, but obeyed nonetheless. Her feet were just about to exit when Madame asked a question, and this time, her voice was like snowflakes: "What would you do if you were as burdened as I, my dear?"

NOVEL WRITING

The young woman's hand faltered on the knob, and her knees felt like they were going to give in to the weight of the world. She made no effort to move, and neither did Madame. They were simply there, one to stay and one to go, trying to converse through a wall that was their experiences. Theresa's mouth opened to speak, but her lip trembled. The chill in the air burned her fingertips, and after a while, her hand was burning alive.

"I wouldn't know what to do," Theresa answered honestly, "but I know I wouldn't go through it alone."

"Neither would I," Madame sighed as Theresa shut the door behind her, "but sometimes even slight discrepancies can make all the difference, hm?"

Now, Madame Llewellyn was alone. It was a strange word: alone. It made her wonder, really, how long had she been alone? Was it when Kathleen fell in love? Was it when she left? Was it when a wall built up between her and those she loved, a wall made of formalities and due respect? When had she created this cage for herself?

She didn't have thoughts of doubt. Those had long since dissipated into thoughts of wonder, confusion, and an understanding that she would always feel that way. She closed her eyes of cloudy sea and she rose from her seat to take a cup of tea. The earth sat undisturbed as the world built itself up only to trip over it and thrust the blame on another.

Kathleen had come to this conclusion much sooner than Llewellyn. She had come running down the street and tossed pebbles at Llewllyn's window till she answered.

"Ellyn." Kathleen smiled with soft brown eyes that edged on hazel. "I've just met the kindest, handsomest man you'd ever meet. Come down! I'll tell you all about it."

She had gone down the steps and winded back around to the narrow alleyway where flower petals scattered the stone path. Kathleen awaited her with a red face and a book in her hands.

"So, who was it?" Llewellyn had whispered, as if they were plotting some fantastical plot to run away from the world and its secrets.

"Griffith," Kathleen responded with hushed words. "He comes from the outskirts of North Le-Varre. He's so *kind* and has this mysteriousness about him!"

"Kathleen," Llewellyn said as she pursed her lips. "The regulators might be checking him out. It's dangerous for someone like you to get too close to someone like that."

"Why, Ellyn?" she pressed. "He means no harm. Just because he's from the Northern outskirts doesn't mean he has affiliation to any Ilvallum."

"Just tread softly for me, alright?"

"For you, I will try," Kathleen smiled.

"Then tell me more about him! What does he look like? What's he like?"

"Oh, he's nothing like the boys here! He's honest and earnest, and I feel like he knows so much more than anyone can learn in a single lifetime. He's incredible and doesn't fear to speak his mind, but I know he has his secrets. And before you warn me, Ellyn, everyone has things they don't want others knowing. For all we know, he could simply be shy."

"He doesn't sound very shy to me," Llewellyn chided.

"He's not," Kathleen laughed, "but he is reserved at times. I think I might—"

"Llewellyn!" cried out a questioning call from the direction of the house. "Llewellyn? Are you in the gardens? Llewellyn!"

"You should hurry back," Kathleen urged. "It sounds like you are needed."

"It can wait," her friend said in return. "What were you going to say? You think you might what?"

"Another day, Ellyn," Kathleen said kindly with a laugh. "Now go, before I do!"

NOVEL WRITING

Llewellyn frowned but nodded anyway as she worked her way back. Kathleen waved, smiling as she walked away down the path which she had come from. That was not the last time she saw Kathleen, but it was the last time the two of them spoke alone.

Now she was the Madame of Ivor, and she would never again be sweetly called "Ellyn." The shouts from downstairs yanked at her sleeves and pulled her gaze away from the warm sunlight that felt cool as it dripped off her skin. She was no longer a child, and the thought of Kathleen alone and remembering her made that fact far more emboldened than it ought to be.

∞∞∞∞∞∞∞∞∞∞∞

"I'm sorry, but you can't just barge through here!" Theresa insisted as the regulator pushed past her like she was simply a veil of light. "Sir, please, do you even know where you are headed?"

Laurence fumbled down the stairs, clearly alarmed by all the noise, and his movements froze as he recognized the blackish-blue and silver embroidery of the hellish group that thought of themselves as the law. Except, a thread of fiery red had been laced through the design ominously and a bronze chain hung purposefully from his breast pocket. The regulator stopped at the foot of the steps and glared up at Laurence with a raised brow. Both men turned to Theresa who had astonished confusion and frustration painted across her flushed cheeks as she cried out for him to not go any further. The regulator promptly ignored her state and turned his back to her.

"The Madame will be in her room, no doubt," he sneered as he took to the stairs. Laurence stumbled out of his way and pressed himself to the wall. Fear had taken hold of his heart.

"What is *he* doing here?" Laurence asked in a whisper with wide eyes that watered softly. He looked as if he had been betrayed. His dread-filled eyes turned up the stairs where the regulator had gone.

Then Laurence repeated himself as he collapsed and stared heartbrokenly at Theresa. "What is he doing *here*?"

"I don't know," she replied, and her voice was even softer than his had been. "But you're safe here; I swear on my life, you're safe here. We wouldn't do anything to hurt you."

✧✧✧✧✧✧✧✧✧✧✧✧✧

The door eased itself open, and Madame Llewellyn did not turn her head to see who it was. She would recognize those steps from legions away during a storm at sea. A soft *click* told her that they were now alone in a shut room with no way out besides crashing out the window.

"Llewellyn," the regulator chuckled softly, and cruel amusement seeped far too deep into his voice. "I thought you were done harboring Ilvallums in the home of Ivor."

"There has never been one from outside the Wall in my home," Madame responded coolly. "And I assure you, Prospector, if there has been, it has come to pass without the knowledge of mine."

The regulator grinned at the use of his title rather than his name. In days long past, she would've softly called him by his given name. If the storms were longer than he could handle, she might've even slipped a "love" or two here and there. But those days grew long and they blinked away before he could grasp them fast enough. Now he was simply "Prospector."

"Well then, Madame." He pressed a stronger emphasis on her own title. "Let me be as brusque as you would have me. We *will* arrest the man who resides here, with or without your permission. He is an Ilvallum, is he not?"

"Algernon?" Madame quipped. "No, I do not think he is."

"The boy you call Laurence," the regulator corrected harshly.

"Oh, Laurence," Madame smiled. "He's a sweet boy. Quite the whittler. His creations more than often surpass that of your own."

"Impressive."

"Indeed."

"Just hand him over, Llewellyn," he sighed as he moved to stand in front of her. Her sharp eyes held a softer shade of the uniform he wore with pride, the uniform she never learned to approve of, the uniform she departed from him over. "This doesn't have to be difficult. We'll leave you alone. Your students, your house-members, and you will have the peace you seek."

"Including Laurence?" she hissed under her breath, standing up to look him in the eye.

"You've a long life ahead of you, Llewellyn," he answered with the same tone. "He is not your responsibility."

"He may as well be my son, Eugene." Madame huffed out his name in anger, his *given* name, the name no one had called him in a long time. "Because I will care for him as such."

"You are barely old enough to be his mother, unless under the oddest of circumstances in another time and place."

"Listen to yourself," Madame scowled. "You used to be sensible. He is not an Ilvallum, and he is not a threat to be worried over by the likes of the regulators, much less the West's Prospector."

"Don't throw everything you have away," he continued to insist. "You will be troubled no more if you simply give us the boy. I do not want to burn this house to the ground, but I will if I must."

"You will not take an innocent man from the safety of my home, Prospector," Madame said, turning away from him. His title took place on her lips once more.

"Have it your way." The regulator sneered the way he had been brought up to and exited the room without another word. His footsteps were heavy on the woodladen floors, and when he reached the first floor again, only Theresa stood there.

"Where is he?" the Prospector demanded.

"I do not know," she answered with a posture frigid with fear. He watched her eyes betray her as they glanced towards the front door.

"He has left," he glared. Then he turned back to her. "Tell your Madame that I will return if I must. I've no reason that inhibits me from such, and her will is no exception."

With that, his dark uniform and the bad omens that came with it left Ivor's home. Algernon stepped out of the shadows and patted the young girl's shoulder, silently telling her that she had done well. Laurence was taken out from the kitchen pantry, and he hurried up the stairs.

"Where will you go?" Theresa whispered as she followed at his heels. Laurence flung open the door to his room and pulled out the suitcase from under his bed. Theresa assisted him in gathering his clothes and neatly folding them despite the fact that they were short on time.

"I've spoken to Madame about this, just in case," Laurence said as he threw his items together.

"The North?" Theresa questioned, though she already knew.

"Yes," he replied, out of breath. His warm eyes met her own. They were more hazel now than brown. "That's where my father was from. There are people there: ones who speak of rioting and freedom, sympathizers who believe Ilvallums have done nothing wrong, even people who say there are grand cities past the Wall. Kingdoms, some say. Places that rival our own. I'll be safe if I go there."

Laurence's eyes stopped at the flowers in the vase. Their petals were dried out, and the water depleted. Then he turned to see Theresa's melancholic expression. She moved to take the flowers and place them upon the top of his packed-away clothes. Her hands shook as she handed him his hat, which he took graciously with a bitter smile.

"I wish you all the luck that can bestowed upon a single person," Theresa said, but her voice quivered into something softer than a breeze. He heard her nonetheless and took her hands into his. She could vividly feel the calluses on his fingertips, and only could she imagine how he got them: chopping wood for the fire, fixing up the roof of his home as his mother stood out and watched, climbing the great Remisire, whittling the figure of a bird, fighting the frost of second spring, gripping Claude's hand as his dear friend passed into a deep sleep.

"I still intend to make good on my promise," Laurence said in a tone that resembled reassurance, but it was tainted with the fear of many things he could not say out loud.

Theresa tore her eyes away from his kind ones and murmured, "I would hope so."

"I'll return. I promise."

She didn't bother to tell him to not make promises he couldn't keep for certain. She was too busy clinging to his words and telling herself that what he said was true, that he would return to her and hold her like this again.

"I'll wait for you."

"I would hope so," Laurence replied with a smile that did not reach his eyes. He brought up her hands and kissed them lightly, as if he were to apply any more pressure to her hands, she would disappear like a mirage in the middle of the night. "I really would hope so."

"They could come back any moment. Hurry away," Theresa urged, though there was no force behind her words and her voice was breaking at the thought of him obeying her command. He let go of her hands and she sat on the stool. Laurence locked his suitcase shut and carried it in his closed fist. Suddenly feeling cold, she wrapped her arms around herself.

"Thank the Madame and Algernon for me," he said with his back turned to her as he made for the door. "I owe them my life."

"I will."

"Farewell, Theresa," Laurence said clearly, lifting his eyes to the ceiling once more. It had not changed.

"Farewell." The door shut behind him without another word, and Theresa was infinitely grateful for it. She hadn't wanted to watch him leave, but part of her wanted to see him one last time. She ignored the ache in her chest as she went to make some tea of Madame Llewellyn. The days would grow longer and blink away before Theresa would be able to grasp them tightly enough.

◇◇◇◇◇◇◇◇◇◇◇◇◇

North Le-Varre differed greatly from the West. Snow crunched beneath Laurence's mud-caked shoes, and the slush of winter came up to his ankles at times. His unoccupied hand was buried deep within his pocket, searching for a warmth that seemed to be missing. The other shivered within the glove it wore. It almost felt like second spring.

"Worst winter in ages," grumbled a man who carried books in his arms. "If only the regulators would leave us alone, we could probably bear snow like this."

Laurence's eyes scoured the bare streets. The buildings were made of a gray stone, much unlike the warm cobblestone and bronze of the West. Instead, iron lined the sky. The only thing golden about this place was the rare sight of a candle burning in someone's window. The sounds of what sounded like shells exploding ricocheted off the walls from some distant area. A darkness loomed over the city, and despite the snow, he found the shadows were more prominent than the lack thereof. Claude's words echoed in his mind. It was dark and loud. The city was a home of death and grenades.

Madame had told him to flee North if the time ever arose, and he would have to seek the aid of a man named Cecil Blanche, not much older than Laurence himself. She told him to find the road of

Geoffrey and follow it down all the way until a steep path jutted off to the side. There he would find the entrance to a safe haven.

The road of Geoffrey was long, and something about it made the weather seem more frigid. It was more of an alleyway, Laurence came to realize as he shuffled past a rusting barrel. His eyes flew shut as an icy breeze sliced through his skin. The path that parted itself from the main one was even more narrow, even more ominous in the falling snow. He felt as though he was going to slip and fall onto the roof of one of the houses below as he crept higher.

"Who are you?" a voice colder than the air hissed from the shadows. Laurence's eyes darted around as his movements halted. He was at a small plateau now, right at the back door of a large house. It was well hidden, in Laurence's opinion, as he continued to glance at nooks and crannies.

"A friend," he responded vaguely. Whoever this person was, they very may well be a regulator who wishes only to send him away to the Gallows.

"Many backstabbing men come through here, only to claim they are the same." The voice was sharp, and Laurence thought to himself, that if he were to see this person, their eyes would be ice.

"I come from Madame Llewellyn Ivor," Laurence ventured. Then he took a leap of faith and lowered his voice to say, "I am an Ilvallum."

The voice emerged from behind a wall, and Laurence saw a man with hair the color of the rust he had seen on his way up the path. And his eyes were black, like daggers or a frozen lake waiting to drown its unsuspecting victims.

"We do not believe in the idea of Ilvallums," the man said with a slight nod. "You are a brother, then?"

"Of Cecil Blanche, I am," Laurence replied, suppressing the urge to turn tail and flee. The man nodded and went to the door, opening it without a care as if he owned the place. A golden light spilled out of the stone building, and it whispered salutations of welcome. His imposing eyes turned back to Laurence expectantly.

"If you are my brother, you have a home here," he offered with a ghost of a smile, but no emotion betrayed the man's heart as he walked in. Laurence hurried after him, desperate for the warmth the light portrayed.

"I'll be blunt," Blanche said as they stepped into an entryway filled with firewood. "North Le-Varre is nothing like the West, where our Madame resides. She fights for the same cause, but in a different way. Here, we wage war with not only our hearts, but our every action. We do not submit to the regulators, and vice versa. It is harsh here, cruel even at times. Will you be alright?"

His words felt like fell blows at Laurence's heart, but his tone was kind and gentle, as if Laurence was a frightened child. He might as well have been.

"Will you be alright?" Blanche said, handing the newcomer a mug of what smelled like tea. *Rosemary,* Laurence thought to himself, *good for staying alert and calming shock*. All that time spent with Theresa speaking of teas and flowers had not been for naught. He silently thanked her as he sipped the warm liquid. It tasted like comfort, and he remembered her favorite tea was rose-ginger.

"I'll be alright," Laurence said calmly, though his hands shook, "as long as we're fighting for something worth the war."

"It's worth it," Blanche said, and a wistful smile appeared on his face: the most emotion Laurence had seen of the man. "Trust me. It's worth it, alright."

<center>~~~~~~~~~~~~</center>

"Will he be alright?" Theresa inquired of the Madame, who sat at her easel after the long lessons she had provided to her students. The windows were thrust wide open, but the crickets' chirps and the rustling of the trees hid the sound of her voice from the rest of the world.

"Of course he will," Madame said without hesitation. She needn't ask who Theresa was asking about, and she needn't worry for him. He would be alright; he had the spirit of his mother.

"Do you think he'll return?" Theresa wondered, setting down the tea cup on the table and sighing at the view of the setting sun.

"He promised you, did he not?" Madame smiled as her brush stroked across the canvas.

"Promises can be broken."

"They become even more brittle if you lose faith in the promiser," she chastised.

"He said he'd take me to see his home," Theresa whispered, but she wasn't too sure whether or not Madame had heard. She had.

"Then have faith in him, my dear," Madame sighed, setting down her brush. "He is not the type to break promises." *Quite like his mother,* she thought reminiscently.

◇◇◇◇◇◇◇◇

The days had grown too long for Theresa's taste. She grasped the flowers budding in her palm with a smile that teetered on the edge between longing and despair. Perhaps it was simply both. Her steps were quiet against the hardwood floor, even quieter easing through the backdoor, and silent as she made her way through the gardens.

Then it was a blur. The bronze sun was warm on her skin. Besides that, everything else became muddled. A bit of stubble and unruly curls of brown hair. Shaky breaths and glazed-over brown eyes. Theresa realized now that they were more of a hazel. The flower is the dawn: a shimmer, that glows against the sky as it grows softer, letting you know the sun was going to climb its way into view: soft tangerine and dried roses and fields of golden wheat. It opened slowly, each warm petal falling into place, soft and cloud-like, orange and pink. His warm eyes met her own. They were more hazel now than brown. Was what he said true, that he would return to her and hold her like that again? He brought up her hands and kissed them lightly, as if he were to apply any more pressure to her hands, she would disappear like a mirage in the middle of the night.

Besides that, everything else became muddled.

"I still intend to make good on my promise."

"I would hope so."

POETRY

Honorable Mention

Eve Bishop, "You." Grade 9. Chadron Senior High School, Chadron, NE. Barb Waugh, Educator.

Eve Bishop, "Meaningless, Meaningless." Grade 9. Chadron Senior High School, Chadron, NE. Barb Waugh, Educator.

Anastasia Brock-Ondresky, "I Am the Earth." Grade 11. Boys Town High School, Boys Town, NE. Beth Sulley, Educator.

Allie Bunjer, "Excerpt 031922." Grade 11. Millard South High School, Omaha, NE. Tessa Adams, Educator.

Ana Carson, "This Town Restrains Me." Grade 10. Doniphan-Trumbull High School, Doniphan, NE. Stacey McCarty, Educator.

Rebecca Ford, "Fester." Grade 12. Freeman Public School, Adams, NE. Brett Sales, Educator.

Rebecca Ford, "Dead Men." Grade 12. Freeman Public School, Adams, NE. Brett Sales, Educator.

Grace Genoways, "I Am." Grade 12. Fort Calhoun Junior Senior High School, Fort Calhoun, NE. Sara Gross, Educator.

Haley Holzfaster, "That Chair." Grade 11. Paxton Consolidated School, Paxton, NE. Mary Vasquez, Educator.

Morgan Lahm, "Poetry Collection: A Love Not Forgone." Grade 12. Raymond Central Junior Senior High School, Raymond, NE. Jenna Winfrey, Educator.

Megan Lambert, "Leave or Be Left." Grade 12. Boys Town High School, Boys Town, NE. Beth Sulley, Educator.

Megan Lambert, "Time." Grade 12. Boys Town High School, Boys Town, NE. Beth Sulley, Educator.

Magnolia Moriarty, "The Overgrown Garden." Grade 9. Millard South High School, Omaha, NE. Amber Wormington, Educator.

If Words Were Poison

Vaishvika Balamurugan

Grade 11. Lincoln High School, Lincoln, NE.
Owen Roberts-Day, Educator.

i've prayed to every god in the world that one day i will know myself.
but no matter how strong the sentiment,
i'm still praying in a foreign language.
i'm still singing a song i don't know the words to,
still a ghost haunting a house where no one is home.
i'm still just masquerading as a girl who recognizes her own reflection.

because no matter how hard i fight reality,
i'm still the girl who hides in the bathroom—
when her dad is on a phone call back home.
home. i know a lot of words, but that one always escapes me,
along with every one i try to speak in the language i'm supposed to love.

i've always had a profound love for words, but these words,
the Tamil ones my grandparents speak from thousands of miles away—
well, these are the words that ruin me.
each one is another crack in my heart,
splintering and tearing and breaking me into eight thousand pieces,
one for every mile that makes it easier to forget who i am.
even with an ocean between us, language is still the biggest barrier.

what's the harm in talking?
the harm in talking is that i've never had enough to say.
and every time we do talk,
i'm left wondering whether they forget that i know what they're whispering,
or if they remember and *want* me to hear.

in *their* language, they tell each other the truth: *she doesn't understand anything.*
as if i'm not on the other end, listening. as if i can't translate every word.
i want to tell them there's a difference between knowing a language—
and being able to fluently speak it.
it's a common theme in all aspects of my life: i always understand,
but i can never seem to say anything back.
so i stay quiet. i let their words seep into my veins like venom.

what i do understand is that blood may be thicker than water,
but it is still no match for poison.
what i do understand is that you can love something without ever truly knowing it.
this is how my relatives love me.
this is how I love Tamil. this is how I love *home.*

my life in America has been a dance with denial,
and i have been skipping and tripping and slipping between the cracks.
the divide between who i am and who i'm meant to be is my one true home.
i *live* in the in-between.

POETRY

my fragmented ideas of India are just figments of a desperate imag-
    ination.
they exist only in the foggy parts of my mind,
walking the tightrope between memory and tragedy,
hoping not to slip into the gaping abyss below.
or perhaps, hoping to deny the fact that i have fallen already.
while i may not want to accept it, i've long since known the truth.

the truth is, you cannot call a place home when you've only gone
    twice on vacation.
the truth is, if acceptance was fire, i would burn just to know what
    it felt like.
not knowing is Hell turned over—yet sometimes, knowing is worse.
i also know that on its own, love is rarely enough.

if love was enough, then my family could do it all.
we could traverse mountain ranges and swim across oceans for each
    other in silence.
we could bridge the gap between knowing and believing,
between doing and dreaming, and we could do it quietly.
if love was enough, my family would hear me before i even said a
    word,
and i could stop holding my mother tongue.
but it's never been enough.

and i know love is stronger than a lot of things.
it is greater than anger, than sadness, than hate, even.
but it is nothing compared to fear.
and it may be thicker than water,
but it is still no match for poison.

Dear Men

Vaishvika Balamurugan

Grade 11. Lincoln High School, Lincoln, NE.
Owen Roberts-Day, Educator.

Dear men,
i bump against walls so you can pass me by in the hallways.
you'd run me over if i let you. isn't that funny?
i listen quietly as you shout every thought in your mind.
why do you speak over my voice like yours is inherently more
    important?
your screams ring in my ears,
like blaring car horns and scratchy policeman radios.
i compose symphonies with the words in my head,
yet you will never care to hear them.
you just yell, and there is no room left over for anything.

Dear men,
you walk a mile and to keep up i must run five hundred.
no amount of work will ever be enough. isn't that funny?
the world fills me up with an anger that i have never known before,
and i hate to admit it—
but i am tired.
a strong woman should never be tired.
yet i am choking on your kicked-up dust,
and i am tripping over all these hurdles,
and i am tired.

you tell me pain does not exist in a world that fills me up with it.
you tell me discrimination does not exist in a world that beats me
    blue with it.
we do not live in the same world, you and i.
to me, this is evident. to you, it's just a joke.
to you, *everything* is a joke, followed up with *isn't that funny?*

Dear men,
sometimes, my comfort exists only in the absence of you.
i heard once that men start wars just to touch each other,
to feel the connection that comes with shared struggle.
women are born with pain carved into our bones.
from creation we are taught what to be,
and everything we're not allowed to be.
you tell me i don't know who i am.
you tell me you know *exactly* who i am.

Dear men,
isn't it funny how i can hold this pain in my own two hands,
yet all i will ever be is a girl who *begs* to be believed?
well, i am tired of begging for anything.
i am tired of wearing these shoes that you could not walk a day in.
and you've looked through me for long enough that i began doubt-
    ing my own existence,
but no longer. i know exactly who i am, and i know what i am not.

i am not glass bones and paper skin.
i am not a doormat, not a punching bag, not a mirror.
i am a person, my *own* person.
i am a woman. i am strong *and* i am tired.
tired of stepping aside for you.
tired of laughing at the jokes you make at my expense,

at the expense of your girlfriend, your mom, your sister.
and *no*, it's not funny.

Dear men,
you tell me the struggles i've experienced are not real.
you tell me my *life* is not real because you have never lived it.
but i do not care if my problems do not exist in your world.
they exist in mine, so they exist.
i do not care if *i* don't exist in your world.
i exist in mine.

i exist.

I Hate the Word Was

Vaishvika Balamurugan

*Grade 11. Lincoln High School, Lincoln, NE.
Owen Roberts-Day, Educator.*

i hate the word *was*.
i hate it with a passion, yet i am doomed to feel it everywhere.

was is every tick of the hands on the clock, every second wasted,
every moment lost.
was is regret.
it is a wake up call, a crash course in growing up,
a lesson on the art of leaving until you know it like the back of your hand.
simply put, it's moving on. again and again and again.

was is time slipping. it exists in final goodbyes,
in fading footsteps on sidewalks with cracks you've never stepped on,
and will never get the chance to now.
was is hugging your mom before college.
was is a closed casket at a funeral, the dial tone on a telephone,
the last stroke of color in a darkening sky.

was is a reminder that time is flying and you are terrified of planes,
that your courage has never been greater than your fear.
was is remembering to forget.
it is self-erasure.
it is taking down posters, selling your first new old car,

getting rid of clothes, moving out,
starting over. it is a beginning and an end and—
everything. *was* is everything.

but the most haunting thing about *was* is that—
it's not everything you've never had.
that would be too simple.
you don't miss the things you've never had, not like you miss the
    things you did.
instead, *was* is everything you said goodbye to,
everything you walked away from.
the moments that turned into memories.

it is sheets over abandoned artwork and—
plywood boards nailed to doors that will never be opened again.
was is the dust settling on each passing moment of your life.
it is every page turning, every chapter ending.
it is every haunting echo, every distant shadow.

was is every bit of longing for what you once had,
and all the pain of knowing you will never have it again.

BLAME

KATIE BOUGH

Grade 11. Northwest High School, Grand Island, NE.
Darbie Mazour, Educator.

I am the mistress in your storybook, no? The tempter, the tease,
The image of mankind's insatiable greed
The living likeness of human nature's unappeasable appetite for sin
Lusty and loathed
You gorge yourself
Growing more gluttonous and guilty with every gulp
You drink in my picturesque resemblance of your darkest desires
Drug up to the surface
To be stretched taut and toyed with
Guilty all the more that you like what you see, no matter how pure
    you pretend to be
And you can't help it
You claim
In an attempt to shrug off your fair share of blame
You feast, you feast
Upon my flesh
Like the body and blood of that Christ you so readily exalt, yet in
    comparison—although sewn with similarities—I am an evil,
    an imp, an unrighteous yet unignorable evidence of all that you
    find desirable, yet disgraceful. Seductive, yet scandalous. Fanta-
    sizing, yet forbidden.
You blame me for a crime it takes two to commit.
Take it upon yourself to point the finger of the hand, which later
    lays on the bible,

Yet you must admit it's undeniable, no matter how hard you try to
    delude yourself otherwise—it was the both of us, two together,
    who took part in this sinful sodomy
Have you forgotten your part in this play?
You do not get to claim innocence and brand my soul as sinful
    when both our hands are stained with soot
A silent slithering, shimmering serpent
The devil in unadulterated form
I am the stray sin you stumble over in the night
Slinking across your path
Do you sleep soundly?
Knowing your heart is just as sullied as mine?
Of course, I am the one who bears it openly. While you deny and
    disguise yours in outward honor. So which of us does sin make
    stronger?
That is the singularity that lies between you and me
I will not admit that I am what I am not
As you so earnestly engage in doing
You play the game on both sides
Unaware that you are losing
As the angel fell from heaven,
I will rise up again, my sweet
To dance this dance, upon the hand, of sinful sodomy

Frozen Summer

Gabrielle Burns

Grade 9. Millard North High School, Omaha, NE.
Marie Severin, Educator.

Those hot summer days,
When the trees stop their sways;
When the world holds its breath ceasing the winds blow,
Creating nervous anticipation that intensifies the sun's glow.
Memories of cool spring days coated with dew,
Have risen to air and changed to humid glue.

Time moves slower with the rising degrees;
Summer took inspiration from Winter's freeze;
But instead of freezing rivers, and letting snow cover grass;
It seems to slow hours and not let time pass.
They say time flies but if time were a fly,
Was it simply caught in a web as it was passing by?

I have so much I want to do before I am done;
Though they aren't completed in these moments stuck by sun.
Should I be grateful for these breaks,
And dread when the world reawakes?
Is it time to savor, or time to stall?
Does it depend on how we decide to view it all?
Should I love these times when the clock ticks are caught?
Or is it that time moves forward but I do not?

Hope and Chance

Gabrielle Burns

Grade 9. Millard North High School, Omaha, NE.
Marie Severin, Educator.

Chance—is a fire,
That burns like a star;
To give warmth or desire,
Or to leave a scar.

Hope—is a phoenix,
To rise from ash;
A soul rising from onyx,
That no one can abash.

Fiery Chance and the phoenix of Hope.
Together they dangerously dance;
They spin upon the steepest slope;
When it seems perilous—they prance.

It takes two to tango they say;
Chance and Hope light the sky aflame.
When they leave people in dismay;
No one knows which to blame.

Like embers they flutter;
Until light fades leaving ash and debris.
They touch one with the mutter
Of the lone word "maybe."

OVERDOSE

ANA CARSON

Grade 10. Doniphan-Trumbull High School, Doniphan, NE. Stacey McCarty, Educator.

We were never meant for each other
I know that
You know that
Hell the whole town knows it
You were destined for so much more
You shouldn't have to fix what you didn't break
You didn't break me
I was already cracking in the womb
Me and you have different paths in life
But why then
Why did your touch feel so natural
It felt as though your hands were meant to connect with me
Most feel sparks the first time their love touches them,
But me
I felt at home
Every little touch
Made up for every hardship in my life
It shouldn't have felt that way
Two people who were made for separate paths
Weren't even meant to encounter each other in the first place
So please explain to me
How those 10 minutes felt more like home than my house ever did
And why am I craving your touch for a hint of normality

I'm addicted to a drug I can't have
You're my morphine
I think I might just overdose

Homage

Rebekah Daily

Grade 10. Home School, North Platte, NE.
Jeannette Daily, Educator.

to Jacob & Wilhelm Grimm:
In the shadowed darkness lay
The Princess of a fallen day.
The world had long since passed her by;
To all its creatures, she had died.

The Knave had ne'er heard the song
Of the Princess lain so long
In the palace—silent, cold—
By the Faerie feared of old.

He felt the ancient spell work near,
An odd sensation, thick and queer.
Unfamiliar to the stripling Knave,
An unsuspecting kiss he gave.

Roiling darkness then broke loose,
Thickly twisting a deadly noose.
He drew his sword—"A useless tool,"
The Faerie hissed, "you brave, young fool."

Her evil sorc'ry lashed him fast
To the Princess, woke at last.

The Knave's defense, ever meager;
The Faerie's wrath: boiling, eager.

The Princess no compunction spent
On the spitting words she lent
To the boy's unweathered ear:
"You never should have come so near!

"As I laid dormant, so did she.
I gave my life protecting thee!"
The Knave went pale; he hadn't known,
Naive and young and barely grown.

The Faerie Queen began a spell,
If bluff it was she had no tell.
The Princess said a desperate prayer,
The Knave clung fast to every care.

With unknown pow'r the chamber shook.
The Faerie's wrath—No! horses' hooves.
Cavalry stormed the cursèd room
The Knight who led them pushing through.

His silver blade with iron inlaid
Morbid hope and fear it bade.
He flung his gauntlet to the stones,
A challenge to her evil throne.

The Faerie smiled with silent pride
At what she saw: an easy prize.
The change was fast and near unseen—
A nightmare rose from Faerie Queen.

The Knight, unaltered swung his sword,
A hiss from Faerie Queen it forced.
She pinned the Knight against the ground;
His fate, it seemed, a burial mound.

The Princess wept in desperate tone,
"My love, for thee, the sun's not shone!
For thee I slept one hundred years!
For thee I'll cry one thousand tears!"

The Knave was touched unto his soul,
Her passion!—guileless, pure, and full—
She loved the Knight, the boy now knew,
It gave him purpose, a job to do.

He drew his sword, took careful aim—
And knew at once, 'twas not a game—
With courage fit for twice a knave,
Threw his sword!—and fainted dead away.

The Knave awoke as Knight looked on,
Princess weeping, Faerie gone.
"I know I have but you to thank,"
The Knight proclaimed, "but I'll be frank.

"'Twas luck alone that saved my life,
But luck you have, I'll not deny.
You guarded my endangered soul
And barred e'en death's untimely toll.

"'Tis with my debt I leave for you
Advice to use at trials new:

In coldest fear or battles hot,
Meet strange young maids, and kiss them not."

to Shel Silverstein:
A prize, a prize
I've won a prize!
The others passed me,
Four, five, six,
And then, to my dismay,
I tripped!
And yet
I pulled it all together.
Picked up my feet,
Light as a feather!
I've won a prize,
A prize, a prize:
A most deserved,
Darn-hard earned,
Consolation prize.

to Louisa May Alcott:
Poetry doesn't count.
    No climax
    No drama
    No horrid
      Awful
    Commas.
    Just words
  And thoughts
In literary knots.

to Ralph Waldo Emerson:
The best things
Are much too big
To understand.
Is song
But sound?
Is paint
But color?
Is clay
But earth?
All unakin to one another?
The best things
Are much too big
To understand.
They reach beyond our flawed, belittling sight,
And bring to earth celestial, radiant light,
That shines upon our human arts,
Turning brushstrokes into stars,
Slip and clay to molten gold,
Fluted notes to stories told.
Aren't the best things,
Much too big
To understand?

Food for Thought

Rebecca Ford

Grade 12. Freeman Public School, Adams, NE.
Brett Sales, Educator.

Here's some food for thought
To nibble while you starve
Ruminate while you hunger
Leave your stomach carved

Let thoughts fill your belly
And nonsense fill your brain
Feast on enlightenment
And fast through the pain

In starvation insanity
Find yourself some clarity
Go on, take a bite
Of abstract delight

Don't think, just consume,
Foresight is great, try common sense too
Wear your skin and bones as a troph
You're thin as a rail but divine and holy

The pen's mightier than the sword
So write it down and record
Your demise from conscious starvation
But with wisdom as your salvation

They'll lower you to your grave
But rest easy knowing you were saved
Mentally satiated and eternally wise
Forget your body, the psyche's the prize

ROADTRIP

Rebecca Ford

Grade 12. Freeman Public School, Adams, NE.
Brett Sales, Educator.

It is hot and smoky and dry
It stings our eyes and makes us cry
Hazy water illusions a lie
This is our limbo when we die

Shriveled scrubland grass and skeletal leaves
Bow and rattle in the blasted breeze
Sun-bleached bones urge unease
Hell-sent omens beckon disease

It smells of asphalt and dust
The air stirs still without a gust
The sun corrupts a metal beetle's hollow husk
We shuttle on because we must

The skeletons in our closet rattle beside us
Memories of sin not to discuss
But eons of age forge forgotten trust
And amnesiac forgetfulness disguises disgust

Yellow plains and infinite prairie
Prompt me infinitely wary
Trapped in a truck with skeletons I cannot bury
A man-made mass grave, a transport cemetery

I hurtle down an interminable freeway
Atoning without night, at the height of the day
My skin will shrivel and gray, my hair thin and fray
And I will join my skeletons in the truck that we all lay.

Hyacinth

Rebecca Ford

Grade 12. Freeman Public School, Adams, NE.
Brett Sales, Educator.

Cry your anguish to the moon
Sob into the sky 'til Artemis sobs too
With your effortless, mournful drive
The hopeful devastation that brought Typhoeus to life

The rawness in your throat and the tremor in your chest
Are alive and fluttering like the toil of unrest
Slamming into the bronze like a mortal who loved
Like a rabid dog, chasing that loss

When that honeyed heat spilled from a lover
From a fallen love to never recover
The ground quivered with the sweetness of the crime—
And the bloodsoaken sorrow, driving blooms from the fists of the divine

Blossoms feast on thick spilled grief and blood
Hyacinths blooming around that grave in the mud
You cage your body over a form that is broken and mortal and raw
There is no honeycomb sweetness to the ichor that drips from your jaw

You tragic, terrible thing
Grief is a selfish song, yet you sing

Disregard fate for your human desire
Drive those spikes into the ground and sound the choir

Beautiful Things

Megan Lambert

*Grade 12. Boys Town High School, Boys Town, NE.
Beth Sulley, Educator.*

when i was little
i used to watch the sun set across the african mountains
i'd sit by the window and take in the colors
and marvel at the orange, red, and pink contouring the sky perfectly
my mama used to come behind me
and rest her soft hands on my shoulders and say
*baby, beautiful things can come
from something going away*
i remember that now
as i watch the sun set across the american plains
*mama, beautiful things can come
even though we are half a world away*
i find comfort in the stars
knowing that they are the same ones you see
and that when the sun sets here
it's rising where you are
and even though we're apart
i know we couldn't be closer
because i am a part of you
and you are a part of me
and beautiful things did happen
despite me going away

ODE TO THE DUST AND TO DUSK

Magnolia Moriarty

Grade 9. Millard South High School, Omaha, NE.
Amber Wormington, Educator.

The sun rises for an audience of nobody,
Like honey
Seeping out of the bear-shaped bottle,
And landing in my tea.
She paints the clouds with textures,
Her favorite shades of amber
I open my window wide
To observe the view.
There is skin that has been set free
Since the last time you held me.
Turned to dust
Being held in the sun's rays.
Around me, they swell,
Happy to be held,
While I sip my honey tea.
Just as always.
The moon rises above my homestead,
Smooth as a child's sled
On a beautiful
    snowy hill.
She holds the light
As street lamps ignite,
Creating an ominous yellow glow
On the fading amber sky.

I close my dusty blinds,
But not before stopping to find
The smallest insects on our planet.
Gratefully they dance in the lamp's glow.
They have come out of their homes,
Happy to dance in the lamp's glow
While I close my window.
Just as always.

Salmon Going Downstream

Magnolia Moriarty

*Grade 9. Millard South High School, Omaha, NE.
Amber Wormington, Educator.*

The other day I got a scratch on my wrist.
I don't know how, but when I found it
I was reminded of all the shit
This achy breaky poet's heart had to wordlessly deal with.
And all that I dealt with
To get rid of it.
Plip—
Plop—
Pitter—
Patter—
Tap/Tap/Tap
The other day I couldn't put food to my lips.
Maybe I'm just sick.
I have no time to panic.
I need to be realistic and realize
That just because I didn't eat once,
Doesn't mean this is who I become.

But out of instinct
I still hold my breath.
Even if I'm okay now I know that
At any moment
The world could throw me back to the sea
Like a fisher setting his prey free.

I need this breath
To save my life.
I need this breath to show myself
That my self-esteem
Must stay as high as the tide
To keep me alive.

Like the salmon going against the stream,
I cannot stop my heartbeat,
Paralyze my bloodstream,
I cannot get ahead of myself yet,
Let my self-esteem
Become the drought.
Plip—
Plop—
Pitter—
Patter—
Tap/Tap/Tap
This river floods
Like an overflowing cup.
With water falling
Over the rim, like rain
Falling on fish as they swim.
Plip—
Plop—
Pitter—
Patter—
Tap/Tap/Tap
And I guess
it always seemed fishy,
How there were so many fish in the sea.
When their blood

is thicker than this flood that is holding them.
Plip—
Plop—
Pitter—
Patter—
Tap—
Blood is thicker than water.
When salmon only have
70 milliliters of blood, worth more
Then the expansive oceans of white water
They have traveled upriver.
Plip—
A salmon only sells for 700 bells
in Animal Crossing New Horizons.
And when you catch him,
The saltwater on his back gleams,
And you're told, "it's only going upstream."
Plop—
How do you expect
These salmon to keep going upstream,
When all of their blood has been sold?
The blood that costs more than the
Expansive waters they've crossed.
Pitter—
How do you expect
These salmon to keep going upstream,
When there are
Thousands of fish with the same splatter?
This one doesn't matter.
Patter—
How do you expect
These salmon to keep going upstream,

When every time a boat passes overhead,
They fill their small lungs with despair
And hold their air?
Tip—
How can I keep holding my breath?
Tip—
How can my self-esteem stay as high as this tide?
Tip—
How are we supposed to reach the end?
I need those fish
To reach the end.
I need to reach the end.
I need to realize that something I can never again be
Is a salmon going with the stream.

I Aspire to Inspire

Katelyn Omer

Grade 8. Peter Kiewit Middle School, Omaha, NE.
Cari Guthrie, Megan Root, Educators.

Dear Humanity
The troubles that tear us apart
can be removed so we can move
into a future so bright,
filled with freedom, love, and light.
If we come together
we'll become one people,
the kind of people who're kind
and understand we've been blind,
but now we see
when we focus on unity
we become a stronger humanity.
Imagine all of us
working to get there
together;
building trust
as we build ourselves up
and help others rise,
open eyes to the possibility
of a better humanity.
If we all strive to be our best self
With no thought to hatred or wealth,
we can all have a place

in creating a humanity full
of wisdom, respect, and grace.
Dear humanity,
let us accept the fact
that acceptance is key.
Let us reach out in love,
so we can rise above
the challenges ahead.
Let us not just face those trials,
but embrace them with bravery!
We can overcome anything
When we come together every time.
I'm honored to be a part of thee,
My dear humanity.

Heroine

You're a heroine in a story,
a bold beautiful benevolent girl
in a wicked whirlwind world full of worry.
Adventure is waiting, though you may not see it.
What then? Oh, our heroine, you must go and be it.
Climb that mountain, see all that lay beyond.
Do not doubt, though there's no doubt, your journey will be hard
    and long.
Go, have hope, though you will face trials, cruel enemies, and scorn.
For it's in adversity stronger spirits are born.
You are just as capable as the fictional women you admire.
Never stop to turn your dreams into reality aspire.
You will fall, but do not be afraid.
It is not a final fate unless you fail to have faith
that you can get up again, call for a little aid.
Every heroine has side characters, even you

on your journey will find friends
that will help you save the world until your story ends.
Do not be dreading the last page,
but dream about how your next story will start.
Your adventures are timeless, not forgotten by age.
Your story will always resonate in my heart.
The best part? You're not just the heroine, you're the author.
No one else can control where your story goes.
Maybe there are things about you no reader knows.
Don't listen to your enemies, they can't decide what you do.
Oh our dear heroine, the only person who can do that is you.
Your fans await with bated breath,
every action, every step.
They love and encourage you to keep going until the end,
then pick up your pen and write again.

Begin Speaking
Words are so much more than words on a shelf.
They are how we connect with things greater than ourselves.
If you don't believe me,
write a bit of truth and see.
Using your voice is a choice
that will be life-changing.
Words don't fade with age.
Once written on this page,
they will stay strong,
create bonds between beings,
cause the change we want to be seeing
in life.
Words testify.
They transform,
form the future,

which goes from yours to ours.
If you don't know what's right,
write.
If you have a choice,
use your voice.
If you are seeking,
begin speaking.

Stained Glass Art
Life
is
making
stained
glass
art

Our
hearts
break
we
take
the
scattered
pieces
of all
different
colors

You
may
not
see

any
symmetry

There's
no
perfection
but
still
beauty

Everything
makes
sense
when
there's
light

So
don't
hide
your
broken
pieces

Every
color
was
meant
to
be

Keep
breaking
creating
waiting
for
light

Today
Maybe you think one must be naive to believe
in better things for this falling world.
So be it.

Maybe you think I'm just a little girl who likes to rhyme
in poems that aren't worth the time
it takes to read 'em.

But I just wanted to say
that today,
hope is light
without cost.
Believing is seeing beyond
all we've lost,
and it's worth it
every day.

We will all make mistakes.
It's whether we give more than we take
that matters
in the end.

Maybe you think you'll never see the light,
that you're set to lose every fight
in this life.

Maybe you think I can never understand
where you stand and what you've gone through.
That's probably true.

But I just wanted to say
that today,
we are here
to wipe away a tear
or if your fear
keeps you on the ground,
we will be around
to help.
You will be found
and you never have to
be by yourself.

We all fall,
but after that comes the flight,
and that's what matters
in the end.

Dramatic Script

Honorable Mention

Semhar Hailesellassie, Grade 12. LPS Arts & Humanities Focus Program, Lincoln, NE. Maggie Elsener, Sally Hunt, Educators.

CRITICAL ESSAY

LOST IN TRANSLATION
The Perils of Displaying Aquatic Life

CALVIN SNYDER

Grade 11. Brownell Talbot School, Omaha, NE.
Matt Low, Educator.

Most animals are relatively easy to contain. With a fence and enough determination, a group of people could conceivably corral anything from horses and cows to lions and elephants into a pen wherein they can be viewed, stored, or killed. However, aquatic life has shown itself much more difficult to contain for extended periods of time, let alone display. This makes the investment in both time and money significant when building something like an aquarium. Because of the larger commitments needed to house them, the expectations surrounding sea life are equally elevated. Unlike a giraffe enclosure, where the limitations of an outdoor enclosure for large animals are accounted for in the viewer's mind; accommodations being made for both the factors of perspective and weather. The controlled environment of an aquarium allows for an easier suspension of disbelief. They facilitate anticipation by removing the need for the tunnel vision that would otherwise force someone to ignore the sight of rhinos from the butterfly house window. However, because these expectations are contextualized by how they are viewed, it stands to reason that they could be dashed. If essayist John Berger is to be believed, then not only is disappointment at the zoo possible, it is inevitable. In his seminal work, "Why Look at Animals," Berger asserts the idea that people are playing God by recontextualising the lives of these animals within a zoo and that, in turn, creates the disappointment fundamental to the zoo going experience. His feelings are similarly acknowledged by actual visitors of real aquariums, in the writings of humorist David Sedaris, and the video game *Subnautica*. By looking at the worlds we construct for aquatic animals and their shortcomings, it is possible to shed light on the truth. Not only do people love playing God, but in this effort we are grossly inadequate, consistently failing to recapture the majesty of what we try to preserve.

There are three things that can be seen immediately upon entering the Henry Doorly Zoo's Scott aquarium: a large shark prop hanging from the ceiling, a tank of the aquarium's less interesting fish, and a wall listing all the donors responsible for funding the building's construction and maintenance. This room exists to serve only one purpose: to attempt to stem the tide of disappointment that zoos inevitably create. The ethos of the room exists in the fish shaped plaques that advertise the building's donors. The wall they adorn promises that despite Nebraska being the most landlocked state/province on the North American continent, there exists ample capacity for exotic sealife. The pathos of the room comes from the decorative shark that hangs from the ceiling. The shark offers the same promise as the donors, only both more tangible and more deceiving, giving a physical representation of the promised animals. The shark makes a promise without need to base itself on either logic or reputation, bypassing those factors by appealing to the sense of wonder that large animals induce. However, the deception of the shark comes into play with its size. The shark seen at the entrance is very large, dominating the initial view of the aquarium entrance. This view of the shark as a figure of awesome power is then brought into sharp contrast by the aquarium's centerpiece, a large exhibit featuring sea turtles, rays, and a few small feeder sharks. These sharks can be seen as emblematic of the great disappointment of the modern aquarium. Not only are they smaller than the promised shark, but they are docile. The general disinterest by the sharks with eating those close to them contradicts the monolithic view of the shark as the bloodthirsty movie monsters seen in *Jaws* or *The Meg*. This view is what the shark at the entrance appeals to: not the reality of the aquarium, but the skewed viewpoint of its visitors.

While the pathos of the room can be seen as in a state of conflict, the great contradiction inherent to the modern zoo-going experience is embodied most in the fish. In order to understand why the placement of these fish is significant, the architecture of the aquarium must first be used as a vector for storytelling. Like most forms of entertainment, the buildings in the Henry Doorly Zoo follow a dramatic curve, with the relative grandeur of the exhibits creating the story. Because there is only one way to walk through the building, the average zoogoer must travel through an open, tropical room into a darker room showing more alien fish, then into a tunnel that intersects the large tank where the sharks are held. By viewing the aquarium's linear path as the desired trajectory, the opening room is then recontextualised as something resembling a prologue and the gift shop as an epilogue where with any luck, viewers will not realize the manufactured quality of their experience and will buy something to commemorate their journey. By putting a relatively small tank of gray, visually plain fish in the first room of the aquarium, those who planned its layout degrade the lives of these fish via presenting them as a preamble to something more interesting. This reduces their lives to mere plot points, living their lives in service to a story that they are not privy to. The logos of the room can be seen in the fact that they are presented as an introduction, their worth being based on their exoticism and color, features which are both lacking. Because the fish are both uninteresting and presented as a preamble to seemingly more interesting fish, that inherently frames the lives of these fish as less than their more tropical counterparts. With its promises of large and exciting fish, the disappointment elicited from the actual contents of the aquarium is inevitable. This creates the effect of not only degrading the fish seen at the entrance to the aquarium, but building up a promise of excitement that can only be broken by a relatively mundane reality.

Keeping the use of design as a medium for storytelling in mind, "Loggerheads" from David Sedaris' *Let's Explore Diabetes with Owls* can serve as a companion piece to the design of the zoo. In "Loggerheads," Sedaris recounts his youth growing up in the suburbs of Raleigh, North Carolina. While on vacation, Sedaris, alongside a childhood friend, captures loggerhead sea turtles and keeps them captive in their homes. He then feeds the baby turtles raw ground beef until they all eventually die. Alone, this story is entertaining. It explores the logical ramifications of a common childhood fantasy of befriending and taming wild animals. However, Sedaris chooses to intersperse his recollections with related stories and these stories work together to build a common theme. The theme that binds "Loggerheads" together is loss of innocence with two smaller stories featured in "Loggerheads" underpinning the combined narrative. In the first story, Sedaris is researching his Turtles when he uses the bathroom in his town's library. "I remember that in the basement there were two restrooms, one marked 'Men' and the other marked 'Gentlemen'" (Sedaris 65). By opting to use the gentlemen's restroom, Sedaris inadvertently encountered two men having sex. This event prompted feelings of guilt in Sedaris, who felt guilty for "recognising" (Sedaris 66) indecency in what these men were doing. He cites this recognition and undue guilt as an early indication of his homosexuality, which he presents as a cause of great pain for much of his adolescence. This only compounds with the loss of innocence that the death of his turtles brought to Sedaris. The second story centers around Sedaris' friend Shaun, whose father dies near the end of the story. When talking to his friends, Shaun universally gives the cause of his father's death as the vague notion that "His heart stopped beating" (Sedaris 69). Eighteen years later, Sedaris broaches the subject once again with his mother, who tells him that "his father essentially drank himself to death" (Sedaris 70). The loss of innocence that Sedaris captures is unique in the fact that it is not his own; while most of his work is autobiographical nonfiction, this deviates from what is expected. Sedaris actively has his innocence preserved by Shaun, whose innocence has been shattered. The thing that drives home the intentional placement of these stories is that none of them is strictly necessary to tell the central narrative about sea turtles. While either one could have been omitted without repercussions for the narrative, the themes would have been obliterated. Unlike the architects of the Henry Doorly Zoo, Sedaris seems to agree with Berger on the futility of holding animals in captivity. Herein lies the primary difference between Sedaris and the Zoo: the zoo is playing god and frames it as adventurous while Sedaris tries to play god and frames it as traumatic.

Unlike the essay, the barrier to creating a video game is very high. The cost is immense, and talent in many disparate fields is a necessity. From programmers to writers, a good game needs everyone involved working together towards a common goal. With this in mind, the indie game *Subnautica* is in many ways a triumph. The game managed to create a unique world with engaging gameplay and story, all while successfully creating a feeling of being underwater when playing and for a relatively low budget of $13 million. For comparison, the game *The Legend of Zelda: Breath of the Wild* has a similar reputation for quality and was given a budget roughly eight times that of *Subnautica*. And while the developers of *Subnautica* were able to make very effective use of their budget, there's only so much an inexperienced team of people can do, regardless of money. Because of this budgetary constriction, the game's story was shaped to fit its design philosophy. Due to the choice not to procedurally generate their world, the vast underwater map of *Subnautica* was limited to roughly twelve square miles, with a sharp drop off into an underwater abyss and intimidating underwater goliaths to discourage the player from leaving. Much like *Loggerheads* and *Why Look at Animals*, *Subnautica* is a game about the aftereffects of unwanted human interaction with animals. In the world of *Subnautica*, humanity has spread across the universe, with corporations spearheading new expeditions for human habitation and resource extraction. The player-character is aboard a mission headed by the corporation Alterra when their ship crashes onto the only habitable part of an almost entirely underwater planet. By the time the player arrives on the planet via the now crashed ship Aurora, an infection has spread throughout most of the planet, killing most of the native life forms. The already small amount of available land left for the remaining inhabitants of the planet is further diminished by the massive footprint of the Aurora, with the irradiated crash zone taking up nearly twenty percent of the map. Those voyaging on the Aurora come to this planet with the purpose of colonization and exploitation, as seen by the habitat building tools and mining equipment brought aboard the Aurora. To progress the game's story, the player needs to actively colonize the planet by building bases and ships using the resources accessible on the planet. This removes player agency surrounding the issue of colonialism by forcing the player to reshape the world around them for the purpose of survival.

Despite sharing the theme of disastrous human interaction with both the works of Berger and Sedaris, the design of *Subnautica*'s creatures serves an almost antithetical purpose, with both interaction and containment of these animals being a near impossibility. Among the planet's most intimidating enemies are the Ghost Leviathans. They inhabit the deepest oceans of the game and are actively hostile to the player character. Ghost Leviathans are massive, can phase through the player's structures and like all leviathan class organisms in the game, are not meant to be killed, only avoided. Due to their utter hostility, these animals cannot be contained and therefore exist as antithetical to Berger's idea of marginalization. They resist becoming *"something that has been rendered absolutely marginal"* (Berger 271). Alongside nearly all other leviathans, they recontextualise every situation they are involved with, forcing the player to keep their presence at the forefront of their decision making. Their design reflects their center-stage presence, with a snakelike body and a head reminiscent of a hammerhead shark. These attributes combine with their translucent appearance to create an apex predator that fundamentally resists marginalization. Despite exhibiting varying levels of danger to the player, all the animals in *Subnautica* share some level of wish fulfillment by their grandiose designs. From the small and bug-eyed peeper to the mushroom dwelling crab snakes, every creature that *Subnautica* has to offer is made with the express purpose of resisting marginalization and satiating the player's innate need for the engagement that zoos cannot provide. The only creature in the game that is not antithetical to Berger's view of zoos is the aptly named Cutefish, which instead serves to vindicate people like David Sedaris, as the fish is meant to be befriended. In effect, *Subnautica* rebukes both Berger and Sedaris just as much as it agrees with them.

 The last time I visited the Monterey Bay Aquarium in California I heard an interesting story. I was with my grandmother at the aquarium's primary showpiece, the open sea exhibit, when a man started talking to me and my grandmother about the exhibit's missing sea turtles. He told us that there used to be large sea turtles in the exhibit, however, they were removed after they ate away the tiling that surrounded the glass window they were enclosed in. Later, when I looked up this event, I found that it never happened. Despite its lack of truth, the idea of this story as a fabrication may be more interesting than if it was true. The original interpretation of the story is nearly parabolic, with the price for humanity's hubris being paid in ceramic tile. But viewing this line of thinking as rationalization rather than reality works very well with Berger's tie between zoos and disappointment. This man was easily able to convince others that rather than the sea turtles at the exhibit being less than was anticipated, they were instead far too interesting to be held captive and requisitely ejected from the aquarium. Through his eyes a dramatized version of *Subnautica*'s ideas played out, with the turtles simply being too wild to live in captivity. However, the reality is much less interesting as the turtles are still there, lying in wait for more hamburger meat.

Work Cited

Berger, John. *Selected Essays: John Berger.* Edited by Geoff Dyer, Vintage International, 2001, pp. 259–74.

Sedaris, David. *Let's Explore Diabetes with Owls.* Back Bay Books, 23 Apr. 2013.

Subnautica. Directed by Charlie Cleveland, Unknown Worlds Entertainment, 16 Dec. 2016.

Sex Ed and *Roe v. Wade*

Charlie Yale

Grade 11. Central High School, Omaha, NE.
Jonathan Flanagan, Educator.

For students at Central High School in Omaha, Nebraska, it's commonplace to graduate without ever stepping foot into a sex education class. It seems like a no-brainer: skip a "useless" class and free up space for an elective or a more rigorous honors class. Who wouldn't want to escape the awkward sex talks and banana condom demonstrations with their health teacher?

But there's a problem with this mindset. After the overturning of *Roe v. Wade*, especially in states like Nebraska where republican supermajorities are looking to ban abortion, sex ed is more important than ever.

Sex ed and/or HIV/AIDS prevention programs are required in 39 states plus DC. But, only 17 of these states require sex ed to be "medically accurate," according to the Guttmacher Institute.

That term is as vague as it sounds. It doesn't specify the content of the course, except for the fact that the educational material must be supported by "the weight of research conducted in compliance with accepted scientific methods," according to a sample piece of legislation from the Public Leadership Institute.

Five of the ten states with the highest teen pregnancy rates don't mandate any sex ed, as reported by World Population Review. All ten are poised to ban or limit abortion in some capacity.

That means one thing: the U.S. needs comprehensive sex education for all students, post-*Roe*, to limit teenage pregnancy.

The US is notoriously bad at sex ed. A University of Georgia study titled "Abstinence-Only Education and Teen Pregnancy Rates" reported that out of the 35 most developed nations, the US ranks first in teen pregnancy and sexually transmitted infections—primarily because of a lack of contraceptive use compared to the other nations in the study. But, a comprehensive, community-based and mandatory sex ed curriculum nationwide will be more effective at preventing teen pregnancy and STIs, especially for African American and Hispanic individuals in their teenage years, as stated in the *Morbidity and Mortality Weekly Report,* a CDC publication.

It has been proven many times that comprehensive sex ed is better at preventing teen pregnancy than abstinence-only programs or situations where sex ed isn't mandated. A Washington University study found that teens who received comprehensive sex ed were 60 percent less likely to get pregnant or impregnate someone than teens who received no sex ed and 30 percent less likely than their peers who received abstinence-only sex ed. This, in turn, reduces the amount of abortions that are needed by teens in the US.

SIECUS, a sex ed advocacy group, reports that 18 states don't mandate sex ed. Nebraska, where I live, is one of them. While my school does offer a sex ed curriculum, students have the option to opt out of it entirely. Because I wanted to take an elective that I missed when we went remote due to the pandemic, I was one of the students who opted out of sex ed.

But learning how to be sexually literate is a basic component of being a young adult in today's world. I should not have been able to opt out of sex ed as easily as I was able to; it is a class that holds equal importance to any other class a student takes during high school. But, unlike other classes, sex ed remains separate because the consequences of a bad sex ed system can be detrimental, and sometimes, permanent.

The structure and premise of high school is to prepare young adults for the real world. There is almost nothing more "real world" than becoming sexually literate, especially in a time where the reproductive rights of those with uteruses have been taken away.

Abortion is a valuable family planning method. Sex ed is important and it will always remain important because family planning is always relevant. Denying abortions to people who need them creates a larger risk of experiencing poverty and job loss, possibly increases levels of abuse and raises rates of single parenthood, according to a study at the University of California San Francisco. An article published in *American Journal of Public Health* goes as far as saying that "Laws that restrict access to abortion may result in worsened economic outcomes for women."

The main opponent to a complete and comprehensive sex ed curriculum in the United States is the same group celebrating the overturning of *Roe*: the religious right.

Both sex ed and abortion have been marker issues for the religious right for over 60 years, according to People for the American Way and *The Guardian*. It is ironic that the religious right chooses to make these contradictory stances their primary issues. If conservatives wanted to limit teen pregnancy, and therefore abortions, they would teach comprehensive sex ed.

The right to abortion and a comprehensive sex ed shouldn't be a trade-off; but to support abortion bans and neglect comprehensive and accessible sex ed is completely contradictory.

Some states have excellent templates for comprehensive sex ed. California, Vermont, and other states such as Maine, Illinois, Oregon and Washington all offer mandated sex ed, HIV/STI training, comprehensive healthy relationship training and contraceptive coverage. Some of these states still fall short; some are still neutral toward LGBTQ+ people, and not as inclusive as they ought to be. But it is a start.

Neglecting sex ed for queer youth is incredibly consequential. AIDS United reports that LGBTQ+ youth are at a higher risk of HIV infection, particularly "youth of color and transgender youth." The National School Climate Survey shows that neglecting queer youth increases school absence and rates of depression while decreasing overall GPAs, self-esteem and "connection to the school community." The path to fix schools for queer youth begins with an inclusive sex ed curriculum.

Sex ed helps to increase queer visibility, normalization and acceptance within schools. The Human Rights Campaign reports that the stigmatization or overlooking of queer children in sex ed standards "contributes to hostile school environments and places LGBTQ youth at increased risk for negative sexual health outcomes."

It is impossible to create a "one size fits all" program for the whole country. But all factors point towards the need for every single state to adopt a comprehensive sex ed program.

We need to do this for our youth. We need comprehensive sex ed for our loved ones who've received abortion care. We need comprehensive sex ed for my great-great grandmother, Elinor, a sex ed advocate for young women who had undergone abortions in the 1920s. This is for the future of our nation.

References

"Abstinence-only education states 2022." World Population Review, 2022, https://worldpopulationreview.com/state-rankings/abstinence-only-education-states.

"A call to action: LBGTQ youth need inclusive sex education." Human Rights Campaign Foundation, May 2021, https://www.hrc.org/resources/a-call-to-action-lgbtq-youth-need-inclusive-sex-education

"Comprehensive sex education might reduce teen pregnancies." Newswise, 13 Mar 2008, https://www.newswise.com/articles/comprehensive-sex-education-might-reduce-teen-pregnancies

Foster, D. G., Biggs, M. A., Ralph, L., Gerdts, C., Roberts, S., Glymour, M. M. Socioeconomic outcomes of women who receive and women who are denied wanted abortions in the United States. American Journal of Public Health. 2018,108(3):407-413. doi: 10.2105/AJPH.2017.304247. PMID: 29345993.

Greytak, E., Palmer, N., Boesen, M. "The 2011 National School Climate Survey: The experiences of lesbian, gay, bisexual and transgender youth in our nation's schools." GLSEN, 2012, https://www.academia.edu/2536128/The_2011_National_School_Climate_Survey_The_experiences_of_lesbian_gay_bisexual_and_transgender_youth_in_our_nation_s_schools

"The harms of denying a woman a wanted abortion: Findings from the Turnaway Study." Advancing New Standards in Reproductive Health, 2020, https://www.ansirh.org/sites/default/files/publications/files/the_harms_of_denying_a_woman_a_wanted_abortion_4-16-2020.pdf

Kosciw, J. G., Greytak, E. A., Palmer, N. A. Reduced disparities in birth rates among teens aged 15–19 years—United States, 2006–2007 and 2013–2014. Morbidity and Mortality Weekly Report. 2016,65(16):409-14. doi: 10.15585/mmwr.mm6516a1. PMID: 27124706.

"Medically-Accurate Sex Education Act." Public Leadership Institute, 2013, https://publicleadershipinstitute.org/model-bills/reproductive-rights/medically-accurate-sex-education-act/.

"Sex and HIV Education." Guttmacher Institute, 1 Nov. 2022, https://www.guttmacher.org/state-policy/explore/sex-and-hiv-education#:~:text=30%20states%20and%20DC%20mandate,appropriate%20for%20the%20students'%20age

Stanger-Hall KF, Hall DW. Abstinence-only education and teen pregnancy rates: why we need comprehensive sex education in the U.S. PLoS One. 2011;6(10):e24658. doi: 10.1371/journal.pone.0024658. Epub 2011 Oct 14. PMID: 22022362; PMCID: PMC3194801.

Stewart, K. "How the Christian right took over the judiciary and changed America." The Guardian, 25 June 2022, https://www.theguardian.com/world/2022/jun/25/roe-v-wade-abortion-christian-right-america

"Teaching fear: The religious right's campaign against sexuality education." People for the American Way, Sep 1996, https://www.pfaw.org/report/teaching-fear-the-religious-rights-campaign-against-sexuality-education/

"2022 Sex ed state law and policy chart." SIECUS, 2022. https://siecus.org/resources/2022-sex-ed-state-law-and-policy-chart/

PERSONAL ESSAY & MEMOIR

Honorable Mention

Megan Lambert, "Origin Story." Grade 12. Boys Town High School, Boys Town, NE. Beth Sulley, Educator.

Calvin Snyder, "The Final Broadcast of Paul Furgison." Grade 11. Brownell Talbot School, Omaha, NE. Matt Low, Educator.

Logan Sylliaasen, "The Girl Who Fell in Love with Stories." Bishop Neumann Central High School, Wahoo, NE. Marisa Grady, Educator.

The Power of a Relationship with Yourself

Jalyssa Caldwell

Grade 10. Northwest High School, Grand Island, NE.
Natalie Starostka, Educator.

Why can't She look like Her? Why can't She have longer legs or ribs that take up less space? Those things are immutable. She knew that. She becomes incensed and castigates herself until She can no longer feel the pain of not being Her. Until She can no longer stand and look herself in the eye. Until She can no longer see through the burning tears She has brought upon herself. Caught in excruciating grief that She cannot be Her, She is glued to the inconsolable thought that She will never be good enough for herself. In public, She smiles to unfamiliar faces, as a dismal attempt to make herself feel better. In public, She uses others as a deterrent from thoughts She tries to keep hidden. But She cannot. She has become obsessed. She is obsessed with Her, stopping to examine herself in every reflective surface She passes. Many times, She does not want to look, but She cannot help it. She inspects the imperfections of herself, comparing them to those of others and wondering once more why She can't look like Her. When She gets home, She studies herself one last time, awarding herself harsh temerity before simply preparing to do it all over again the next day. Yet, She does nothing to change it because in some way She is satisfied with herself.

From the Point of View of "Her"
She will never look like me. She has shoulders that are too broad and a face that is too round. She will have to contort and extract bones to

look like me. She will never look like me; it's an Irrefutable fact. She is different from Her. I am Her, yet we are not the same. We have mismatched complexions and mismatched lives. I am beautiful, affable, and well-liked. She is not. I am poised and polished. She is the opposite. I have unmatched confidence, and I am fervent towards what I believe in. Others emulate me and many want to be me, but She will never reach me. She will never be able to see herself in the way I see myself. She will never be able to think of herself innocuously unlike me. She finds it imperative to be like me but she will not concede to the idea of change.

From the Point of View of the Mirror

She does look like Her. Nothing needs to be changed or contorted to fit the unrealistic expectations that no real human could ever reach. She accepts the derision in the form of lies and slander She receives from herself. Truly, She shines like an iridescent stained glass window hit by the sun. She is full of great placidity and aptitude. She is incomparable to Her. She is better than the idea of Her. She casts negativity onto herself that She does not deserve. I am hurt each time she passes by me and ignores the beauty of her own reflection. I am nonplussed each time beleaguering words about herself are dispensed from her straight, white teeth. However, I say "herself" because I have realized something more. I have come to realize that She is Her, and they are in fact, the same person.

Stained Glass

Rebecca Ford

Grade 12. Freeman Public School, Adams, NE.
Brett Sales, Educator.

I have always been made of glass. Beautiful, colored glass. Ugly, clouded panes. Crystal that refracts the light into a thousand shapes. I am made of glass, and everyone else I know is a mural, each pane a memory or characteristic or lesson, every shard something unique or congruent.

Everyone I knew was a mural of stained glass, and I wanted to copy their mosaics.

In 4th grade, I would flap my hands when I was excited. Or stressed. Or afraid. Or whenever I felt a strong emotion. It was a relief to express the tension from the buildup of emotion. To hear the tinkle of colliding glass fragments, like crystal windchimes.

In 4th grade, I was standing in line for lunch. The cafeteria was cold, beckoning goosebumps and frosting each pane, and the air was thick with the scent of boiled broccoli. The fluorescent lights washed out the area in a watery glow, reflecting off the tile. The sunlight from the door reflected brighter, blinding, brilliant. The volume of the lunchtime conversations was almost too loud, wildly distracting, and wildly exciting, and I had just received incredible news; we were having a cookie with lunch. As a 4th grader, this was the best news I could have received, so of course I flapped my hands, bounced on the balls of my feet, exclaimed my enthusiasm to my friends. The clatter of crystal rang in my head. Another classmate stared at me.

"What are you doing? Stop it, you're being autistic, you weirdo. Only Seth does that."

I don't have autism, but Seth, a boy a grade below us, did. And whenever he felt a strong emotion, he flapped his hands too, and I'm sure whatever panes of glass or crystal he had twinkled and glittered too.

Every child tried to break his glass, destroy the panes that made him different. There was no greater crime than the crime of failing to align oneself with the impossible standards of everyone else. Seth was thus a criminal, and his sentence was social ostracization and otherwise solitude. The silent decay of vitric in isolation. They were cruel to that boy, and anyone like him. It was found in Seth's solitude at lunch. It was in the threats and insults hurled at him when no one would hear. It was the constant slew of toxicity, from any student, from any grade.

"Little autistic bitch." Perhaps it was a snicker in the hallway, a shove in class.

"Stupid fucking retard." It was snarled, a lash of irritation.

"God, don't talk to him. He's incompetent." A quick summary. Straightforward. Exasperated.

"Don't be autistic." A warning.

"You're being autistic." An observation.

"Stop being autistic." A threat.

They hounded him like wolves, and I was desperate to escape their snapping jaws. I never knew 'autistic' or 'autism' to be anything but a slur, the gravest insult. I never knew it to be anything but bad, and I was desperate to be normal and accepted. I was desperate to copy their mosaics.

I slowly lowered my hands, and slowly flakes broke off, decaying in winter sunlight and fluorescents. They glittered in the air like suspended snowflakes, and slowly fluttered down in larger and larger fragments until entire crystals broke away and shattered on the floor. I turned away and let the chatter of the cafeteria fill my ears. I didn't flap my hands again. They were too fragile, then, to clang together and make their lovely windchime song, so I instead shoved them into my pockets, and I fell silent. God forbid I be lumped in with the "others." The freakshows. Kids were cruel. We were cruel.

It was still freezing in the cafeteria, with brilliant sunshine reflecting off the tile, reflecting off glass. I shattered a pane that encased a chamber of my heart. It had still been soft and warm, malleable from the glassblowing heat of youth. Something brittle and grey replaced it, etched with spiderweb veins and the skeletal fingers of an elementary winter. In 6th grade, I would hold my sister's hand. I always did, even before 4th grade, when we first started going to public school. I always held her hand, because why wouldn't I? I loved her. I went with her everywhere, holding her hand. We were each other's moral support. She struggled with navigating the school, so I walked with her. I was clingy, so she walked with me. In 6th grade, I was walking with my sister to one of our classes. Our hands were pentagons of pale pink glass, her fingers prongs of still-glowing crystal while mine were rough stumps, and sometimes I thought our digits to fuse together, each of us a part of the other. I swung her hand and bounced a little, grinning as I made my way down the hall. I was stopped by a few classmates.

"Why are you holding her hand? That's weird. It's like you love her."

I did. I said that I do. I was confused. I didn't understand what I was doing wrong. Which standard I failed to conform to.

"No, it's like you, LOVE love her. Are you guys going to get married? That's so gross, you guys are sisters."

I was embarrassed, suddenly awkward and ashamed that I held her hand. What a shameful display. I gave her hand a little squeeze, but a few shards of glass broke off and fell away.

I still held her hand often. Through the halls, as we left classes. Still, we got comments.

"That's weird."

"Are you guys lesbians?"

"That's actually gross. Imagine holding hands."

What a crime.

We held hands. I held her hand tight. I never let go until I once let her hand drop from mine. I let her hand go and didn't hold it again. I didn't want to be made fun of anymore. Kids were cruel. We were cruel. The glass of my palms ground down, powdery and fine. I snapped off my crystal stumps and left fragile wire in the ragged planes. In junior high, I wore t-shirts and shorts. Everyone did. I was always cold. But in junior high, I was wearing a T- shirt. I started to receive comments.

"Do you eat?" Curious.

"Are you anorexic or something?" Concerned.

"Dude, you're so thin. I could literally, like, snap you in half, y'know?" Taunting.

"Oh my God, your wrists are so little, they're like toothpicks. I could just crack you over my knee." Derisive.

"Who's that flat, fuckin' alien girl over there?"

That one hurt.

I started wearing sweatshirts. I covered up. I wore sweaters in June, and jeans in July. I didn't take pictures and I didn't look at them. I couldn't stop looking in mirrors, but I felt sick seeing my reflection. Carefully, I tinkered away at the glass on my extremities. I removed each fragment with tweezers, took a blowtorch to the stubborn shards, and I melted the glass into something wicked and sharp. I slotted in different shades of stained glass, and some of it was wild with a bubbled pattern, with angry and jagged lines and breaks, and sometimes it was dark, deep red, sometimes it was dark and muddy, sometimes it was pale and ghostly, but never a lovely shade.

My senior year, I was in class. I'd grown into my stature. I was thin, still, in that way that makes one wish that heroin chic came back in style, but I no longer felt shameful. Senior year, I stopped receiving comments about my weight, and I thrived in the absence. I had started to replace those ugly, cracked panes I had from years ago, lovingly tinkering away at the awful to create something lovely. Everyone had forgotten about that awkward, gangly phase of a youth growing into her height. All but one.

"Do you remember when everyone used to think you were anorexic?"

I did.

"They literally talked about it all the time, behind your back."

Few comments were made to my face, but I figured as much: people always talked.

"You don't actually have an eating disorder, do you?"

I don't. This is just what I look like.

Someone made a comment, about how eating disorders can kill.

"She's not that far along yet."

I was no longer insecure enough to be hurt. Rather, I was indignant, outraged, and the glass I had lovingly, tirelessly replaced was melting down my forearms and trickling down my spine, molten from a pyre in my chest. Why would someone say that? What drives someone to reach so deeply, to root out the deepest insecurities and expose them, just to hurt?

Kids were cruel; it was normal, surely, to retain every bad habit and every insult ever received, to base my identity on it and resign myself to my lot. I continue to retain these habits, so deeply instilled in me. I contain my emotions. I shy from touch. My arms are always feeling too exposed. But as glass can be wicked and sharp, it can be beautiful and lovely as well. I remember the hurtful things I've been told, but likewise recall the kindness I've been shown and the loving things I've been told.

"Oh, dear, your hair is so pretty."

I'd been working my shift at my job, letting an older woman into the fitting room. I shied from the compliment, smiling, hot in the face. She sighed ruefully.

"It isn't fair. You're so fortunate to have such beautiful hair." The woman had smiled, melancholic and bittersweet before disappearing behind the door. And so, I keep my hair long, glass threads that captured the light and reflected it, golden brilliance.

"Your hands are so lovely." It was many years ago my mother had told me this, and I was no older than nine. She clicked her tongue and shook her head.

"If you grew your nails out—they would be so pretty, honey."

So, I grew my nails long, taking care when cutting and trimming them. Like icicles, they became delicate and beautiful, daggers of glass with frail beauty.

"Do you work here?"

I did, and I smiled and nodded at the woman as I rushed to help her.

"Really? I was just looking around and I was just taken aback: you're very pretty! Now, if you could help me find the pharmacy ..."

And as I change my parts for other people, I take parts of them as well. I click my nails together as my mother does. I amble aimlessly when brushing my teeth or speaking on the phone like my father. I laugh like my sister. I write like a hundred nameless faces across the continent. I shake my head to clear hair out of my face, even when there is none, like a boy I used to know. I take on the speaking cadence of my friends, families, associates. I copy these small pieces and slide them into place. I take these habits and make them fit.

I am a mosaic of every hurtful comment, every compliment, and every insult. Bad habits linger with me as fissures in the panes, as does someone's kindness and encouragement—a strengthening element, staining the glass something brilliant. I have been cruel, and others have been cruel in return. I am stained glass, and pieces of others color the panes. I am a sum of my parts and more, and I am a sum of everyone else's parts. I am a mosaic of everyone I love and hate, people I've never known. I am stained glass, and my pieces have been broken or cracked or melted by others, and in the same way, I have taken pieces from others and cherished them.

    I am made of stained glass, and I am a mosaic of everyone I know.

Silvermist

Hannah Tang

Grade 11. East High School, Lincoln, NE.
Sarah Staples-Farmer, Educator.

Like the average first grader, I had a peculiar lunchtime routine.

At 11:24 am, the echo of the school bell pervaded the air. The sound was my cue to plant myself in the center of the cafeteria, where the warmth of my classmates embraced me. The envelope of bodies simultaneously shielded me from the glare of bullies. I then made a dramatic display of opening my American cheese Lunchables, an effort to eradicate the *chow mein* effluvium from my breath. At recess, I pranced around the playground with my friends. Our monkey-bar calloused hands held sticks we envisioned as magical wands. Tiptoeing out of our teacher's peripheral vision, my girlfriends found solace under a maple tree. Solace was, however, not the only reason for our gathering. The day's agenda was momentous: each girl would receive the fictional fairy she was to play-pretend.

The ceremony began with a clandestine deliberation among last year's fairies. The former fairies flitted away to a faraway fence. I studied the discussion intently. Their faces were as clear as nebulous blobs, but I remained undeterred. Never once did my eyes glance away—I prayed for a divulgence of their sentiments. After several minutes of surveillance, I had no interpretation of their stoic expressions. Deciphering their gestures proved similarly inconclusive. Limbs swirled in secrecy, arms flew in stupefaction, and palms concealed thinly-veiled anger for seemingly no reason. My ears too joined my investigation. To my dismay, the fairies' voices were shrouded by the wind's whispers, obscured by our classmates' chatter, fell silent on fascinated ears. I could only hypothesize the words dancing off their tongues. At last, the former fairies seemed to reach a consensus. Their return to the maple tree quelled my unease. The newly appointed fairy leader, Carla, flung torn pieces of notebook paper around the fairy circle.

"On the count of three, open your papers."

"3." I traced the ragged edge of the slip with my finger.

"2." My breath shallowed.

"1." The air swelled with the synchronic sound of papers pulled taut.

Almost instantly, a cacophony of squeals overwhelmed my ears. Only my cheer was not among them. I was relegated to the fairy no other girl wished for: Silvermist. Silvermist's only remarkable quality was her icy blue gown, for she possessed no other qualities the other fairies could remark of. Even her eye-severing dress could not overshadow her dreadful character. In Pixie Hollow films, she was often silent and dispirited. I perceived her as an obscene excuse for a fantasy's fairy, a pitiful onlooker of all the other fairies fraternizing. Now, she was me.

"Are you okay?" Carla asked, blue eyes in bewilderment. "You're supposed to be happy, silly."

Oh goodness, I sighed. *Pretty please don't ask me what's wrong.*

"Disappointed with the fairy you got?"

"Yeah."

"Be realistic. Silvermist's the only fairy that you look like. Her narrow eyes and dark hair are just like yours." Carla toyed with a strand of my black hair. "Nothing will change that."

My initial apprehension materialized into actuality. Was I as insignificant as Silvermist's minuscule eyes? Was my fate icy isolation from my vivacious counterparts? Was I solely the sapphire-clothed subordinate?

I did not grace Carla with a response.

Silvermist, I contemplated. *The subservient fairy who tolerated everything.* Witnessing Silvermist's reticence infuriated me. She held the same standing as all of the other fairies. Despite her status, she seldom spoke. I did not want to be coerced into her same quietness. I dreamt of being outspoken like Carla or revered like the senior fairies. Even being recognized as somebody beyond Silvermist would suffice. Silvermist served as an incessant reminder of my place: I didn't have one.

In the following weeks, my attachment to Silvermist assailed my self-worth.

Perhaps Silvermist's superficial characteristics would liberate me from having to play heir, I pondered.

I colored my tresses with neon pink hair chalk, concealing the black that lay beneath. I conditioned myself to resent her slit eyes. Thanks to the discovery of my mother's cosmetic collection, I began implementing makeup into my morning routine. I smeared black pencil eyeliner on the periphery of my eyes, reinventing them to be round. In hindsight, I looked more like a raccoon.

As the school year continued, the frilly pink skirts, identical pigtails, and Twinkle Toe sneakers became my disguise. These guileless garments served a far more conniving role: they became my facade to conform. Each time I ran out to the playground, I carried the guilt of a knowing naivete, a perforated pretense, a conviction-filled incredulity.

For my eighth birthday, my mother promised me an American Girl doll. I sat criss-cross applesauce on the living room rug, absent-mindedly flipping through the doll catalog. I chose Marie-Grace, whose caramel curls and hazel eyes entranced me.

"Really? You don't want one that looks like you?" my mother questioned. She shook her head in confusion, as if she could not fathom spending one hundred dollars on a gravely inaccurate replica of her daughter.

"No," I insisted. To my mother's chagrin, I wallow in denial. Denial of her genetics, denial of her heritage. Still, I held firm. "It doesn't look like the ones the other girls have. It wouldn't even be an *American* girl doll."

Seeing my mother's disheartened expression, I did not proceed further. However, what I told my mother only scratched the surface of my self-doubts. American meant pure, pale flesh. American meant Carla's blue eyes; American meant Marie-Grace's dirty blonde ringlets. Despite any amount of persistence, their captivating characteristics could never be mine. Owning an American Girl doll was the closest I could ever get to being American.

While my mother's compliance initially seemed to be a blessing, it was a curse in disguise. My marionette served as my masquerade. I forced myself to mirror Marie-Grace's exterior. I caked on pink blush to obscure my yellow skin, in fear of my classmates' yellow peril. I concealed my monolithic monolids, drawing a shaky crease to separate my single eyelid into two. Marie-Grace stood atop my bookshelf, her hazel eyes casting a glare at my fraudulent face. Though I wished to escape her tormenting eyes, it was those very blue eyes that I wished to have.

"Your face looks like a pancake, like it got run over," my classmate pointed out to thirteen-year-old me, his face contorting with an uncanny look of disgust.

Even my existence is a discordance, a clash of dissonant chords to a musician. Yet, the reverberations only make their way to my ears, because no one glances up from their phones. Although my classmate did not lay a finger upon me, my face was still kneaded like dough. The homogenizing pan grilled, shaped, and splattered my facial features—and my exhausted spirit was the sole witness.

The comments will cease. So I encouraged. *The day my pancake face would too fit the cookie cutter.*

An eternity passed. Despondent in the gravity of my silence, I giggled to compensate for my speechless state. I regained my calculated composure, plastered on an unaffected smile, and subconsciously traced the bridge of my nose with my fingertip. I would have rather his words been a scalpel, performing a rhinoplasty. At least then I would get beauty from my pain.

Bile rose to my throat. I pushed it down. Guilt accompanied the bile. That was certainly harder to ignore. Nausea seemed like an appropriate price for my moral debt: I hid my indignance and humiliation. His "pancake face" insult only proliferated because I remained silent. Again. Though I could hardly blame my classmate for his contempt. By tolerating thinly-veiled racial ridicule, the uncanny valley stare was not foreign to me. First and foremost, *I* perceived myself as less than human.

The same night, I peered into my bathroom mirror. In the fashion of a seance, every instance where my past self was a bystander—and a betrayer—surfaced. Emotions as innocent and insignificant as insecurity transformed into something far less benign, far less easily dismissed. Insecurity proliferated into infidelity to my family, my culture, and most importantly, myself.

I am an infidel because my features are too youthful, too provocative, too striking, too inconspicuous, too dissenting, too accepting. My eyebrows are too thick, uncomfortable, and unworthy of taking up space. My Silvermist eyes are so narrow that I almost see my first-grade friends' narrow-minded worldview through them. My fat cheeks never allowed me to swallow my cultural regrets.

I still do not know if being assigned Silvermist was an enchanted accident or a mythical malice. When I drive past the maple tree, glance at the Silvermist costume hanging limp in my closet, and flip through elementary school yearbook pictures, my self-doubt of being seen as Silvermist still churns. Ridding myself of such diffidence remains a journey in progress. Yet, through acknowledging and addressing my insecurity, I have found the sliver of silver in the mist.

BOOM! THE SOUND OF HELL CHOSUN CONSTRUCTING TO ITS DOOM

DANIEL YOO

Grade 8. Scott Middle School, Lincoln, NE.
Kimberly Ridder, Educator.

"We all Have the Right to be Rich!" proclaimed a banking commercial's chipper voice that blared across my grandmother's living room in Seoul, the capital of South Korea.

It left a bitter aftertaste in my TV experience and a resentful sigh escaped my mouth as the ever-evolving channel had already begun another round of delusional advertisements.

Those eight words seemed to be mocking young people's struggle. Many young South Koreans, including me, call our nation "Hell Chosun." Drawing parallels to Chosun, an old Korean kingdom dominated by feudalism that had simultaneously made advancements in science, technology, and the arts, to young men and women cheated out of a chance at a better life our country is simply "Hell," where "bumo jal matnanda," meeting wealthy and influential parents, is the key to survival. Once, forever ago, following the Korean War, South Korea was a land of opportunity, where hard work and effort were met by success and impressive upward mobility with access to a life that their parents only dreamed of, hence the name "A dragon that came out of the humble ditch." Many South Koreans in our parents' and grandparents' generations, including my father, are those dragons that fiercely climbed their way out of the oppressing ditch of poverty. South Korea truly was a place that provided a better life for anyone that was willing to invest in dedication and determination.

But not anymore.

In the 21st century, things have gotten impossible for those of us in South Korea. A model of hard work gave way to an abusive educational system, where endless labor at expensive tutoring sessions is a must to even have a shot at getting into even an average, low-key university. Then, per academic elitism, your degree goes to govern your life forever, a label that wholly represents who you are, disregarding the fact that you are much more than your diploma.

Living in wealthy areas of the capital city Seoul, like the world-famous Gangnam District, has somehow become impossible without "meeting good parents," in terms of their wealth and influence, not their character or love. Somehow over the course of its rapid economic development, South Korea degenerated to a nation that judges its parents by their financial abilities, a country that came to call itself "Hell" and became the foundation of many sarcastic twists to famous sayings, with one exemplar denouncing success as 99% corruption and 1% talent.

Those were the things that were on my mind on our first trip back to South Korea for summer vacation after moving to the United States four years ago. I was exhausted from my life, one of running continuously toward the promise of a better life in the United States that never seemed to be happening. The aftermath of the sprint, which I had temporarily paused in favor of a visit back home, conveyed a gloomy future and made my family wonder if it was a mistake to move to the United States. I felt like a desperate, naive teenager that idolized the United States without even knowing how it worked.

It was no secret in my family that I loved living in the United States. My parents jokingly called it *Migookbyung*, or American Disease, which is used in South Korea to describe pro-American sectors of the community. But I saw one thing about the United States that brightened my life. I did not ever again want to relive the Hell

Chosun-style hopelessness that I witnessed among the young scholars as fruitful as nine. But here, despite all the inequality, racism, and other critical issues like healthcare and gun violence that plague the United States, it is still possible to advance through the social ladder. If I couldn't make a life for myself in South Korea, I was determined to do so in the United States. I would get a quality education here in America, and as a lawyer, I would come back to Seoul, and, by settling into an upper-class lifestyle of my choice, show everyone that I had made here success despite bypassing the traditional path.

But I couldn't help but wonder if that dream had already been dashed to pieces. Maybe I really was a naive teenager who idolized the United States without knowing anything.

As I walked down the long corridor to the Korean Airlines flight departing for Seoul, the events of the past few years flashed before my eyes.

September 2020. Lincoln, Nebraska. Covid had blocked international travel. My grandfather had just died of cancer in South Korea. Unable to attend the funeral, and not having seen him for over two years, our family had no choice but to gather at our living room table and cry as my mother's beloved father departed for the arms of God.

February 2022. In a set of unfamiliar clothes from school that had replaced my original ones soaking wet with milk, me, with my shaking hands, pouring all my outrage and frustrations onto paper.

May 2022. Scott Middle School. I swerved around groups of people playing football, basketball, and Four Square, in a game of not-quite-tag real life chasing game at recess. As the bell rang and it was time to return to our classes, I sprinted to the door—and ran straight into a group of girls on the sidewalk, promptly knocking one of them down.

Damn it, I muttered, and then quickly mustered a feverous apology. As usual.

My old sixth grade pod was what I passed by that day, and every day on the way back to class. Wondering what my life had become in the last few years, that day, I choked with tears with a smile, reminded of a time where there was much more to life than worrying about grades or getting to classes on time.

Welcome to my life. Swerving people, crashing into people, and reminiscing about the past.

Welcome to my life, of me pretending to be a normal American teenager when I know that it is the first thing that I am not.

Welcome to my life, one of me panicking over math tests, getting stuck in traffic, rushing to classes, hanging out with friends, playing wiffle ball, wondering what my life has become, and trying to maintain a facade of normalcy.

Therefore, there were a million and five things I thought about as we fled to Seoul that summer.

1. Why do people love me so much?
2. What happened on the last day of school?
3. Did we make a mistake by moving to the United States?
4. Am I fleeing from all my problems on this plane?
5. What's for lunch?

But no matter how hard I attempted to think through those million and five things on our 12-hour flight from Los Angeles to Seoul that seemed like eternity, I just couldn't get myself to think. The truth was, I desperately needed a break from our life in the United States to figure out who I was, who I am, and ultimately who I was going to live as when I got back. I just wanted to be done with everything for the summer. After four years of words and actions floating above my head, I needed the time to chill in my "own nation" and understand the direction of my life. The person I saw myself as wasn't how others regarded me. The public viewed me as a strong, energetic leader in my community when I saw myself as an unimpressive A student scraping by at the bottom of my middle school who had just begun to understand the social hierarchy and continued to make dumb mistakes. When I looked at myself in the mirror and saw the mastermind behind all unintentional incidents, others saw a kind, lighthearted 14-year-old that they could rely on and talk about their minds.

Who am I? I asked God as we flew over the Aleutian Islands. *By the way, I need to know soon.*

I could feel myself being captivated as our plane flew over the Seoul Capital Area, called *Sudogwon* in Korean, a hardworking metropolis that was just getting ready to wake up to a holiday of local elections that would eventually end in victory for the conservative People's Power Party. This sprawling, ever-growing region used to be my home four years ago. The hard work and the spirits of millions of people made this Miracle of the Han River possible.

But somehow, those efforts have backfired.

Somehow, every answer to every problem became, "You are just not trying hard enough."

Somehow, effort was the only thing that we were lacking yet were deprived of.

But no matter how much I was frustrated about the fact that I couldn't advance in the South Korean society, I felt proud to be from this nation. I had spent the last four years shaming my Hell Chosun passport and all the disadvantages that came with it, but I suddenly felt a sudden surge of pride for my homeland and all its people that lifted themselves out of poverty and more controversially, oppression, after the end of the Korean War in 1953. I knew that my homeland of South Korea, in spite of all its faults, had come a long way the past seven decades, going from a war-wrecked nation in poverty and military dictatorship to a top 10 world economy.

As our flight landed at Incheon International Airport and the landscape around us became fully visible, I looked around and was struck by a wave of realization. This was what frustrated and angered me. It was the fact that I, and a lot of other talented young people, couldn't contribute to this nation and society. It was the fact that we couldn't help run this country only because we weren't born into the right families.

This didn't make any sense, that I was speaking in riddles, but it made sense to me.

Our hate, our distress, and our anxiety came from our love for our country.

We were the true patriots.

JOURNALISM

Making a Wish

REBECCA FORD

Grade 12. Freeman Public School, Adams, NE.
Brett Sales, Educator.

After a life-threatening battle against liver failure, Ms. H celebrates her road to recovery

HICKMAN, Neb., June 30—When Mrs. J took her daughter, Ms. H, to the hospital in mid-January, liver failure was, quite possibly, the last thing on her mind. She quickly learned that it was a much more plausible possibility. In fact, it wasn't even a possibility. For Ms. H, liver failure was her reality.

Ms. H, 11, is the first child of Mrs. J and Mr. A and the sister to two younger brothers. Until January, Ms. H had always been a relatively lively, healthy child, making her sudden and severe decline in health not only a mystery to medical professionals, but also a horrible shock to her family.

Mrs. J first realized something was wrong in mid-January, after her daughter came down with extreme nausea, lethargy, and acute sickness. Hospital staff gave Ms. H a COVID-19 test and a flu test, but without any lab work, the first signs of liver failure went under the radar. It was only two days later when Mrs. J realized that something was seriously wrong with her daughter. Something deadly.

"She could not stop throwing up for two days," Mrs. J says. "Two days after I took her in the first time, she was up in the middle of the night, completely delirious, and I noticed the whites of her eyes were completely yellow." Jaundice, a yellowing of the eyes, is perhaps one of the most notorious signs of liver failure. Mrs. J wasted no time in rushing Ms. H to the hospital, and Ms. H, delirious from sickness, remembers none of it.

"All I remember is fainting in [the] hallway," Ms. H recalls.

Rushed to the Saint Elizabeth Regional Medical center, Ms. H was finally administered lab work, and with an astonishingly low blood sugar level, it became clear that Ms. H was facing a deadly battle with liver failure.

Immediately, she was taken to the University of Nebraska Medical Center, or UNMC.

"It was just terrible. She was unconscious for days, they didn't know if she had brain activity, she was on a feeding tube and a breathing tube at the same time ... Her whole body was just bloating, and she just looked awful," Mrs. J says.

While Ms. H is unable to recall any of it, the line she toed between life and death is not something her family will soon forget. Even breathing without medical assistance in her unconscious state was impossible, leaving Ms. H in a fragile position before she received a liver transplant.

However, after being placed on the transplant waitlist, good news came in record time. After only a few hours on the waitlist, Mrs. J received a phone call informing her that the liver transplant would be shipped to UNMC in only four hours.

The surgery, taking place on January 20th, was a grueling seven-hour procedure with three surgeons alternating throughout, and about halfway through, the family received a very simple, very significant phone call.

"All they said was, 'The old liver is out, new liver is in.' That's all they said," says Mrs. J.

The next few days after the surgery, Mrs. J reflects, were difficult. While Ms. H was tremendously better off, even managing to breathe at times on her own, the emotional turmoil the family faced was at an all-time high as Ms. H fought to stabilize and recover.

"One day, she just barely opened her eyes, but she was looking around, and she whispered, 'what happened?' So that's when she found out she had a liver transplant," says Mrs. J.

There wasn't even a conclusive catalyst for Ms. H's seemingly spontaneous liver failure. At the time of her liver failure, Ms. H also had COVID-19 for the second time, and while the family and medical professionals suspect her liver failure was brought on by multisystem inflammatory syndrome in children, or MIS-C, which is a rare inflammatory illness, nothing has been confirmed, leaving them baffled.

Some days throughout Ms. H's hospital recovery, she was unable to speak or make expressions, leaving her nearly entirely unresponsive. However, during one such occasion, something happened that Mrs. J remembers particularly fondly.

"They have a music person come in and they handed her ... a ukulele ... and Ms. H's lying there in the hospital bed, unable to speak, no facial expression, and she's just playing her little instrument in her hospital bed, and it was so sweet," says Mrs. J.

From there on, progress moved exponentially. Ms. H could soon speak regularly and, from that point on, regained her memory, but expressed some issues with regaining her ability to speak.

"I forgot how to talk because I was trying too hard to talk!" Ms. H expresses.

In the coming days, paperwork became another struggle, but there was a silver lining to the clouds the family had to face. Make-A-Wish, a non-profit organization specializing in creating "life-changing wishes for children facing critical illnesses," as their website describes, contacted the family, offering them hope and a very welcome respite in the difficult circumstances they were faced with.

Ms. H was at no loss when it came to her wish. Fueled by her love of avians, Ms. H initially wished to build a bird sanctuary, and was consequently given a cockatiel as a pet. However, the medication Ms.

H took seeped through her skin and hair and was toxic to the bird. The cockatiel tragically perished as a result, and Ms. H was given another cockatiel, still not realizing the medication she took was toxic to birds.

The plan to create a sanctuary soon fell through as the second cockatiel also nearly died, and after giving the bird to a family friend, Ms. H went back to the drawing board and plotted her second choice for her wish: a "she-shed." However, it soon became another plan that fell through once Ms. H learned the shed would lack air conditioning.

Finally, Ms. H selected her wish: a $3000 shopping spree.

With a shopping list containing everything from a mini fridge to a hoverboard, Ms. H had the wish of any kid's dream, and on July 23rd, it came true. With a limo ride to and from Lincoln, Ms. H was living the dream, spending $2000 at Target and $1000 at Walmart. A manager at the latter franchise even gifted her with an extra $400 gift card.

Returning home in Hickman at around 5:20 p.m. after a day of shopping, Ms. H was escorted to her neighborhood in a limo surrounded by police cars, fire trucks, and even a motorcycle gang. The community had all lined the streets in support of her, sending her home with quite the shopping haul and the support of everyone around her.

Recovery hasn't been easy for Ms. H, despite her tremendous progress. A month in the hospital has left her with significantly reduced muscle mass which has been difficult to gain back. Her weakened muscles leave her shaky and susceptible to fatigue even from simple tasks. Due to her more fragile physical condition, Ms. H has also been barred from participating in many of the activities she once enjoyed, such as swimming, biking, and horseback riding. She couldn't play on the playground or go up steps at school due to the risk of blows to her abdomen. Her medicine leaves her susceptible to cancers such as skin cancer, and she is unable to swim in large bodies of water such as lakes due to her compromised immune system.

Recovery looks to be a long process, but as kids tend to do, Ms. H is bouncing back. In fact, she's in high spirits when it comes to her situation. When it comes to the severity of her life-or-death situation, Ms. H touches on it with all the nonchalant laxness one might use when talking about something as inconsequential as the weather.

"I feel like nothing's happened!"

The Rise of South Asian Representation in American Media

Ashmiza Shaik

Grade 8. Millard North Middle School, Omaha, NE.
Patrick Miner, Educator.

For decades, South Asians in American media have been depicted by characters such as Baljeet from *Phineas and Ferb* and Ravi from *Jessi*. These characters fulfill the stereotype of the South Asian Nerd. However, the representation of South Asians in American media is taking a turn. People are getting extremely sick of viewing South Asians as scammers and weirdos.

The number of television programs and visual media featuring more realistic South Asian characters has significantly increased over the last couple of years. The number of South Asian actors and hosts on television has risen drastically. Examples include *Patriot Act*, which features Hasan Minhaj, an American television host of Indian descent, and *Bridgerton*, featuring Simone Ashley, a British actress of Indian heritage. The Disney film *Spin* supports breaking down stereotypes of South Asians by focusing on Rhea, an American-Indian teen girl who discovers a love of music and incorporates her South Asian culture into the music she creates.

The popular Netflix series *Never Have I Ever*, stars Tamil-Canadian actress Maitreyi Ramakrishnan, who plays Devi, a 16-year-old Indian girl attending a regular high school in California. *Never Have I Ever* centers on Devi's life and highlights her struggles with culture, love, and friendships, and challenges the stereotype that all South Asians are merely nerds. When writing *Never Have I Ever*, Mindy Kaling thought about some of the comments against South

Asians. In one episode, Devi makes fun of these "non-whitewashed" Indian girls dancing for Ganesh Puja and says: "They seem cool here, but can you imagine how dorky they would look doing this anywhere else?" After commenting on her own culture, Devi gets schooled by a performer's sister who responds with "Her Bollywood dance group was in the Macy's Day Parade on a float sponsored by Ziploc. Who looks dorky now?"

Previous media depicted South Asians as close-minded, as though they would consider their profession a complete failure if they did not become a doctor, lawyer, or engineer. New shows and films are beginning to showcase more than one element of South Asians' lives. They are developing fresh narratives that reveal the genuine nature and values of a South Asian character. New stories are emphasizing the importance of mental health, which was previously seen to be a "waste of time" for South Asians to consider because according to the stereotype, all they cared about was getting into Harvard. The public is observing an entirely new perspective watching people of a different race deal with day-to-day life.

All these new shows and movies featuring South Asians received positive reviews from people all over America. They proved to be successful in their performance and the diversity they bring to the viewers. It's become clear that times have changed. South Asians are not portrayed as being tech support or absolute weirdos who have no friends. Fair representation in media sends an important message to people of all backgrounds that being different is normal and diversity is necessary to make our country truly beautiful. This ongoing craze for television featuring South Asians will promote a further reach of representation and bring forth a new era of television consisting of minorities and bending the stereotypes.

Transgender Nebraskans

Charlie Yale

Grade 11. Central High School, Omaha, NE.
Jonathan Flanagan, Educator.

LGBTQ+ individuals living in rural Nebraska have many barriers stopping them from getting proper physical or mental healthcare, according to Nebraska healthcare organization OneWorld.

Jane Joe, a Nurse Practitioner, and teen/young adult healthcare provider at OneWorld explained that there is no clinic that offers transgender hormone therapy west of 130th street in Omaha. She talked about how her clinic sees a lot of patients from western Nebraska.

"Before I was at OneWorld I was at a nonprofit that was called Associates of Reproductive Healthcare," Joe said. "It was just for transgender care. At that location, I had patients coming from all over western Nebraska and Central Iowa, but even at OneWorld I have one patient who is out at Chadron."

The drive from Chadron, NE to 130th and Center, the location of OneWorld's clinic, is just below seven hours. The patient that Joe referred to meets with her over Telehealth. Joe said that creating follow-up appointments for patients in western Nebraska is incredibly difficult.

"For the first year or two, we have to watch labs pretty closely while we're adjusting medication," Joe said. "Out in western Nebraska, they either have to drive into Omaha to get labs or find a clinic that I can fax labs to that will then go ahead and get the labs drawn for them and get the labs sent back to me."

Joe explained that finding labs in western Nebraska often creates extra hoops for a patient to jump through.

"It takes a lot of work on [the patient's] part. Trying to feel safe contacting a clinic and explaining the situation. Usually, they have to make an appointment to go in and there's some charge. You get into more money because they're paying to have a visit with me via the phone and them there to have labs. It's like being charged double," Joe said.

While most of Joe's experiences with labs and practitioners in western Nebraska have been positive ones, she reflected upon a patient she served whose pharmacy made it hard for them to obtain hormones.

"I had a patient who was out in the Kearney area, and they had originally used one pharmacy ... that was giving them a really hard time, so they called and switched to a different pharmacy," Joe said. "They were not very helpful with insurance and those types of things."

John Johnson, a transgender man living in Omaha, said that even in Omaha, getting labs and appointments to obtain hormone therapy is an incredibly difficult and arduous process for trans individuals.

"I go to [the University of Nebraska Medical Center's] clinic for my care. It's not great. I do all of my meetings online because it is very difficult to get to everywhere in a timely fashion," Johnson explained. "There was a lot of scheduling issues to where I didn't have an appointment for nine months, and all of my levels were messed up." Johnson said he didn't know many practitioners in the state who provide hormone therapy. He said that they attract patients from states in surrounding areas as well, creating a high volume of individuals for a small number of doctors and practitioners able to provide these services.

"Every trans person in Nebraska plus neighboring kind of places go to these handful of clinics, it's so swamped," Johnson said.

The volume of patients that these clinics deal with create problems, such as scheduling errors and missed appointments by clinicians or patients. For patients, this can mean missed hormone prescriptions, missed labs and missed doses. Consequentially, patients' hormonal levels will fluctuate, which brings about negative side effects.

"I just had a meeting a week ago, and even then, I had one scheduled for two months ago and they didn't show up," Johnson explained. "I couldn't get my lab work done because they wouldn't set up a time for me to come in and get it done, so I was out of it for like nine months. I don't blame them for it because there's only one doctor at my clinic. There are so many people that do it [at UNMC] because we don't have a surplus of clinics."

James Doe, who is sixteen, believes that the process of starting hormone therapy is intentionally hard to discourage transgender people, especially transgender youth, from starting hormones.

"It's way too long, the process. I get that they want people to be sure and one-hundred percent ready, but I was ready in 7th grade, maybe 8th grade and I've been ready for years and like, they still need to do a whole bunch of assessments and all these appointments that I'm on a long waiting list for," he explained. "I feel like that's all to provoke a sense of hopelessness into people and just make people give up. A lot of people don't want trans people to be happy, especially here in a red state."

Doe was disgruntled with the lack of transparency and communication he has received from his hormone specialists. Doe, who is trans-masculine, started taking testosterone at the UNMC Gender Care Clinic in August.

"I've heard that they're overbooked, I've also heard that there are not a lot [of practitioners]. I get a lot of mixed messages which also I feel like, it's just people don't want me to go on testosterone. I don't know the facts because people don't really tell me," Doe explained. "I'm kind of mad. Like, they've just slapped on a waiting period without telling me why or if they have a limit. I've asked and they don't ever give me a solid answer."

Furthermore, Nebraska requires individuals to wait until the age of 19 to get hormone therapy without parental consent, which can be incredibly taxing for individuals with transphobic parents. An anonymous transgender man (who will be going by X for the sake of coherency) shared his experiences with dysphoria because of a parental reluctance to put him on hormone therapy.

"My parents are transphobic. I was outed to them at a pride parade. My mother told me a few weeks later that 'I would always be her daughter.' Unfortunately, due to that, I can't get on T (testosterone) because I don't have my parents' permission," he said. "I have to wait till I'm 18, and it's just like, you count down the days, because there's nothing I can do to change my parents' minds. You deal with a lot of dysphoria."

Joe Public, a transgender man living in Colorado Springs, CO, touched on some of the effects of being denied hormone therapy.

"It's had severe effects on my mental health for sure and causes a lot of anxiety and dysphoria," Public said. "A big reason that parents are hesitant about HRT is that the side effects are often permanent, but I'd wish they'd realize that allowing your child to go through a natural puberty is also permanent. Hormone blockers on the other hand are completely reversible and not at all permanent or damaging so as long as you keep an eye on bone density levels and hormone levels, [it's healthy]."

Karen Koe, a Nurse Practitioner at OneWorld, said that for trans patients, it can even be hard to find a primary care physician who they feel comfortable around in rural Nebraska.

She explained that "People think when we say trans care we just mean HRT. Primary care [for trans people] is a big thing too." Koe said that she has "heard some pretty bad horror stories" from trans people about primary care experiences.

Koe detailed the story of a colleague she had a conversation with. "My colleague—not at OneWorld—called me in talking about a trans woman, and she was saying stuff like 'he gave himself little boobies' and just having to correct them a bunch of times on this person's pronouns," she said. She expressed concern that many trans people may avoid going into a primary care physician's office because of transphobic experiences, making them more likely to have a disease or disorder go undiagnosed or unchecked for long periods of time.

X said that his experiences with binding have caused uncomfortable experiences at his physician's office.

"Most people bind until they can have T or get top surgery. You have to be careful with that because you're binding a chest and that's where you have all your nerves. People make a lot of risky decisions and I've made that mistake myself, which is binding with something that is too small and you can potentially damage the nerves, and I've caused myself bruising on my ribs because of it," he said. "When I'd go to my physician, you'd just see like some bruises sometimes there and like, it's hard to explain. It's very awkward to do."

Smith said that his primary care pediatrician neglects to answer many of his questions, which causes him frustration because he feels as there are no good sources for him to ask.

"With my primary care they just kind of ignore it, I guess," he explained. "It's almost like they're like 'maybe if we don't address it, it won't be there,' which kinda sucks when like I have questions about stuff that revolves around that like physical activity and all that stuff and they're just like 'eh, bring it up with your hormone doctor.' But their job is just hormones."

Smith also attested to misgendering and deadnaming during a stay at a mental hospital.

"I had to stay in a mental hospital for a while, and Nebraska's rules are that they can call you by your name, but the name from your birth certificate has to be on your bracelet as well as your sex and they can't change it unless you go through legal stuff, so that's what they call you because it's on your charts," he said.

Mark Moe, a transgender man, said that even with his strong support system, his pediatrician and other specialists still fail to use the correct name and pronouns for him.

"My old pediatrician saw that I used he/him pronouns in my chart and didn't even look at it or address it at all and still misgendered me," Moe explained. "I go to Children's Hospital, and like, they're okay, they do good with pronouns but sometimes they make it very apparent that they don't care. My mom will correct them, and I will correct them, and they will continue to use they/them pronouns instead of he/him pronouns and it is very frustrating. If they were to use my correct pronouns, I would feel more comfortable."

Doe said that even in transgender specific care settings, the environments are uncomfortable because of the lack of trans people in the profession.

"At the gender clinic that I'm doing testosterone at, there is not a single trans person there, which kind of freaks me out. I don't want my gender journey to be overlooked by cis people, because I don't really trust them," he said. "No offense, but they just don't get it."

Not only do trans Nebraskans have to deal with transphobia inside of the physical healthcare system, but many trans individuals have had bad experiences with mental health specialists as well.

WPATH, the World Professional Association of Transgender Health, is a nonprofit that helps identify trans-friendly and LGBTQ+ friendly providers in an area. In Omaha, there are only thirteen WPATH certified physical or mental health providers. While not all trans-friendly providers are listed on WPATH, many make it a point to get certified and approved by the organization because of the rigorous standards they hold providers to.

"My last therapist wasn't exactly, well I've had a lot of therapists, I've gone through like all of them. My last-last therapist, I had to explain what gender dysphoria was to her," Doe explained. "She wasn't anti-trans, she just did not know anything, and she would tell me like 'that sounds like body dysmorphia' and like maybe, but it's gender dysphoria. And I just had to explain what I was going through."

Smith talked about a series of micro-aggressions that he has faced in therapy. He explained that a lack of understanding and education is what causes problems within these settings.

"I've had therapists say before like 'I have experience with transgenders' and I just kind of look at them and I'm like 'Oh! That's fun.' I feel like a lot of it has to do with like if you are transgender a lot of times if you have mental health issues, they think putting you on hormones will solve it all," Smith said. "That's not really how that works."

Koe explained that the combination of transphobic experiences and lack of access may add on an extra layer of complexity to an already overly complex healthcare scene for trans western Nebraskans.

"There's definitely a stigma," Koe said. "Mental health is a big problem. There's some statistic that 41% of Transgender Youth have attempted suicide." She explained that "Finding a [mental healthcare] provider who is friendly" is much harder in the western part of the state.

X believed that it would no doubt be harder to exist as a trans person in the western part of the state.

"I think it'd be a lot harder [to be trans out west]. I live down in Dundee. It's mixed—you get a lot of liberal people, but you also get a lot of right-wing people. I haven't dealt with a lot of bad reactions, but I can imagine out West it'd be a lot worse. I can imagine it'd be hard to socially transition, and even more hard to medically transition," he said.

Moe believed that a lot of problems within the health setting arise from a general lack of understanding of trans people.

"I one hundred percent think that becoming educated and like being willing to be educated is so much of the problem. A lot of people are educated, but they're not willing to like act upon that education," Moe explained.

Quintin Qoe, a transgender nonbinary person, furthered Moe's point.

"Even when we try to inform older generations, they don't really care," they explained.

Smith explained that to make transgender healthcare more accessible in Omaha and surrounding areas, it must be made more visible.

"My clinic is behind a wall of buildings, and the place I went to get my testosterone, I pick it up at a different location, but that one was very tucked away," he explained. "You can't really see it. At least having a sign that's like 'hey this is here' because we just circle for a long amount of time and you just kind of give up. If I can't see it, how can I know that there is something there for me?"

Joe explained that there are not very many accessible and outwardly visible clinics for hormone therapy in Omaha.

"Overall, I don't think most clinics have that welcoming atmosphere that immediately someone can walk in and feel safe," Joe said. "When I go to conferences or events where there are other practitioners there, you just talk about 'what do you do at your clinic?' or 'what kind of patient population do you see?' and you kind of make connections. I always ask 'are you seeing trans folk? Are you seeing the LGBT community?' and then kind of get into the conversation of 'do you have literature? Or a pin on your shirt? Or a rainbow lanyard?'

that you can wear that can make someone feel safe to talk to you. When we do that outreach with other clinics it's really helpful."

Smith talked about the value of being able to ask questions and have a safe space inside clinics.

"It's such a gut-wrenching feeling to be in the dark about it and you can't ask questions, and no one really knows and I can't ask my general practitioner because she just kinda ignores it," he explains. "I can't really look it up because a lot of times sources come from very blue states or very accessible states."

The bottom line is that transgender healthcare is healthcare. There are many barriers across the state, implicit or explicit, that prevent many transgender Nebraskans from receiving the care they need.

Doe explained how he feels that his time is being misspent.

"Yes, they're like irreversible changes, but people, especially people like me who've been out for over a year, well I've been out as not cis for three years, that's enough time to decide," he says. "The time that I'm in my body that I have been in since birth is like, it's just wasting time that I could be so much happier, and I think that's what people want."

Qoe stated an essential truth.

"Trans people have been around forever," he says. "It's just a matter of safety and coming out."

Smith wants people to realize that trans people are just that, people.

"We just wanna experience life and live happy lives that we feel fits us best. We aren't monsters. I've been called a monster by full grown adults. I just wanna f**k around and have fun in my high school years and into college. I want to be able to access my care like anyone else would go and access their healthcare. Trans health care, it really is just healthcare, and it doesn't affect you in the slightest," Whalen said. "But it does affect me, and I just want to live a happy life."

SENIOR PORTFOLIO

Honorable Mention

Addison Bryant, "4 Poems, 2 Stories." Grade 12. Anselmo-Merna Public School, Merna, NE. Shelby Saner, Educator.

Nathan Ertzner, "The Fruits of a Weary Mind." Grade 12. High Plains Community High School, Polk, NE. Keith Killion, Educator.

Megan Lambert, "No One Is Coming to Save Me." Grade 12. Boys Town High School, Boys Town, NE. Beth Sulley, Educator.

Hannah Wooldridge, "The Pieces." Grade 12. Gretna High School, Gretna, NE. Mary Bennett, Educator.

Circumstances

Olivia Achtemeier

Grade 12. Beatrice High School, Beatrice, NE.
Kathryn Glenn, Educator.

Through My Hands

"And then, I said to Hailey that I didn't even like movies. I was more into TV shows and that sort of thing." The cashier returns my card. "But Hailey said that she didn't watch TV, so instead we ..." I don't know Hailey, so I pull to the next window.

"Howdy!" a young man greets me. "Did you have a chicken sandwich and small fry?" I nod my head, and he hands me a grease-stained paper sack. "I should probably mention that one time I had the flu and showed up to work anyway," he says. I determine it would have been better off not mentioned, and I pull out of the drive-thru. With one hand on the wheel and the other rummaging through the sack, I check that my sandwich and fries made it into my keep.

"I hadn't heard of the band before, but I wanted to go to the concert," a woman's muffled voice says. I look up as she walks down the sidewalk. She is alone and without a phone. The sight never becomes easier.

In my apartment, I toss my finished meal in the trash and throw myself on the bed. I take a deep breath and close my eyes.

"When will this end?" I picture myself writing the words in my journal. "I thought the news said we all had a day, but it's already been a week. I'm afraid they are wrong. What if the storm never comes? What if we still have another month, another year, another decade? Surely the chatter will stop. Surely people will learn."

"Pat. Tata. Pat. Tata." The rain taps my window. I reach for the journal on my nightstand and flip through the pages until reaching the entry titled "July 20th, 2023"—three years ago. This is the one.

"Ben told me that in fourth grade he stole two dollars from me," I continue to recite in my mind. "I don't know why he said that. It's two dollars. I don't care. Mother said I should visit more, but then she told me about how she never visited Grandma when she was younger. She never talks about the past, yet that's all she's talked about this week," and it's all anyone's talked about since. My eyes rest on the last sentence: "I haven't said a word." A door clicks in the hall.

"That was the day I flushed my goldfish," I hear my neighbor's muted voice through the wall. "I didn't want to tell Frannie." I furrow my eyebrows. Yesterday he said his father was the one to tell Frannie. I prop up on my elbows and flick on the television.

"In other news, the storm is set to come tomorrow. During August a few years ago, I gave a friend some tomatoes and said that I grew them, but that was a lie. I didn't have the green thumb for ..." I flick it off again and flop my head back. Tomorrow? I sigh and roll under my quilt. It's always coming and never here. At that, I nod off to sleep.

"I got this chip in my tooth when I was seven." I wake up to the sound of my neighbor's voice. Sweat soaks my pillow. I get up, splash my forehead with water, and pat my face dry.

"The first time I got in a fistfight was when Ronald stole this pebble from me. I had found it at the lake," my neighbor continues.

"Click. Click. Click." Feet meet the pavement outside. I stand motionless. "Click. Click." I listen closer. "Click. Click. Click." I set the towel on my bathroom sink and walk to the window. Pulling back the shade, a man walks steadily. I'm puzzled. His feet make a sound, but his lips are still. *Maybe I'm not the only one.* I turn away, but the clock catches my eye. It's Saturday? I'm free until Monday.

The face of a man flashes through my mind, and the blood drains from my face.

Jumping around again, I peek through the window. The man still moves down the street. *It's him.* I run out of my apartment, scurry down the stairs, and burst through the lobby doors.

"Click. Click." I scramble towards the sound. "Click. Click. Click." Turning down a different street, I see him: dressed in sweatpants and a black t-shirt. My feet patter to his side and match his tempo. Footsteps later, we wait for the crosswalk. I glance up at him. His eyes are fixed on the long stretch of buildings. I glance down again.

"Got somethin' to say?" he murmurs. My head swivels to meet his blank expression. Sure, I've got a lot to say. For once, I'd like to wake up to my alarm clock and not just my neighbor's voice. For once, I'd like to see my brother without his list of long-kept secrets. For once, I'd like to walk down the street without hearing about someone's antifungal cream. Yet, what I really want to say is I'm sick of living in a world where everyone thinks they need to get out their last words and final confessions before everything ends. And as to what I'd like to do, I'd like to slap the guy beside me who lied, who told the world that the storm would come tomorrow, and tomorrow never came. But I don't say any of this, and I don't slap the man.

"Hmf. Lost your voice?" he asks dryly. My throat burns. I've lost a lot, but I haven't lost my voice.

"No matter. I know what you would have said." He pops a stick of gum in his mouth and tosses the wrapper to the ground, "You would have said that I'm such a *villain*, and you would have told me about how your uncle died because of me, or something like that. Or, maybe you would thank me. Tell me that I really did you a favor. Is that what this is?" I shove my hands in my pockets. The man stops smacking his gum for a moment.

"Listen, I didn't mean nothin'." He shrugs. "I was wrong about the storm. That's all." We walk past a warm cafe. Coffee grinders buzz, useless conversations are partaken, and the man resumes chomping his gum. "Take me for my word, I really did believe the storm was coming that day. It was an anomaly on the radar. I tried to ignore it, but as a scientist, I had to report it. *It was my job.*" We walk three more blocks in silence. He pops a bubble. His gum is already pale and he spits it on the cement. I stop in my tracks, and he slows his pace.

"What, kid? If the world's gonna end, what's a wad of gum matter? For all I care, I'd smoke if I had a cigarette on me." He walks back and bends down, as if going to pick up the chewed glob.

"What—" My voice is weak. "What are you going to do?" He lifts himself slowly

"What kind of question is that?" he scoffs.

"What are you going to do?" I swallow hard. "The world's done listening."

"Well aren't you observant?" he mutters. "At least you've still got yu'r head on. The world isn't done listening because it never started. That day I came on the news report was the first and last day anyone's ever listened to me." He heaves a sigh. "What are you gonna do about it?" I bite my lip.

"That's what I thought," he chuckles. "Everyone's got a voice until they've got to do somethin'. Tell you what, I was just going to check the radar. News says the world'll end today, and for once they might be right. You can come with me if ya like." My heart drops.

"What do you mean 'they might be right'?" I ask.

"This'll be the third appearance of the storm on the radar, and you know what they say? Third time's the charm. I think it's finally gonna show itself." Around the corner, we turn into a stark black building. The entryway is quiet and we enter a dark, cramped room. In the center lies a flashing monitor. The man leans over the monitor, placing his delicate hands on the sides of the device. I squint as the screen lights up. The whole device suddenly burns orange. With a scuffed fingernail, the man taps the glass screen. His cheek pulls coolly to one side, his lips curl, and his eyes keep distant. I can't read him.

"What is it?" I ask.

"It's all I could hope for and more," he says. He flicks off the monitor and turns away. "The storm'll be here tonight." I fight back a cough.

"Tonight?" I say. He exits the room. "Wait," I shout through the doorway, but my voice gives way.

"You think I'm gonna wait on you, kid?" he says over his shoulder. "If you've really got yu'r head on, you'd stop wasting time in that lonely room." He opens the door to the street and disappears. I never see him again.

That evening, I sit alone on my bed with the window open and talk to my mother through the phone. I don't have time to drive home to her.

"It's been ages since I've heard your voice, dear. You know, if that man is right, I hope you know I love you so. I wanted to tell you about this time when I was five. I've meant to get this off my chest. It was during the ..." I set the phone down, but don't hang up. I let the mumble of her voice drone on and walk to the window, which is fragrant with the smell of muddy air. I start at a large boom. It sounds like thunder. The clock on my wall rattles, and the line on my phone goes still. I fold my quivering hands. Another boom rings through my ears, closer this time. My knees quake and hit the ground. I've run out of time for an apology. I've lost the hours with my brother. The time with my mother has fled. My last chance slipped through my hands. My throat burns, yearning to cry out, and for the last time I whisper:

"I love you too."

The People You Meet

"Thyme Café ..." I murmur. "2032 Machine Street." I look up from the scribbled note to see the cafe's sign resting above its brown and olive-green awning. I step from my car and check the curb.

"Hello?" My head jolts up to see a young man on his phone. "I said we'd discuss this next Monday." His briefcase is as full as his current state of mind. "No. I'm meeting a client." As the words fumble from his mouth, the leather strap snaps; his attitude follows.

"Got to go. I'll call you back." I gather the notepad that scattered. It's filled with names, numbers, and doodles.

"Thanks," he mumbles and hurries on. In the cafe, the smell of roasting coffee and light chatter fills the air. After ordering, I find a table in the back corner.

"That's exactly what she said," a woman says and leans over the table. A smirk is hidden in her face as she searches for a reaction. She's charmed her audience. I'm not her audience, so I look away. I think of Anthony, the one who recommended Thyme Cafe. *Perhaps I should talk to him more ...*

"Is this seat taken?" I meet eyes with a woman who appears a bit older than me. A teal purse sits on her hip. I'd nearly purchased that same purse, but it was costly. *Maybe it's gone on sale since then.*

"No. You're welcome to sit," I reply, despite immediate instinct.

"Is this your first time?" she asks with a smile. I nod, about to reply, but she continues, "I love this place. There's something about it ..." she trails. "I think it's the atmosphere. I must admit, the coffee doesn't taste as good as it smells, but I suppose that's how it is with coffee." I smile; I've often thought the same thing. An employee approaches with my club sandwich and tea. He holds a second drink in the other hand.

"Delilah?" he asks. I nod, and he disappears.

"You drink tea?" I notice.

"Yeah," she lifts the tea bag and examines the label. "Ginger Reset," she reads off. "I enjoy trying different teas depending on the occasion."

"Same," I say. I read the label of my own tea bag: *Fragrant Past*. The menu had mentioned it has floral notes to it. She blows on the water.

"Actually," I begin, "it's strange, but I don't believe I like tea." She nods, unfazed. I continue, "I think I drink it because my sister loves the stuff." I chuckle and add, "It's cheap too."

"I feel the same." She takes a sip. "My sister drinks it, but it's never been my favorite. I've no idea why I still order it." She laughs.

"Must be a sister thing," I say with a grin. We chat while the hour passes.

As we stand up to leave, she says, "If you're interested, we should meet again next week—say, six-ish? I hate drinking tea alone." I agree.

Starting my car, my thoughts pick up where they'd left off. *I'll have to give Anthony my personal review of Thyme Cafe.*

✧✧✧✧✧✧✧✧✧✧

"I think you're capable of filling both positions. It will benefit the company to make these cuts, but I want to ensure you're able to do so." I sit across from my employer and grip my hands lest they shake. I peer at him from behind his hulking desk.

"Yeah," my voice falters. He raises his eyebrows, though his eyes below remain disinterested. "In a week I can give you a more decided answer."

"Hmf," he nods. I collect myself and leave, but my mind is jumbled. Down the hallway, I pass Joanna and Anthony's office. *I can't do it. I can't cut their positions.*

"Delilah?" I pivot to face the shared office. I suppress my thoughts with a smile. "Joanna and I were just talking about Thyme Cafe. Have you stopped by?"

"Yeah! I'm going again this week. It's nice," I reply.

"You have to try their avocado salad," Joanna chips in. "I always go in with the intention of getting something else, but never do."

"You make up for the blandness in your crazy drink concoctions," Anthony says and explains, "Joanna always mixes her coffee and smoothie." I frown with a smile at the idea.

"I better get back to work," I say.

"I better do the same," Anthony mimics and rolls his chair to his computer.

The day drones on as I bounce between the looming decision and work. By the end, I want nothing more than to take a nap, but I remember my previous arrangements. In my apartment, I scramble to fix my hair and grab a snack. Then, I head to the cafe. As I turn the corner, the woman from last week opens the cafe door.

"Hey!" I say to catch her attention. She turns, and I wave to meet her. "We have perfect timing," I remark.

"I'll have the Turning Tides tea," she orders at the counter. After ordering, I meet the woman at the table.

"You okay?" she asks with a slanted smile, "I mean—you look tired."

"Oh," I say. Her eyes look so familiar. "Work has been stressful." I look down, but back up for reassurance to continue. "The company has to cut people, and, well, the way things are set up, I have the final decision." I search her face to see if I've said too much.

"Hm," she says. "Do these people deserve to get cut?"

"No," I reply curtly, but correct, "one of them has a family to support, and Anthony is a hard worker." I blush at the slip of his name.

"Anthony?" She pauses. "Anthony Michaels?"

"Ye-yeah, actually. You know him?" I ask.

"Yes," she says. "Not that I'm in any position to give advice, but he, well, he's," she stutters, "he's not a good person."

"What?" I ask in shock.

"Oh, I don't want to gossip, but you should stay away from him; that's all." I stare, dumbfounded. "Please," she says with great earnestness, "stay away." A waiter hands us our drinks. I stir my tea bag around the rim of my cup. She stirs her tea in like fashion.

"What'd you order?" I ask.

"Turning Tides," she says. "You got Pivotal Petal, right?"

Examining the label, I exclaim, "Why, yes!"

"I'll let it rest after this," she says and meets my eyes. "Don't let others take your job. You need it as much as they do." My expression is blank. I consider her words but find my decision growing farther from her guidance. She sips her tea, and all the tension in her face disappears. I do the same. There's a sour note, yet I'm not sure what tea should taste like.

⋄⋄⋄⋄⋄⋄⋄⋄⋄⋄⋄⋄⋄⋄⋄

Monday morning, just before 8:00.

"I've decided I can't fulfill those duties, sir," I say to the empty passenger's seat. "I've thought about it, and I don't think I'll fill the positions," I rephrase. "No," I mutter, "too passive." I'm interrupted by a build-up in traffic.

"I quit! That's it. I quit my job. Then what're you gonna do? You'll have to keep Anthony and Joanna's positions. That's right." My fictionalized employer doesn't respond.

"Or ... or ..." I stammer on with great emphasis but never finish the thought. *Don't get worked up. Everything'll be alright.*

"Actually, Delilah," I imitate my employer's deep voice, "I'm no longer making cuts. Everyone's a hard worker and the company doesn't need the money." I heave a sigh. My stomach burns.

In the office, I log into my computer with a glance at the clock. An email notification pings. It's from me, and it reads:

You Got This

I need to fill this position because if I don't, someone else will. I can't afford to get cut. Without this, my savings will only go so far. I have to support myself. If someone else gets cut, they can figure things out as I would. Don't worry.

It's the way I write, but I don't remember it. I must have been tired when I wrote it. Skimming it again, I find comfort. I was tired but right about one thing: I don't need to worry. The ticking of the clock becomes all I hear. I swallow hard. It's time for a meeting with my boss.

"Enter," I hear from outside his door. Inside, my employer rests his head on folded hands.

"I've—" I steady my voice. "Come to a decision." He gestures for a seat. Once more, I'm made small behind his lofty desk.

"The company's already made a decision," he says to my surprise. He leans back and straightens a stack of papers.

"Someone else will be filling the positions." I smile and relax my shoulders.

"Who?" I ask.

"Delilah." There's a twinge of sympathy on his face. "I'm sorry, but—" He rubs his wrists. "Your position is cut." Silence rings through my ears. *What?* I squeeze my hands until the knuckles turn yellow. *How?*

He goes on to say, "Joanna. To answer your question, it's Joanna." I stare at my feet. "Please have your things cleared by tomorrow," he says. I stand, and he picks up the phone to say, "Anthony. Yes, I'd like to speak with you." I close my employer's door for the last time.

Reaching my office, I choke on the sudden lump in my throat and collapse in my desk's chair. Glancing around the silent room, I turn on my computer. My eyes sink to the email's last line: "Don't worry." With great effort, I stand, close my laptop, and bend to put it away. The initial shock begins to wear off, and warm tears build in my eyes.

"What was I supposed to do?" I mutter.

"You did all you could." I inhale sharply and straighten to see Anthony leaning in the doorway. I open my mouth, but no words come. Abashed, I look into Anthony's eyes. Standing still is all I can think to do. The rush of fear and the clatter of thoughts grow quiet.

Click. The hour hand startles me, and I resume gathering my things. Anthony remains silent, so much so that I wonder if he left, but his voice cuts through my rustling.

"I'm glad I got fired with you," he says. His eyes dart to the side. "I guess," he pauses, "I don't think I'd enjoy it much without you." Warmth floods my face. Again, I open my mouth to speak, but nothing is said.

"I'd better get packing too," he says. He gives a disheartened smile and leaves.

By noon, my desk is cleared and ready to be forgotten. I start the car, but can't bring myself to drive home; if I go there now, I'll do nothing but sob the entire afternoon. In the past, I've been reminded time and time again it's good to cry, but for now, while it's still daylight, I want nothing to do with it.

I enter the streets, ostracized. All these people are on lunch break—leaving work to return—but I have all the time in the world, and then some. I plot no course, but wind through the busy streets. The radio murmurs, but none of it reaches my pensive state.

"I wouldn't like work without you," I recite. *That wasn't it.*

"I couldn't enjoy work without you," I try.

"I don't think I'd enjoy it much without you." The words fall into place. Another voice interrupts my thoughts.

"The company's already come to a decision. Someone else will be filling the positions." *Why didn't I see it? Why didn't I see sooner* that I was being cut? I jolt forward to a screeching halt behind traffic. Thoughts of this morning disappear as a woman walks down the street. She scrambles through her teal purse and slams into another distracted bystander. The man's briefcase scatters. She helps gather his papers before touching her own belongings. Then, she steps under a familiar brown and green awning. The traffic inches forward, and I squeeze into a parking space.

I clamber out of my car and cross the street. I too step into Thyme Cafe. The line is long, but I'm not hungry. I scan the room and hasten to the woman's table.

"Why, hello!" she greets with alarm. I give an unenthused smile and sit. Her eyebrows lower, and a calm expression washes over her.

"Everything alright?" she asks.

"I—" I hesitate. "I lost my job."

"I'm sorry," she says. Neither of us speaks as burning tears well in my eyes. I swipe them away and inhale a choppy breath.

"I'm sorry. I should've gone straight home," I ramble. "I saw you come in here, and I thought that, well, I thought ..."

"It's okay," she assures. My mouth twists in pain.

"Delilah?" a waiter interrupts with two cups. One is set before me.

"This is very kind, but I don't have any cash," I say.

"I've already paid, so please take it," she insists. I read the label: *Citrus Storm*.

"If you don't mind, what happened?" she inquires. I talk her through the meeting.

"So Joanna took your position?" she asks bitterly.

"No." I scratch the back of my head. "I don't know what happened. The company could've forced her to." Her head shakes.

"No, she definitely did," the woman determines. I'm taken aback. She continues, "trust me, I know." This provides no reassurance.

"Pardon, but how would you know?" I question.

"I know Joanna Darner." She frowns. My eyebrows spring up. "She took your position intentionally—and Anthony's too." She winces at his name. I jump up, ready to leave.

"Wait," she implores. "I can explain how I know all this." I shake my head. I turn from her, but she blurts, "I'm here because of Anthony!" I twirl around and scrutinize her.

"Who are you?" I whisper. She pulls out a card. I don't move.

"Please," she pleads. "Look." I step forward and scan over her license.

"What about it?" I ask. Her eyes pierce through my own.

"I know you see it," she says. She's right. I read the name again: *Delilah Michaels*. The pieces are here, yet the picture is fuzzy. One single piece twists everything: the year.

I hold the card. It says the year is 2032. *Ten years from now.*

"I don't get it," I murmur. She gestures, and I cautiously take my seat. She returns her license to a wallet similar to my own, though hers is weathered. Her unpainted fingernails are of mismatched lengths, her arm has two freckles that connect in the shape of a snowman, and her eyes—they remain just as familiar. These similarities become all I see.

"Before anything, please hear me out on this one point." She pauses, and I prompt her to continue. "I don't expect this to make sense, but please do me one favor: stay away from Anthony. It's crucial that you don't interact with him. If you see him, ignore him. If he calls you, let him go to voicemail. If you run into him while trying green tea for the first time, leave." Her breathing picks up. "And ... and I want you to know that you've every right to be angry with Joanna. In fact, I don't see why you shouldn't hate her! She's taken so much from you, and for so long you've let her walk all over you. If you don't hate her now, if you don't *hurt* her now, you'll never get the chance again." I take a long sip of my tea and consider her words carefully.

I inhale steadily to reply, "I don't like jumping to conclusions. It rarely leaves people unscathed. However, I've come to one conclusion quickly—I love Anthony. He's always been kind, and I hope that someday I'll return the favor. And, I know it's easier to hate. It's so simple and natural, but I can't stomach it. Anger is already a beast. Why let it hatch into hate?" It looks as though a new woman fills her spot. Her figure looks hollow as if another breath will blow her away. I swallow my words. I am afraid that I've said too much.

She murmurs what sounds like, "Why did I lose you?" She buries her face in her hands, and I sip my tea. Minutes go by, and I wonder if she'll ever recover.

A faint whisper protrudes from her lips. "I know you understand." Finally, she lifts her head. "I was trying to protect you—*me*—from Anthony's diagnosis." Her lip quivers. "I thought I died that day, right there with him." A stray tear trickles down her cheek. "But I think I've only forgotten myself. Perhaps I'm still in there," she pauses, "somewhere ..."

I take another sip of tea. Comfort replaces its sour taste.

◇◇◇◇◇◇◇◇◇◇◇◇

A winter's evening, 2035.

A harsh wind sweeps across the window. A flurry of pillowy flakes brushes across Thyme Cafe's decal, then wistfully settles.

"Now you're telling stories!" an elderly woman says with a grin. The two old friends sit across the table.

"No," the other responds, "that's exactly what he said!" The other shakes her head, no longer deceived. My phone pings. For now, I swipe away the fundraiser notification. I smile. Before Anthony had passed, he always joked that he put the *fun* in fundraiser.

"It's all theoretical," I overhear. "We'd know if someone traveled through time. It'd be all over the news!"

"Come on," the boy defends. "Maybe they haven't worked out the kinks yet, but they've done some sort of trial."

"Really? And who'd volunteer to be the guinea pig?" the other retorts.

"Maybe someone wanted to be first," the boy reasons.

"Right! If anything, it'd be someone desperate." The other chuckles. A memory begins to resurface.

My phone pings again. I read the name: *Joanna Darner*. As bundled humans shuffle outside, I smile. A bitterness melts in my heart. Suddenly, I'm reminded of what I'd forgotten; within my soul, I hear the voice of compassion return.

To Love and To Leave

"What's all this?" Frederick's grandmother asks with the bob of her grey hair. She snatches the brown paper sack from my hand. Without my reply, she squints into the bag filled with rare and exceptional flour (as noted on the packaging), the most bitter chocolate I could muster, the sturdiest looking spatula in the whole market (which, unfortunately, is still a poor replacement), and a box of microwave popcorn.

"You don't have to repay me," she says with a small glare.

"No, no," I correct. "It's not repayment. It's just a gift." One corner of her mouth pinches.

"Fine, but I know you can't afford this," she murmurs and places the sack on the faded kitchen counter.

"I budget my money well enough," I answer in justification.

"What's all this?" Frederick repeats the question as his wide and buoyant stride enters the kitchen. He too scrutinizes the bag.

"Janet, you don't have to repay Grandmam," he says as if in imitation. "But," he pauses to scoop out the dark chocolate, "you're always welcome to repay me." I glance out the window to see the vast vineyard stretching beyond the human eye. A wooden bench is nestled between two clean-cut cypress trees—something I hadn't noticed before. Frederick joins me at the window and points a finger at the bench.

"That's what I've been up to," he says and adds under his breath, "moving it certainly isn't a one-man job." I smile softly.

"You should ask next time. I could help you," I say and look back at Grandmam putting the flour away. "Should we go and admire your moving skills now?"

"Well, I certainly hope someone will enjoy it." He snaps off a piece of chocolate and pops it into his mouth. "I suppose I'd consider it worth the work." I shuffle through the bag and pull out the popcorn and spatula.

"I'll put these away. You two head out there," I say and receive no objections. Grandmam shuffles out the door with Frederick guiding her arm. I flip through a few cupboards until finding one with potatoes precariously stacked on canning supplies. There, I balance the popcorn box on a cluster of glass jars. Then, I flick on the faucet and scrub the spatula after spotting the dish soap. My heart is warmed by the sound of Frederick's boyish chuckle, and I peek out the window to see him leaning against the armrest of the bench where his grandmother sits. Drying my hands upon my shirt, I make my way out the door.

"For you," Frederick says with a gesture towards the bench. I nestle next to his grandmother, and she keeps her gaze steady on the vineyard. I admire the way she rests her wrinkled hand on her grandson's lap while giving it the occasional pat. I admire her slumped shoulders that bring her head forward in such a way that her chin hovers above her knees. I even admire the way her droopy face frowns at the darkening orange sun, which sets upon the soft green hills. I breathe in the sweet evening air and take note of the two generations sitting beside me.

"Janet." Her voice is low and wispy. "Must you leave?" I close my eyes, knowing the answer very well.

"Yes."

"Janet," she repeats. "Do you *want* to leave?" I desperately try to grip onto the wonderful feeling I had, but it slips through my fingers. I suppress the thoughts that battle within me.

"That's not a fair question, Grandmam," Frederick says in my place. He lifts her hand in his own and tenderly rubs it with his thumb. "You're a blessing, Janet, but you're needed elsewhere." I blink and look away as if I could forget this good in my life—as if by forgetting this picture, my troubles wouldn't seem so bad.

For a long while, we sit there and watch the ribbons of color set from the sky. As the first speckles of light appear on the canvas of the night, Frederick's grandmother pats his knee once more and sends him off to start the popcorn. A subtle breeze brushes upon my cheek.

"Why must you keep him here?" she asks. "You could travel to the driest desert, and he would follow you at the drop of a hat." She swallows, and her tongue clicks in the stillness of the night. "He could help you with your brother." I close my eyes again with the wish that I had never known such happiness.

Her lips part as she utters, "That boy loves you." A heavy weight pulls in my chest. Perhaps I love him. Her shriveled hand brushes against my own limp fingers. A strand of familiarity passes over me. Her hands remind me of another, but I can't yet place its owner.

"Thank you. Thank you for your great kindness," I say, and my voice gives out.

"Don't thank me," she says with a light squeeze. "I'm the one that owes you." I shake my head.

"Are you coming?" Frederick calls.

"You don't owe me a thing," I say into her ear and lift her from the bench.

The next morning, we set off for the train station. Grandmam dons a blue shawl and wilted sunflower, which I find to be fitting for the somber occasion. Frederick sports a suit that I much fancy, and, for once, his unruly hair is tamed. We approach the station, and I see the train coming in from the East.

"That should be the one," I say. Neither of them makes a sound. Stepping from the car, our heels click upon the brick pavement. Frederick studies his shoes as we walk, unable to meet my earnest expression. How can I comfort him? What solace do I have to offer? He loops his arm in my own and lifts his face.

"It'll be good," he says with a smile, though his eyes betray him. "Theo's lucky to have a sister like you." My feet hesitate at the mention of his name.

The train pulls into the station, and I say my final farewells to the gentle hearts. As I board, I find a seat in the back as the sole passenger of the train. Outside the glass, Frederick lifts a lanky arm and waves. His other arm is slung over Grandmam's shoulder. Her eyes don't meet me but remain fixed on the door of the train as if I'm already gone. I give Frederick a weak grin and return his wave.

There's a holler in my ears, and the train's wheels start to chug. I watch the two figures adjust themselves to leave and notice the grandson pull out a small velvet box. His fingers ball up around it, and he shoves it back into his well-dressed pocket. I lose sight of them as they part from the station. With a sigh, I lean my head against the booth and let my eyelids sink. The bandage has been ripped, but the wound stings.

Last I saw my brother, every vein in his body was visible. His skin was cold, his forehead damp, and his gaze always kept distant. I press my eyelids tighter together.

"Remember the boy he once was. Don't ever forget that face," I think to myself, but all I see is the young man who's leading his grandmother home. All I feel are his hands caked in dried mud from the field. All I hear is his bright laughter.

"Miss Night," a man says and enters the passenger car. I reluctantly open my eyes. "Mister Seven's on the other line. I nod to dismiss him. I slide out the briefcase from beneath my seat and pop it open. With the nail of my ring finger, I scratch at my jawline and rip the rubber-like material from my face. Once the material is fully removed, I toss the mask into the briefcase, slide the briefcase under my seat, and walk to the other side of the train car. I remove the phone from its hook.

"Miss Night, this is Seven. The sample will need to be transmitted as soon as your location allows. For the time being, there is new information to be relayed." I nod along as he paints my upcoming assignment. With my hand in my pocket, I fidget with the sample of hair I had collected from a seamstress in the market. She had seemed so courteous; it is hard to imagine the foul activity she's been involved in.

"And Miss Night, there's something else," he says with a pause. "It's about Theodore." Pictures of the boy's hollow form flash through my mind. "He's no longer with us."

I clench my jaw and return the phone to its hook. My feet feel for the ground with every step that inches me closer to my seat; I fall into its cushion. With my gaze absently towards the sky, I change my demeanor with a small smile because of a small hope. Perhaps, as with the softening of skin into wrinkles, these hard moments will soften with time. I pat my thigh, then ball my hand into a fist. My neck strains as a bullet-shaped lump slides down my throat. No longer will my heart pound, my fingers quake, and my tears rain down at the thought of my brother and the things I've left behind, but maybe, perhaps, I'll learn things, forget things, and laugh as the memory resurfaces under a whole new light. A glint of sunlight strikes my eyes, and I release the breath I'd unconsciously held. Maybe—just maybe.

I swipe the tear from my eye and let the time pass as I return to a lonelier place.

The "Alpaca"lypse

"Thump. Thump. Thump." The pencils on my desk fall to the floor. The lights turn off, then immediately back on again. It's here; the monster from all over the news.

"Get going ..." I mumble to myself. I have to retreat to a safer area. Hoping for the best, I grab my bag and head out the door of my apartment.

Somewhere on the Outskirts of Town ...
"William, you started this," an employer at S.S. Laboratory chastised, "and now you're gonna get us out of it." A little over a week ago, William's branch of research (genetic engineering) was assigned to the task of solving a large scale problem. Well, okay, it more or less became a large scale problem. They were asked to create clarity in today's society between the llama and the alpaca. For the scientists, it was an honor to hear they would be dealing with this epidemic struggle.

From day one, they had a meeting in the department over reasonable solutions. "We just need to genetically enhance it in some way," a coworker of William said.

"What about giving alpacas a bald spot?" someone suggested.

"We could make llamas' eyes blue and alpacas' eyes brown," another chimed in.

"What if we had alpacas be left-handed, while llamas could be righties," another said. This continued for a few minutes.

"We could give llamas extra teeth," Amanda suggested. You must know that William has never been very fond of her. She always seems to come up with genius ideas, which, in turn, makes him feel meager. He knew he had to beat her at brainstorming.

"What if," William spoke hesitantly, "llamas become smaller than alpacas?" Everyone's chatter stopped to look at him.

"Sounds good to me," Amanda said, although he knew what she really meant was, *"Outstanding job, William. That is an amazing idea!"* The rest of the group agreed to give it a try.

So, for the next couple of days the group got to work. By the third day of strenuous research, they had a prototype. William watched as some of his fellow researchers entered a room while carrying a capsule of blue liquid. They gently poured it upon the patient plush toy, and sure enough, it shrunk. William excitedly started to enter the testing area, but, to his dismay, it jumped back to its original size. It, alas, was only temporary.

Many days went on like this, until the scientists had another meeting. "We need to come up with a better solution," the discussion began. It continued much like the preceding group consultation. That is, until William had another idea.

"Rather than making llamas smaller, what if we make alpacas larger?" he astutely reasoned. Much like before, everyone agreed. The meeting was once again followed by a few days of testing until they had created a green liquid. This worked better than they had originally predicted, and honestly, too well. William had been watching from behind a wall of glass. By now, the group was able to get a live alpaca to try the serum on. William fidgeted with his pen as the serum was injected into the animal.

"Um, William?" one of the men in a hazmat suit said through a small microphone.

"Yes?" he responded.

"I don't think this formula works either." Before William could feel much sorrow, the alpaca shot up a foot or two.

"It works!" he gleefully remarked. "It actually works!" The man within the glass scrambled backwards. "Is something wro—" Before he got the chance to finish, the alpaca sprouted a couple more inches. Then, it grew a few more feet. Eventually, its head softly brushed the ceiling. William knew what he had to do. His hand reached over and yanked the trigger to evacuate the building. As people rushed out, he heard a large crash, and as he glanced back, the animal had reached preposterous proportions.

Back in an Apartment Building Downtown ...
"Code Thirteen," the speakers above me muffle. "I repeat ... Code Thirteen." I continue walking as apartment doors fling open, and people of all ages flood the hallway. Although chance of survival is unlikely for most, the odds are stacked further against me due to my severe llama allergy. I make my way to the congested staircase as the speaker comes on again: "The Beast is on 7th street and heading towards 5th street." It's only a matter of minutes until it reaches 2nd street. I'm shoved towards the door, and I burst it open.

The people around me scatter. *Where did I park my car?* Before I have a chance to answer, the streets grow dark and the air is filled with the smell of a petting zoo.

To my left the monster stands; it's still two blocks away. The streets are swarmed by people, and I follow in the direction they run—away from this monstrosity. It's no use. The Beast towers more than seven stories high. My two legs are no match for its four. I fumble through my bag, and sure enough I find what I am looking for, though at the expense of a slower pace. Something soft touches me, then consumes me: the Beast's leg. I jump to face it and spray all of the llama repellent I have left in the cheap container. To my disappointment, it remains unperturbed.

I panic. I was never taught what to do in a situation like this. I grip the curly fur of the animal, ready for it to move. I hold my breath, but nothing happens. I gradually lift my eyes, afraid of what I might see. It's head, a massive thing of fluff, is cocked downward, and its eyelids are closed. The throng goes silent.

"Incredible!" a woman exclaims in disbelief. "It's asleep!" Her voice comes from within the mass of frozen humans. In shock, I stumble away from the wild animal. *Why hadn't I had an allergic reaction?*

A gigantic snort echoes through the buildings, and I see the llama's eyes shoot open. It begins to stomp, shaking the cement below my feet. Screams are heard all around. *My car is in the alley!* I recall. *That's not too far off.* I head into a narrow street, grab my keys, get in the truck and drive fast. As I am exiting the alleyway, my vehicle comes to an abrupt halt. Cars are all over the street and going nowhere.

"Why must traffic be so bad at a time like this?" I cry. The creature is only a block away. Getting in my truck proved to kill time, not buy it. Throwing my purse in the back seat and hopping out of the car, I dodge automobiles, bikes, and human beings. Then, much like before, everything stops. The llama leans its head forward and into the street. I can hear its steady breaths. In and out; in and out. A strange moaning sound emits from the Beast. Is this some sort of battle cry?

From here on out, things can only get worse. A clear, slime-like liquid spouts from its mouth. Within minutes, this repulsive-smelling goop is everywhere. It splatters all over me. Although I can't identify the substance, I know it to be a biohazard. So, I do all I can: wipe it off with my hands and keep sprinting. The Beast progresses down the street, and I cannot keep up the pace I'm running at for long.

"Swishhh. Swishhh." I glance behind me to find that the llama is shaking from side to side. "Swishh. Swishh." It looks like a dog leaving a bath. Looking farther up, I see a small helicopter with buckets full of blue liquid. The fluid is being poured onto the llama's fur coat. And, just like something out of a storybook, the animal shrinks. I'm baffled. It is still humongous but, nonetheless, smaller than before. I'm frozen in place.

Another helicopter swoops overhead, and, like the first, it has numerous buckets of the same liquid. The people, who from a distance are just small specks, empty the buckets' contents on the now sleek fur of the llama. The same astonishing thing occurs. It is now half the size it was! Two more helicopters arrive. They follow the example of the others. The creature becomes roughly one story high, but before more liquid can be poured, it darts away and is swifter than before. It speeds past me and turns left down a different street. The tables have turned; I start to chase the animal and am eager to see how this will play out. It gracefully gallops, but something changes. It appears to grow an inch or two.

A white van swerves in an attempt to corner the llama. The animal makes that same peculiar moaning noise and runs in the other direction. More vans drift into the street. The creature is trapped, but still growing. A woman in a lab coat steps out of the first van with an important-looking briefcase. She bends down to her knees and pops the case open. From a distance, I can see what appears to be a syringe with a bright orange substance inside. A huge needle is at the end of it. Just the look of it gives me chills. The woman, with the syringe in hand, walks closer to the animal and makes shushing sounds. Her hand gently touches the soft, curly fur of the llama and jabs the needle into its shoulder. It starts to shrink back to an average size. A zookeeper comes into the scene with a rope. He gently ties it to the now normal zoo animal and walks with it into a van.

"Hey! Where did that llama come from?" I shout to the woman.

"It's an alpaca," she shouts back. Then, she gets in the van without truly answering my question. As the vehicle drives off, I can't help but contemplate all that just occurred. *So that's why my allergies didn't flare up.* I trudge back to my truck to find that traffic has sped up again. When I arrive at my apartment, I turn on the television and watch the news report. The headline says that a disproportionate porcupine is on the loose.

A man from S.S. Laboratory waves his arms and yells from the background, "It's a hedgehog!"

Just Okay

Frozen, I sit with my forehead upon my knees while holding the legs close to my chest. Drop by drop, water plops from the shower head at uneven measures like musicians missing a conductor. My tears flow steadier than the plumbing.

"Please ... please," I mutter, unable to finish the request. My arms droop to my feet and the fingers attached fidget with the toenails.

Plip. Sqwip. Plip. Sqwip. Sticky, bare feet walk across the tile. I swallow my snot and listen carefully. *Plip. Sqwip. Plip. Sqwip.* The sound meets me and stands beside the porcelain-covered tub.

"Ellie?" I pull up my head (though it's the weight of a stove) in response to my name. A small girl stands with curly, strawberry-blonde hair. Her eyebrows are pinched together in sympathy and concern, but her lips are stretched into a smile. The girl's innocence strikes me; she grips the corners of her well-worn nightgown and is unafraid of the skin that clothes me. I blink hard as tears sting and my eyelids swell.

"Why're you crying?" the child asks. I wrap my arms over my knees and rest my head in the palm of my hand. I am incapable of forming the right words. Her eyes meet my own and urge me to answer. Fighting back a forceful cough, my lips twist and curl into a frown. I shake my head. With determination, the girl flicks out her hand, extending it to my own. I stare at it through squinted eyes until finally grasping the pudgy fingers.

"No one can hold your hand when you're locked in here," she says while squeezing my thumb tight. She goes quiet, and I feel the sticky hand, much like the sticky feet. *Tip. Tip.* More water falls from the showerhead and crashes upon the faucet. With a sudden burst, my throat crackles into a loud cry. My chest is thrown up and down with each sob.

"It's gonna be okay!" the girl pleads. "It's gonna be okay!" She clutches my thumb even tighter. I lose my breath and am powerless against the raging storm within me.

"Ellie, are you 'fraid of spiders?" she asks. I shake my head between breaths and little care where she might lead.

"I think I won't be, too, when I get older," she says. I don't understand. The girl plops to her knees. "And, and," she stutters to continue, "maybe you won't be 'fraid when you get older."

"When will I stop being afraid of his—his," I whisper to myself as mental images silence my voice.

"He's gonna be okay!" Her chant changes. "He's gonna be okay!" A fire bubbles to the surface and burns my face.

"Ellie," I call the girl by name. "Never will this be okay! All I want is for it to be okay: not good, not great, just *okay!*" I scream. At the sound of a sniffle, I look to the girl's face. Tears rain down upon her cheeks. She clasps my thumb so tightly that I wonder if it's lost circulation.

"You don't know that," she says through a booger-filled throat. "Be patient."

My heart drops inside my chest; it doesn't shatter in a moment— it drags through the space. I feel each individual shard fall to my stomach.

With a gasp, I jump to my feet and observe the empty bathroom. Everything is still: the locked door, the white tile, the fluffy towel. I sigh and release the tension in my fingers, which had mercilessly suffocated the thumb. I release what tears remain and turn on the tub's faucet to splash my face clean.

"It's going to be okay," I urge.

Tea, Gloves, and the Abandoned

Crack. A flash in the window illuminates the darkened room. The sound reverberates through the old wooden hutch and shakes the trinkets nestled inside. A figure sits towards the window with attentive ears that follow the rhythmic patter on the roof. She slouches while one bony elbow rests on the table. There's a hot tea set beside her, but it has long since cooled. With eyes that still follow the trickling water on the glass, she reaches a wrinkled hand towards an empty chair. She feebly clutches the air and heaves a sigh as another flash of light reveals knitted hats, fleece gloves, and wool socks strewn about in miscellaneous places.

◇◇◇◇◇◇◇◇◇◇◇◇◇◇

A ferocious gust causes tears to build in my eyes. While I blink them away, the wind playfully dances through my hair, as if to say, "It was only a joke! Why are you so serious?" My feet struggle to find the ground within this stormy breeze. *Crack.* I jolt back and look down. Beneath my feet, a small twig lies injured beyond repair; nevertheless, I scoop it into the palm of my hand and examine the scraggly piece of wood. Before I can brush my fingers against the rough bark, the twig is swept away. I choke while swallowing the parched air, and I set my gaze behind me at the distant skyline. The dark clouds that hover above the city contrast with the vibrant sun, which brightens the empty field. As I turn away, the taste of paper smacks my mouth.

"Are you kidding me!" I shout while brushing away the weathered newspaper. The only response I get is the wind screaming in my ear. A small smile breaks from my lips at the paper's bold print heading:

Timing is Everything— Plan for a Storm. A woman's twisted lips form a smile just below the text. *If I'd looked at the forecast, I would've left town sooner.* I release the paper and continue to trudge forward. *Green mittens, er, maybe gray?* Yeah. She'd said gray ... right? I'm reminded of her twinkling eyes: so hopeful, so reminiscent. A pin strikes my heart. Something tells me she's fading.

The turbulence takes a momentary, hard-earned break. Catching my breath, I dart my eyes around the field. *It might have blown away.* A bright green speck attracts my attention. I gather my impetus and make headway across the field.

A half-hour later, I toss what was treasured in the backseat and slam the car door closed with two arms. Rubbing my frigid and chapped hands together, I note the sound they make. The sound is so easily muted outside but amplified within this small space behind the wheel. The car sputters to a start, and I soon find myself whisked back towards the towering buildings. The sunlight gradually turns its warmth from me as I enter the shadowed city.

I start at the buzz of my phone against the dash.

"Hello?" I answer. There's a crackle on the other line.

"Uh, yes. It's Carmen Niting." I smile. She's the only Carmen I know. The grainy voice continues, "Did you remember to go to the field today? It's the one east of town. If you see a small blue windmill, you've gone too far. It's about three mi—"

"Yeah, yeah," I gently interrupt. "I'm actually on my way back." There's a pause. I wait for a stop light to turn green.

"You found something?" her voice asks softly.

"Yeah," I glance at the back seat. "It's a green mitten." Another pause.

"You're coming over now?" I hardly make out her question.

"Yeah. I'm only a few blocks away."

"Oh! The tea," she says beneath her breath.

"Well, I'm gonna let you go now. I'll see you soon."

"Oh, okay. Buh-bye," Carmen responds absently. I hang up the phone. After a few turns, I reach the suburbs near her home. The incessant squeaking of my windshield keeps me attentive until the small yellow door, dimmed by the clouds, comes into view. Turning the key once more, the car steadily relaxes. I reach into the backseat and tuck the mitten beneath my elbow. With a deep breath, I burst the door open and scuttle to the front step of Carmen's abode. I press the plastic doorbell with my pinky. From where I stand, the smell of damp, mineral-filled mud fills the air.

"Alexandra?" With two shaking arms, the stout woman presses the door fully open. "Come in!" I do as I'm told. "Are you cold? What kind of tea would you like?"

"Whatever you'll be having," I answer the latter of the two questions while sliding off my shoes and setting them aside. I turn to close the door for her and, as I face her again, she's already begun to shuffle away. I meander behind her and peek at the different pictures on her wall until she finally reaches the kitchen. I loosen my shoulder and place the mitten beside stacked Tupperware. As she adjusts the stove, I pry open one of the lids to find oatmeal raisin cookies nestled inside. Carmen turns to see me peering into the container.

"Those are for you," she says. With a cough, she adds, "If you don't want 'em, you can share 'em with friends."

"Thank you," I say with an appreciative nod. She turns her attention to the tea. I cross the room and stand beside her. The water begins to whistle, and I scan the counter for the cups. Finding none, I pull two mismatched mugs from an upper cupboard. Carmen turns to see if I'm still behind her and finds it isn't so. Her squinting eyes grow a little wider, and her thinning eyebrows raise.

"You—" She struggles to part her lips. "You found it?" Abandoning the tea, she scuffles her feet to the other counter. I find the tea bags beside the stove and look over the package for how long it should steep.

"Yep," I reply while setting a timer, "Is that what you were looking for?" I read the tea bag label: *Jasmine River.* "You know, I love Jasmine in tea," I comment. Still, no response comes. I turn my head over my shoulder to see Carmen holding the mitten to her cheek. A lost tear finds its way rolling along the fabric. My eyes are fixed on her warm expression; my heart takes a while to follow. I tug my sights away from her and back to the tea.

Grabbing the two mugs, I carry them to the small dining table. A teacup catches my eye—*it's still full.* I sit in the chair across from it and stare into my own tea, which warms my chin. The liquid ripples as I blow into it. An abrupt gust pelts the kitchen window. *Plop.* A small leaf escapes my tea bag and lifts to the water's surface.

"Alexandra?" I jump a little to see Carmen standing beside me. The bright green mitten shakes in her hand as she tries to point something out to me. I meet her eyes. "It's Howard's. This is my signature." I note the scribbled red stitching near the wrist of the fabric. *Bzzz ... Bzzz.* I hurriedly stop the alarm on my phone and pull the tea bags from both of our mugs. As I do so, she finds her place in the other chair. With the tea ready, I blow on it a second time. Carmen slouches into the chair and grasps the lost belonging with two hands. Her face steadies itself on the window, and her nose follows a single drop weaving down the glass. I suddenly notice her hand reaching over the table. She balls it into a fist, then gently sets it on the stained wood. Instinctively, I fold a warm hand over her own.

"He would be so happy you found it," Carmen whispers. *Crack.* Carmen's tea splashes inside her mug.

Lullaby for This Broken Time

Camila Gomez

Grade 12. Lincoln High School, Lincoln, NE.
Christopher Maly, Educator.

Sharpen Me Softly

there's a dullness round my edges
where I fancy I used to gleam

a cutting smile
worn into a press of bitten lips,
faint impression of my favourite lies

a luminescence
bouncing off windows,
dancing round mirror mazes

a vitality,
flame licking up my limbs
taunting the whirlwind

of colour kaleidoscope
fair rides distorting the universe,
bright blurs focusing on

buoyant laughter riding
the orbits around me,
finding ourselves in suspension

shining eyes flirt with the edge
and oh, how we've fallen

words stumble as mouth lags
into the shapes of harsh vowels
of unpracticed mother tongues

textures roll flat as I strain
to pick out faces against
the dimness from the heavy curtains

simpler to be stationary
encased in slow swirling warmth
it is nicer here, beneath the covers

there is nothing beautiful,
golden ichor run deep crimson
has dried up black blood

while hollow, we perform
this stuttered social dance
to the barbed traps of unforgiving audience

look into my eyes
I was brilliant once, I promise

flay me,
I want to see the red meat dripping

cut me,
snip my tendons so I sag like a marionette

break me,
snap my bones in two and suck the marrow out

and then what is left of me?

just blood and flesh and bone
in the wake of the carving knife slipping from my fingers,
dull and dim and hollow
scraping and clawing and coming up empty

shaking hand draws a smile on my lips
rubs my eyes together until they shine
shoves the words back into my throat

I spit a fire into my veins and bask in its sickly glow
and all the brilliance burns around us

so sharpen me softly, my love

What We Tell Each Other As We're Drowning

"Le vent se lève! ... il faut tenter de vivre!"
Paul Valéry, Le cimetière marin

"*I have beaten you to the bottom of the sea, love*"
say your bloodshot eyes and wry grin
and I am too far to throw a rope or lend a hand so I jump in after
    you.

This is as much as we can offer each other:
company as we sink.

It's a metaphor we throw around so freely,
upon which our camaraderie has built
a generation of drowned youth.

There was a cliff once,
where we were told to get up and keep marching.

I stood on the precipice
too far down to fly, too far up to fall,
you cannot get your bearings in the endless blue.

And as we reach the ground the sea gives way to sky gives way to
    sea,
and the wind gushes and the currents churn, and we all plummet
    one after the other
and you grab my hand and you say *"the wind is rising! We must try to
    live!"*

Pendant, Pilgrimage, Paradise

pendant
I slip gold chains over my head in silent ritual,
seeking refuge in an icon I'm not sure I believe in.
still, I will carry her pendant on my neck
until I make the pilgrimage back home.

sacred is the feeling of safety

sitting at the table with the matriarchs,
trading the secrets of life and death,
conversations confined to kneading dough,
pouring tea, and peeling potatoes.

to women I pray

I kneel by the mounds and lay down the symbols—
never decided if they were for respect or resilience.
until time comes and I can be with them again,
I shall close my eyes and dream of paradise.

pilgrimage
distant memory, suspended
in moonset and sunrise.
there are no hours here,
blood orange seeps into velvet blue.

I miss that perfect purgatory,
hanging in limbo,
between sleep deprivation
and adrenaline alertness.

and when the world trembles and falls,
my palms clasp gold.
lungs burning, heart bursting,
don't know when fear gives into faith.

in the seat behind me someone whispers,
"is there not a more beautiful way to go?"
every time, I marvel that I've seen
the other side of the clouds.

paradise
the garden sprouts
from where her fingers
touched the earth.

life-giver, it is a power she carries silently
as she sets the table in the dining room
and builds the hearth in the house.

there are empty places
but always more mouths to feed.
I take my seat amongst them,

waiting for the ground to take me,
deliver me to the place of my birth.
the road doesn't travel this far

and there is such a distance
between us, the sky, and the earth.
I feel it all in my breath and my blood and my bones,

so I hold you as close as I can.
nestled in your arms again,
I've come back home.

This Rotten Head of Mine / Trial by Fire

laying on a pile of leaves, golden-red and smelling of dirt, I made my bed among the detritus. sun-swath, wind-lulled, caressed by soft grass, the ground rocks my cradle as I drift and doze and the haze blooms all around me

Silence,
then a snap.

I am fed in the way I am feed; they take me in the little ways this time, nibble at my skin, burrow into the cavities of my bones—devoured and regrown, gone are the days when they took me whole—and here in the mercy of numbness, I am warm and I am held and I can rest

A face plunged into icy waters

> biting and gnashing,
> clawing behind the eyes.

I look up at the world in this way, drawn out and broken by branches, and for a second I see so clearly the inferno before me, rolling out in the distance, taunting and beckoning in a pale imitation of pure, vital energy and when it roars, I hear it sputter and I laugh in its face

> A body plummeting into pool of sulfur,
> crackling and hissing and blazing and burning.
> Baptism by fire, surely.

there is no pain in this place, just peace or there is no peace in this place, just pain or it's all the same washed-out colour on the backdrop of agony or maybe it's all this smoke clouding my senses, and I am forgetting if I came here to find myself or lose myself

> Do not try to abscond,
> you will not be absolved.

no amount of scrubbing can clean the fog, and I know that in the last polished clearing I'll find I haven't got a single good thought in this wretched, rotten head of mine upon my shoulders

> Awaken.

Snowing in April

It's snowing in April again. Though I suppose it always is. Flurries forever falling—spun into whirlpools by the wind, coating newly green grass for just a second before being kicked back up again. The cold creeps into my hands. It's an old friend. I'm sitting on the wooden step of my back garden, trying to think of what to say to you. The thing is, right now, on this very step, it is snowing a year ago in April, and I am hearing these words I am trying to weave into an explanation. Now, a year ago in April, I do not yet see how futile it is to use these measurements—these invisible lines we've tried to carve into an ever-changing abstract river, these tenses, these *words*.

Time. I have not. Too little. Too much.

You don't know how it lords over you, commanding my movements from sleeping to waking—the very conditions of my living. You don't get it, I know. I am confused and I am explaining and I am listening and I am telling. It goes like this:

Everything happens all at once, always.

We are acting out *Romeo and Juliet* in 9th grade English class, standing in the center of the classroom, smiling through Shakespeare. I am Juliet on the balcony, arms out gesticulating wildly to my audience, my love. "*O Romeo, Romeo, wherefore art thou Romeo?*" I am Romeo at the tomb, kneeling above my lifeless lover who giggles from behind her book. "*Arms, take your last embrace.*" I blow my poison kiss, clutching the pages to my chest, as slowly I collapse onto carpeted linoleum. "*Thus with a kiss I die.*"

I am standing in the middle of the aisle, breath fogging up in my glasses as I examine the barren shelves. I read the sign they have posted to answer for the emptiness; "*Due to high demand we are limiting purchasing quantities of bath tissue to 3 per purchase. Thank you for your understanding.*" I look out at the sea of shoppers, orbiting each other in a 6 foot radius, half with new cloth over their mouths and noses, the other half flashing their naked sneers. Their carts are as full and as empty as ours. I stare on with a strange sort of detachment seeped in surreal hilarity. *What kind of dystopian film have I stumbled into?*

I am bashing my head on my desk, trying to dislodge the helpless procrastination that has taken root in my brain in place of analysis on Kurt Vonnegut. It is Friday, the last day of spring break. I am useless, I decide. So I run over to my friend's house where we gorge ourselves on her mother's rice and chicken while watching *Thor: Ragnarok* and catching up where our lives diverged to different high schools. "*We should do this more often.*" I grin. When the school calls canceling for a week, we both whoop, toasting soda in celebration. I have more time to work on my Vonnegut. "*So it goes ...*"

The WHO calls it a pandemic and President Trump calls it "kung flu" and dread pools in my stomach.

I walk into American History to see my classmate sitting at his desk, a blue-green surgical mask covering his smile. He's the only one wearing it. I try to open my mouth but the sound doesn't leave my lips. "*I distanced myself from the Chinese community in Lincoln as a precaution*," he assures me, and my heart breaks. His China is not my Kazakhstan. I am afraid I am ashamed I do not know what my Asia means to me.

There is a new language we must learn. It is a tongue of awkward silences broken by overlapping crackling static. We are both Echo and Narcissus, our words playing back through dodgy internet connection that always lags a second behind, as we preen ourselves in the reflection of our inverted square pools, stacked together, caged. Performing for camera, we sit silently muted. *I will never get used to being boxes on a screen.*

I am watching in anger and in pain. On the screen people are screaming "*I can't breathe!*" There's a fire in my blood as I wish to join them. The police are firing tear gas into the crowds. We have seen white police officer's knee on black man's neck. We watched George Floyd be killed. We are furious. We are grieving. Minneapolis is burning on the TV. America is bleeding.

Bullets fall again after a long absence. I promise not to forget the drop in my stomach, as they lower the flag for another day. Three days in I am already desensitized.

We are sitting in lawn chairs on our driveway, necks craned at purpling sky upon which a colourful battle is waged. The coach unleashes pompous red, white, and blue and the doctors retaliate with a barrage of shimmering gold. The booms die down and our ears are ringing with the remnants of bursting bombs and exploding stars and burning money. We take a sip of our not-quite-coke and observe the phenomenon we aren't half-a-world away to miss.

A week I am caught in a cycle of blue red blue, stress churning my stomach until there is nothing left. A moment of hysterical catharsis. I laugh all morning. My body collapses in relief when four years are finally over.

I sit in front of the TV screen and I watch in apathy as a mob storms the Capitol. They are waving their Confederate flags in the seat of democracy. I am aware that I am witnessing history. I'm exhausted. Vaguely I can make out a CNN anchor saying he feels like he's speaking to a correspondent from Bogotá. No, sir, these things happen in the United States of America.

January is warm as we walk the streets of Bogotá. Cousin hitches a ride on my back, her little feet sore from striking the cobblestone paths around Parliament and Casa de Nariño. She flaps her arms like the pigeons feasting at our feet, trailing us to see if we drop seeds like pieces of pre-Columbian gold offerings to the gods, now on display in the museum. Behind me I hear Grandmother and Grandfather, heads bent together murmuring in Russian amongst Spanish chatter. I smile, *we will be on their home turf soon enough.*

I don't know what day it is when I stop counting. Perhaps it is the day April rain showers fall as snow. I am pacing, eroding the grass of our empty garden. None of it makes sense and I am tired of trying to understand it. It is, in the end, too monumental. And I am, as always, too insignificant. *And therefore it can never touch me.*

I am washing the dishes. Parents are standing outside looking at the stars. Grandfather is dying.

All the words I keep repeating, trying to beat them into my head, trying desperately—*always trying*—to wring out a conclusion, a lesson. There is none. So it goes.

It is noon and I wake to a pounding on my door and Father saying *"get up, Mom has tickets."* But all I hear is *she is leaving and I am staying* and I finally break.

Spring blooms with apples and peaches and cherries where Mother plants her Eden. Inside, lemons and oranges, tomatoes and peppers, mint, cilantro, celery, and salads. Now, I pace through green neighbourhoods as I regale my new friends with my sorrows and to my surprise *they grow and grow and grow.*

It is a small stab, soft press into my left arm, not even painful. It is everything and nothing I have built it up to be. It is a tentative question, *could this be the beginning of the end?*

I am sick of the news and I don't want to be sick again. I let out a shaky breath as the judge reads the verdict. It feels as though I have been holding it for a long time. Still a long way to go.

It is late now. Midnight for me; midday for her. I am selfish and she is sick and I am afraid to look at her. I cannot sleep. Forty days is a long time for the house to feel so big. I'm scared I've adapted to it. So I sing and dance and scream to fill it. I clean, I haven't cleaned in months.

I have never felt more alone.

She is home.

We meet the decade with cumbia, clinking champagne, fireworks and ¡*Feliz Año!* We hug and kiss and my bare feet slip on the cold grass of the football pitch. My cheeks ache and my throat is scratchy from laughter. I want to jump into the swimming pool and watch the flashing lights floating. I am floating. I look at my family and think if I jump in they will jump with me and we will dance in the sky. I don't want to come down. The air is fresh and it feels like anything is possible.

April showers turn to April snow. *It is snowing in April again. So it goes.* I am Romeo and Juliet and I will never get used to being boxes on a screen. *"Thus with a kiss I die."* She is leaving and I am staying and I have never felt more alone. *The air is fresh and it feels like anything is possible* and we will be on their home turf soon enough and *could this be the beginning of the end?* The WHO calls it a pandemic and President Trump calls it "kung flu" and dread pools in my stomach. It is too monumental and I am too insignificant and therefore it can never touch me. I am selfish and she is sick and I am washing the dishes and Mom has tickets and Grandfather is dying and I haven't cleaned in months. I am always trying and I am ashamed I don't know what my Asia means to me and America is bleeding. I sit in front of the TV in apathy and I am watching in anger and in pain and three days in I am already desensitized. Due to high demand we are limiting purchasing quantities and I am caught in a cycle of blue red blue and what kind of dystopian film have I stumbled into? I regale my new friends with my sorrows and to my surprise they grow and grow and grow. "We should do this more often." I grin. ¡Feliz Año! You don't get it, I know. It goes like this. Everything happens all at once, always.

Letter to My Future Child

My child,

It's a strange kind of longing, born in the dark of night, burrowed under my covers, clutching fabric as it pools around my waist. I can feel you—the soft press of your phantom palms on my face, the slight tickle of hypothetical hair against my nose. It scares me, as I curl into a ball, wrapping my arms tightly around myself, that I can imagine holding you in my embrace. Imagine combing my fingers through your hair—is it silky soft or fluffy curls?—tucking it behind your ears, where I whisper sweet nothings. (By and by I wonder if your skin is an exquisite mixture, like mine, and if you feel the burn of unwanted touch, too.) I don't know what to tell you. I can't sleep, counting cases instead of counting sheep. The numbers are staggering, too many, have not enough. In my mind, a litany of доча, hija, daughter. "You're precious," I begin.

I trace my finger down the slope of your nose, cup your cheeks in my hands and press fluttering kisses on your eyelids. My darling, I cannot begin to fathom the world you have seen. Would I even be able to recognize it? What horrors lie waiting that I am unaware of?

I feel a terrible lurch in my stomach, and I already know I would give every remaining second of my life to you. Every last atom of my body to protect you. What from? I feel the weight of your trust, the crushing expectation rolling off your tongue in a soft whispered plea, "Mama, I'm scared." And there are tears rolling down my face because you believe in the lie that I have all the answers.

And I want to jump out of bed and run to my mother, curl up in her arms and whisper, "Mama, I'm scared. I'm scared of this massive gaping emptiness where people used to be. I'm scared of this world on fire that just keeps turning and turning as we keep burning. Screams drown out the words, but the fire isn't extinguished. And I'm scared of missing friends, of missing the simple feeling of touching skin instead of screen and seeing a smile instead of a mask. I am scared of loving this broken world, of the bright elation and wonder for such a painful place. But Mama, I am more scared of the nothingness, the flatness, the nagging stillness of waking up and going through the motions, of blocking out the screaming, of sitting there as life piles up and piles up and piles up on my shoulders. Mama, I am so small to bear such a burden but too big to hide in your arms."

When I force myself to look back at you, somehow I find—inexplicably but inevitably—my own eyes staring back. You, my child, have my eyes. And in them I can see the fierce hope for a return to innocence. When I feel my heart breaking open inside my chest, I know the warm blood staining your nightshirt is my own. "Hush, my darling," I placate with promises I don't believe. "Baby, it's alright." I brush the tears away, grasp my little hands, and place them to the blooming red spot above my heart. "You're alright, my love." I murmur made-up reassurances of a day in which I can feel the outline of a grin against my lips, restart my bleeding heart and calm the pounding from disillusion back into contentment. And there are no fires here, just a rainbow garden where we all dance among the flowers. Family new and old, reunited with those we lost and those we left behind.

I feel myself relaxing in my arms. Young daughter nestling into the crook of my neck, my world is so uncertain, how can I even begin to think about yours? More seems to fall apart each day and you can't see me breaking. But tonight, buried under my sheets, I mother myself in the second person. I smooth over your stress lines and reaffirm the immensity of your existence. "It's alright," I promise. "I am here to protect you, to rock you to sleep and coax you awake in the morning, to try it all over again." But how can I be mother and daughter? What do I learn from this dynamic I carve out of myself? What do I achieve by allowing me to break but having to be strong enough to hold myself together? My child, I hope you never have to learn this comfort.

All my love

Finding Peace in All the Strange Places

Carmen Marley

Grade 12. Lincoln High School, Lincoln, NE.
Christopher Maly, Educator.

Being Left Behind

My family and I moved my sister into college over Labor Day weekend. Sunday afternoon we packed up all her things—her ten-foot long extension cord and collection of young adult fantasy novels and brand new posters recently acquired from Gomez Art Supply—all the possessions that add a sense of home to her stuffy dorm—into our smoky topaz Honda minivan and drove six hours to her rural Minnesota university town. Monday night, after organizing her clothes and putting sheets on the bed, we started towards home; this time, with one less passenger in the back seat.

It was our second time at this move-in rodeo, so the goodbye didn't feel nearly as heavy and hard as it was when she was a freshman. Last fall, I cried ugly tears as she gave me a tight squeeze and a quick *I love you* in the auditorium after convocation, just before hurrying off to find her orientation group outside on the lawn. I felt so worried about losing her—about no longer having the connection, the friendship, the sort of silent communication that only a sister can provide—but now I know better (or maybe I feel less attached): she will always be there.

As we drove away, and I watched the dark green northern landscape fade into the beige corn fields of Iowa and Nebraska, all bathing in a distinctly September glow as the sun dipped below the horizon, I tried to feel something—nostalgia, sadness, melancholy—but if anything, and I hate to admit this, I felt free and relieved. Indeed, sometimes I think that there is a sort of identity I am able to embody only when my sister is not at home: someone who is more independent, who is fiercely taking on the world, not waiting for somebody else to lead the way. It is not that I don't love Janna, that I do not yearn to be with her; it is simply that there is a greater self that I am unable to fulfill when she is present.

I spent much of my childhood putting my sister on a pedestal. (I still do it now, though at least I am self aware.) She was and is one of the most intelligent people I know. She is incredibly thoughtful and only chimes into discussions when she has something worthwhile to say, always careful not to speak on topics that she isn't well enough versed in. During dinner table debates I watch her eyes and the slight tug of her lips to deduce her opinion, though often to no avail—she doesn't pick sides in the senseless debates that my father and I get into at the slightest convenience.

My parents don't pick favorites, but even *I* can understand that my sister is easier to love than me. I have moods and get frustrated easily and fall into a somewhat polarizing personality in family settings; where I am loud and impulsive my sister is kind and passive.

I think it's a somewhat unsettling experience to suddenly be an only child during the late teenage years. All my life, I have expected to share everything and constantly be compared, but also to have a partner in crime, someone to gang up on my parents with. Now that I am home by myself for at least eight months out of the year, I feel like a fish out of water, like I am reaching a dead end in my life: completely lost and unsure where to turn.

I have this memory from when I was really little, probably just four or five years old. It was a rainy Sunday in Spring and my sister and I had just baked sugar cookies with our mom. Mother was searching in the cupboards for frosting and sprinkles to add decoration with, but immediately when Janna saw the icing, she made a sour face and said in a disgusted tone of voice: *none of that for me ... frosting makes things wayyy too sweet!* Without even really considering my own opinion, I followed suit and rejected the glaze; whatever Janna disliked was objectively bad—who was I to disagree with her?

By the time I reached middle school, I at least understood that people can have separate preferences—that to blindly agree on matters as simple as frosting is immature and childish—but I continued to find myself, consciously and unconsciously, trying to be her in many areas of life.

My sister is and always will be my greatest friend and role model, but as she sets off on her own journey and I too find my own direction, I feel her existence weighing on me and my decisions less and less. There is much in my sister that I hope to embody in myself—but I am trying to recognize that where she is a shining star, I have my own light to share. I can recognize the goodness in her without slighting myself—I just wish it hadn't taken me seventeen years and 400 miles between us to figure that out.

Summer Camp Sadness

I mean what the hell, the world will be over in 70 years anyways. This was a thought that ran through my head quite frequently this past summer, occasionally even springing off my tongue jokingly to my sister and friends, though I was always a little uncertain whether or not I was serious. Indeed, for much of my adolescence, I allowed climate change to be a little bug in the back of my mind. Its high-pitched voice occasionally squeaked up to tell me to walk to school or shop sustainably (often after a conversation with family or an especially moving headline in the *Washington Post*). But it had suddenly transformed into a full fledged figure in my life, following me around, pushing me toward a much more nihilistic view of the world.

This shadow appeared during my family vacation in Italy, as I experienced a record-breaking heatwave first hand. It attended my archaeological internship in Virginia as well, as I listened to discussions of the impact of sea-level rise on the field—how there are entire sites that have been eroded and washed away due to global warming, entire windows into the past gone.

Despite this, I continued with my life as normal—working, seeing friends—but I felt, underneath it all, hopeless and extremely sad. I couldn't imagine my life decades down the line; the world existing on my 80th birthday seemed unthinkable. Even worse, I felt there was nothing I could do: a well known study I had heard about years prior concluded large corporations make up 70 percent of emissions, and in my mind, humanity would never turn its back on capitalism in a way that would be effective.

One day while at my summer camp job, sitting in a meadow as a few seven year old campers braided dandelions into my curls, I considered this predicament. It was unseasonably cool; a chill of spring was present that was normally far gone by mid-June, and had the sun been behind a cloud, I may have been cold. It was beautiful, yet I couldn't help thinking of how days like this were fleeting, how sad it was that these children would grow up in such a cruel, transient world.

But as their giggles surrounded me, their banter making me laugh despite myself, I thought of my own childhood, growing up at this rural Midwestern summer camp. I saw myself in the kids around me: barefoot with dirt between their fingers, wearing dresses simply because that's what they liked, but not letting that stop them from climbing trees and playing tag. I thought about how gingerly they held butterflies in their hands, and the strength they used when pulling bindweed from tomato plants in the garden. I saw how fiercely and independently they experienced the world, how much they truly were *kids*.

As I sat there in that field, feeling the soft tingle of little girls playing with my hair, their bright eyes looking up at me with gleaming adoration, I felt at peace for the first time in a while. I thought, *the world is ending but children are still children; the world is ending but life goes on.*

Suddenly that shadowy figure felt like someone I could befriend, someone I could face and work with, not someone I should hide from. I felt that there was a truly beautiful world around me, and I felt that it would still be beautiful even if everything I feared came true, even if I couldn't do anything about it, because people would still be people, and their kindness can be the most breathtaking wonder of all.

Ignorance Is Bliss

So this is it, a moment that feels both sudden and unexpected, yet at the same time marks the culmination of a decades-long struggle: *Roe v. Wade* has been overturned, and just a little over a month shy of my seventeenth birthday. I know it seems funny and ignorant—putting those two events together, side by side, as though they hold equal moral and political gravity—but in my small world, the one where I am the center, the sun, it feels as though they hold the same weight. Indeed, these two entities, one that marks my liberation from moody teen into an almost-adult, the beginning of the end of my childhood, and an exciting time of learning and discovery, and another that conveys a new era of oppression in the lives of myself and so many others, feel very at odds at this unique point in my life, like two magnets pulling me in opposite directions.

This summer so far has felt so special to me, every day like the opening credits of a coming-of-age movie. I wake up each morning feeling inspired and rejuvenated, as though the sunrise has provided a new opportunity for me to reinvent myself and explore the possibilities of who I am and what I want to become. In the past few weeks, I have spent long, never-ending hours in the car, gotten caught in the rain more than a few times, started my first ever job, flown half-way across the country by myself, met new people, and watched countless sunsets, and yet nothing, no singular experience from a laundry list of firsts felt more defining than the moment on June 24th when I learned that my reproductive rights have been stripped from me. It was like after a precious era of basking in my new found independence and freedom as a soon-to-be high school senior, my senses finally caught up to me. I remembered that I am a woman in 21st century America, and unfortunately that means that no, I may not explore my sexuality, or date around, or be rebellious, or make mistakes, because instead, I must live with the constant and gut-wrenching fear that with a pregnancy, my goals, my identity, my passions, and my plans could all be stripped from me, just like that.

While on the one hand the recent Supreme Court decision makes me angry and hurt and pushes me to protest and fight, another, less courageous part of my mind simply wants to go back to being the kid I felt like a few days ago. I want to sit by the pool with my friends. I want to worry about college applications and how much money I'm spending on overpriced lattes. I don't want to think about humanity's impending doom, and how in many ways, my rights are more restricted now than they were for some women 50 years ago. And I also recognize that I am able to do this: if I wanted to just "stay out of politics" and pretend sexism doesn't exist and go about my life as a naive high school student, I could, and that comes from a place of great privilege. I was born into a supportive, progressive, upper-middle class family. If at any point I needed an abortion but could not be provided with one in my current state, my parents would pay for me to travel to get one; I know this with absolute certainty. In this way, I understand that this ruling does not impact me in any comparable way to the way it impacts women of color, women in low-income communities, and women in the South.

But despite not being impacted in a practical sense, I am still struggling greatly to come to terms with this new reality; I feel almost as though my life has been split in two. Every day, I struggle to choose what world I want to live in: do I wallow in fear and hurt as I watch the government demolish the small fraction of equality women stand on, or do I go about my life as normal, excited for the future and content in the present moment?

Chaos in the Absence of Routine

College. This was the only thing on my mind the August before senior year and yet at the same time I was in a constant state of avoidance of the topic. Essays, recommendation letters, transcripts, interviews—they all felt so overwhelming that whenever I sat down to do anything about them I felt about to be sick. Simultaneously, college was keeping me alive. I loved my hometown in a special way—I felt a unique sense of belonging and safety within the city limits of the liberal midwestern enclave of Lincoln, Nebraska—but I also knew that the next term at my high school might about kill me, and I was dreading it profusely. The only light at the end of the tunnel, at least the only one my sunsick eyes could see, was moving somewhere far, far away and creating a new identity for myself at some small leftist university, probably in the East.

Everyone I knew had a different idea for what they wanted in a school, a fact that surprised me as I expected everyone to want the exact thing I desired, so I got a sort of thrill out of the uniqueness of my goals. Kennedy wanted to go to California, Julia a state school in North Carolina, Kaitlin to Michigan, and others craved the societal prestige of the Ivies. It was like we were all about to jump off the same cliff, hoping to land in drastically different places, but no actual control, really, as to where we ended up.

It was around this same time that I was beginning to enjoy starving myself again. This had been an issue for me the previous summer and I had worked hard to get away from the routine, but with the clockwork of a chain smoker, there I was, back at it again. I was suddenly gaining a strange euphoria from lying in bed for hours in the morning, unaware of the time but for the color of light streaming in my windows, feeling a deep hunger in my stomach as I turned pages of something by Sylvia Plath. When I saw myself in reflective windows on walks I wouldn't quite recognize the figure staring back at me and would feel a jolt of dopamine as I saw that the woman in front of me, with a spine rising from underneath the skin of her back and ribs peeking out of her stomach, was actually myself. As awful as I know it sounds, I felt elated as I familiarized myself with just how thin and sickly I was beginning to look.

Unavoidably of course, I felt a slight guilt over this resurfaced obsession of mine. Not because I genuinely cared about my health, but because, subconsciously, I felt as though I was doing something wrong—breaking some unspoken rule—and knew my parents would be disappointed in me if they found out. During a walk one cool summer morning my mother made a comment about how she felt that I wasn't eating enough—that she was worried for me, worried I wouldn't be able to attend college or be successful in my education if I continued on this way. I hated when my mother got emotional like that—it gave me such intense anxiety I simply wanted to jump from my body and run—so I said whatever I could to get her to drop the subject, all the while ignoring the substance of her words. Nevertheless, the conversation came back to me again and again as my mental health regressed.

A few weeks before the first day of school, I decided on a whim to bike over to a bagel shop downtown to get lunch. The shop was near the local university campus and was filled with students who had stayed in town for the summer. I absently observed their biker shorts, Lululemon tank tops, Nike sneakers and straight, untangled hair—in other words, the way their whiteness and all-American upper-middle class wealth flooded over their appearances to mold them into the most bland, basic version of themselves. The students were an embodiment of the life I was at a never ending war with to escape, so I was reminded how desperate I was to leave Nebraska the following fall.

After some consideration, I realized that I must not look much younger than the students surrounding me—I was but a year their junior—but nevertheless, I felt immature and small compared to all of them. I remember a girl walking in wearing a body-con pink dress and six-inch nude heels attached to a boy with a muscled linebacker's body wearing athletic shorts and an oversized red t-shirt. I assumed they were on a date (this was confirmed later when I watched him pay for her meal), and I felt bad for her because she was clearly dressed for a much different lunch. Somehow, though, she played this off with such effortless confidence that I felt more intimidated by her than anything else. Her facial expression somehow seemed to say that she meant for this to happen—this was her plan all along. She was attractive, attractive in such a way that made me overlook the sorority girl appearance in her that I detested, and when we made eye contact as I stood in the corner, sipping my ice water waiting for my sandwich, I saw something in her face that made me feel she had an edge to her—more intelligence and cunning than my internalized misogyny had originally given her credit for.

I waited a while for my order to get made. When my name finally did get called I collected my food with a smile and then asked the girl there if I could get a lid for my water, but apparently I had said this so quietly that she did not hear me and asked back to me, *a lid for your what?* In a very sing-songy voice that made me think she must not have imagined me to have a brain. I found this slightly insulting but mostly interesting. I didn't see myself as the sort of person that came off seeming very stupid and enjoyed getting to know how I was perceived by others. As I collected my things I decided, if nothing else, this outing had taught me that I was woefully unprepared for the social rigor of a public university and needed to change something about myself to become more appealing.

Afterwards, I sat outside eating my bagel in very small bites between reading blurbs of *The Bell Jar*. As I baked in that humid, late summer heat, I was beginning to realize I was rather uninterested in consuming the thing I had spent most of the morning thinking about. Every time I lifted my sandwich to my mouth I thought about my reflection in the window—the woman I was becoming—and all that was tied up with the uncertainty of the time.

With the sun beating down on me, sweat moistening the meeting between my scalp and face, I felt terrified for college and school and senior year—but I was beginning to realize that most of all I was scared I would look awful in front of all the people I wanted to impress. That was the truth, wasn't it? As much as I tried to appear unbothered, I wanted to impress everyone in my life: my mother, the girls at the cafe, all my insufferable friends. I hated saying that I was afraid to be fat—I was too much a feminist to logically believe in such a patriarchal disgust with weight—but I was. I was afraid to be fat because I was so obsessed with attaining the perfect picture of my life.

I folded my sandwich into its paper wrappings and put it away. I sat there a moment longer, pondering all of these subjects swirling in my mind: college and people and my body and food. I felt terrible. I felt as though I should hate myself when my mind goes a mile a minute the way it does but I didn't—I actually liked the way I saw the world, the way I existed. I thought to myself, *what should it matter about all of these things when I enjoy my own company?* Then I laughed—I laughed at myself because that was the sort of nothing phrase that a motivational speaker would say and I rejected myself for attempting to feed such a trite piece of advice to my mind, but deep down, I think I felt a quiet sense of comfort from it. I swung my bag over my shoulder, grabbed my bike, and rode home, but secretly, somewhere in the innermost chambers of my heart, I felt that I would be okay.

Sisters

Akmed. This was the name my sister gave to me while stationed with two friends of my parents, Morrie and Rebecca, as my mother and father rushed to the hospital for my arrival. Evidently, at the age of one year and three hundred fifty-two days, Janna simply could not put together the syllables to pronounce my actual name, but I often wonder what image she had in her mind as she said Akmed. Did she find this name beautiful—would she have wanted me to have a beautiful name? What did she think Akmed would be like? Did she realize it was her sister she was talking about, did she realize what that meant? When I think about that day, I laugh at my sister's innocent stupidity, but I also see it as a moment of quiet importance. I feel that in many ways that was the beginning of our connection: Janna was forging the way for me, deciding what sort of person I would be before I was even truly a person; our souls were slowly reaching out to each other, intertwined before we had even met.

I grew up believing that my sister was a better person than me. I suppose one could read that to be a somewhat sweet expression of my love for her, a testament to her positive mentorship throughout my childhood, but it was always a thought that passed through my mind in a much more self-deprecating manner. I think, for a long time, I felt that Janna's existence simply exposed my fundamental inadequacies as a person: I was a failure while my sister was a beacon of all things good. But our dynamic was not nearly as dramatic as I'm making it out to be; I loved my sister and generally felt valued by my parents growing up. My idolization of her was simply the beat underneath the melody of our coming of age.

My sister was a quiet child and mostly bottled her emotions inside—my mom always said this about her. She'd look over at Janna at the dinner table, perhaps moving her pesto noodles around her plate with the caress of a fork, an aloof expression gracing her features, and she'd comment something in an amused, tender tone like, *I think Janna has something brewing inside of her, I wonder when she'll burst.* But my sister never did: even in the throes of depression when she was 13, she was never one to communicate with words or volunteer information. In many ways, I felt this aspect of her character put her on a separate, more refined plane than me. I sometimes still feel this way.

Occasionally, I wonder if this masking of emotions was a product of her mental illness showing up early on or some sort of trauma response from infancy, but at the time, it simply provided objectivity to her superiority over me. Unlike myself, who threw tantrums often and was an overall angry child, Janna was a portrait of composure. At times, I became jealous over the excessive attention she received from my parents whilst trying to unravel her emotions, or felt cheated by the undue praise she received for her self-control.

When Janna and I were little we had this book meant to teach us to love one another, I suppose. Aptly called *Sisters*, it was a delicate, short thing with big, dreamy sketches and a sentence, at most, of writing on each page. It was about these two girls, siblings, who were similar in some ways and different in others, but loved each other through it all. We could spend hours staring at the thing before bed—comparing ourselves to each daughter, laughing at how similar the characters were to us.

Recently I found the book lying around the office of my house and, feeling a sense of comfort in the dusty pages, absently flipped through the story. As I examined each page, giggling at the memories

I recalled, letting the nostalgia wash over me, I realized I no longer felt the resentment towards my sister that I did as a young child. Truly, I know now that Janna was hurting as much as me—that we were both struggling to deal with the prospect of growing up, aching to find our places in the world. At the age of seventeen, I think I am just beginning to take *Sisters* for what it was worth; I am only now understanding the yin and yang that Janna and I truly embody, that our identities can ebb and flow without infringing on one another's worth. We are two rivers joining and meeting and joining again—etching out our silhouettes in the mountain side.

The Things We Don't Talk About

In November of my senior year of high school, I found, after months of non-stop creation, I was struggling to write. I knew why: I could not feel. In many ways, I could tell I had let go of my once incessant internal monologue, and without that lifeline of white noise in my head, I found myself floating through life like a stray balloon: helplessly uncertain of where I was headed and filled with nothing but air.

I suppose other things had taken priority and I had simply forgotten to think, forgotten to process my existence. When things get hard for me that is how I cope, and man, things were hard. My eating disorder is not a secret but I do find it quite difficult to talk about. Tears or nervous laughs often come along as side effects when I am forced to discuss it. I don't really know why—I have no issue bringing up my anxiety or certain self-diagnosed depressive episodes, but my eating disorder is a bit of a gray area in my mind. Like a parasite, it is separate from my body, but it grips my nerves, my heart, my lungs, hoping to pass undetected, and it takes what it wants. That chilly gray November, I had given it less and it had wanted more; as the cold set in, I found myself too weak to fight.

Earlier that year, in late August, I had read Roxane Gay's memoir, *Hunger*, and found it to be evocative and insightful. It told the story of her childhood rape, subsequent eating disorder, and resulting experiences as a fat woman. I related to some things and found most others to be very much removed from my life, but I suppose that's what I wanted from it. I wanted to know what it is like to be fat—what it is to experience what many would consider my illness's opposite; that was precisely what I received.

During my reading, I felt a guilty curiosity in the details of Gay's disorder. I perceived, whether this be false or otherwise, that I was doing something wrong by reading her work; I somehow decided the narrative wasn't *for* me, and that therefore I should have nothing to do with it. Simultaneously, I understood the feeling came from the taboo I felt around my condition—that it denoted some deep-rooted flaw buried inside, and I could not bear to let it out. Engaging in literature that could help dismantle my internal fatphobia and inform me on the struggles of others, or, if taken the wrong way, feed into the fears that motivate my disease, forced me to face myself in new and uncomfortable ways.

We all have those things we don't talk about. Veterans don't talk about war, widows don't talk about husbands, and I don't talk about my eating disorder. I vividly remember sitting on a cold metal foldable chair in the main athletic center of Doane University, my mother's voice echoing through the microphone while delivering the keynote graduation speech, and learning, for the first time at the age of 11, of her long-term battle with depression. I felt shocked and caught off guard that this space—this appearance in front of thousands of people—would be where she would choose to discuss this topic. I recognize now, though, that there are parts of life that simply feel like too much, that appear unbearable, so we tuck them away in all our secret places and hope we can hide from them in plain sight.

Indeed, sometimes it is easier to speak to strangers in hoards than to a family member one-on-one.

But important things get lost in the crossfire when we choose not to experience ourselves in full honesty, and that is where I found myself that November. Slowly but surely, I realized being human is about grappling with the hard stuff, and grappling starts with communicating, whether that simply be with my own consciousness or an entirely separate individual.

As a freshman in secondary school, I was obsessed with Luca Guadanino's *Call Me by Your Name.* The Italian imagery and dreamlike atmosphere was immensely comforting for me, but I don't think I truly understood its core theme until now. It can be summed with a quote from one of the final scenes: "but to make yourself feel nothing, so as not to feel anything—what a waste."

Twisted Fairytales

Logan Sylliaasen

Grade 12. Bishop Neumann Central High School, Wahoo, NE. Marisa Grady, Educator.

Cruel Reflections

Ada stared at the mirror, her breath coming in short, panicked gasps. A young girl with gold eyes in a red gown stared back at her, her expression hauntingly terrified. Ada pressed her shaking hands to her chest, willing herself to calm down, to breathe in and out. *I'm going to be fine,* she told herself, then choked out a broken laugh at the blatant lie. *No, I won't. I have been second best to her my entire life. Always. So why now, when my life depends on it, do I expect anything different?* Ada shook her head, banishing the thought, and straightened, tamping down the roiling flames of her magic.

"It's time, miss." Ada turned and saw a guard standing in the doorway. She glanced around her room one final time, her eyes hungrily devouring the space she likely would never return to. The guards outside her door flinched as she passed. Although it had been years since the last incident, the damage was irrevocable. They did not even try to hide their fear, their hate.

Ada stopped in front of pair of grand double doors and waited, her entourage of guards halting behind her. A soft pair of footsteps padded against the cold stone floor, halting next to Ada, who simply lifted her chin and stared forwards.

"How are you feeling?" the sweet voice of Ada's twin, Arwen, questioned. Ada's breath caught slightly, but she remained silent. She wouldn't give her sister that satisfaction of seeing how thoroughly her actions had broken her, alienated her, isolated her. She wouldn't show how alone she was, how desperate for love she knew she would never receive.

Arwen plowed on, unperturbed by Ada's silence. "I'm terrified," she whispered. "Ada, there are so many things I wish to tell you—"

Ada stiffened. "Please don't," she whispered.

Arwen's face turned pleading, a desperation flickering behind her emerald eyes that made Ada pause. But she simply turned away, facing the doors as they swung open. There was nothing Arwen could say that could make a difference now. Nothing that could atone for the past.

Both sisters stepped forward, equally enthralled with the grand room within. Massive windows lined the walls, letting in golden rays of sunlight that rebounded off of the vast amounts of wealth and treasure decorating the hall. Although the beauty was breathtaking, it made Ada sick. All the riches and power had been leached from the deaths of girls. Girls like Ada. Clusters of finely dressed nobility whispered and sneered, eyeing the sisters hungrily as they approached the throne and the figure perched upon it. Both girls stooped into deep curtsies, their eyes cast to the ground.

"Rise," Queen Adeline said, her voice imperious and void of emotion. Ada rose and stared at her mother with cold eyes, relishing the flicker of fear she witnessed. Good. The Queen switched her gaze to Arwen, offering the other girl a soft smile. Ada's fire boiled within her, and she shoved it down. *Second best. Second choice.* Ada had never quite discovered why her mother had never loved her the way she loved Arwen. Perhaps it was Arwen's perfect smile and pretty nature magic. Perhaps it was the way Ada had let her emotions run free like wildfire.

Perhaps it was the way Ada seemed to burn everything she touched, both figuratively and literally. Or perhaps it was jealousy. Ada possessed raw power her mother could only dream of. And although Ada had worked so, so hard to control her power and emotions, to seal them behind ironclad bars, it had not been enough. She had not been enough.

"Welcome to the Choosing," Adeline said. "Since the beginnings of our kingdom, this most sacred ceremony has determined the future of our great nation," she paused, turning towards her daughters. "One for the throne and one for the blade. The Mirror shall choose."

"One for the throne, one for the blade," the court echoed. In Ada's queendom, every ruler gave birth to a set of twins, both blessed with magic. On their eighteenth birthday, the twins were presented to the Mirror, an enchanted artifact that judged their spirit and power, and chose. One twin to be queen, and the other to be slain, a sacrifice to fuel the magic of the queendom for another eighteen years. It was cruel and ruthless, but it was tradition, and it had brought the crown vast amounts of wealth. None dared to question it.

The crowd quieted as the Queen beckoned her daughters onto the dais, placing them in front of a veiled object mounted on the wall. Ada started, unable to stop the brief jolt of surprise. The concealed object, which had to be the Mirror, had not been there moments ago. A slight tremble wracked her body, but she tamped it down. She had worked too hard, sacrificed too much, to be afraid of a simple object. It would choose her, right? She was the most powerful princess in generations. That had to be worth something.

The Queen pulled the veil from the Mirror, letting the swaths of fabric drift to the ground. Ada's gaze locked onto its polished surface. It was not nearly as big as she had imagined, and yet it was all encompassing, its gilded frame expanding and pulsing, pulling her into its depths, down,

  down,

    down ...

Ada gasped, her head spinning. The throne room and its occupants were gone, and in its place was a simple wooden stage surrounded by pure, unending darkness. Ada stood on one end, Arwen on the other, both girls dressed in simple ivory slips instead of their ceremonial red gowns. A simple full-length mirror stood in front of each girl, glass was empty, void of the reflections it should have held.

Magic mirror, on the wall ...

A chant, made of one voice and many all at once, seemed to echo from everywhere and nowhere.

Magic mirror, on the wall ...

Arwen turned towards Ada, her expression desperate. "We don't have to do this, Ada. You and I, we are powerful enough to fight this. We can end this cycle of bloodshed. We can free ourselves from the roles they forced us to play. Please. We were friends. We can be friends again." Her voice broke, and Ada shook her head in disgust.

"*You* made them hate me! *You* shoved me into my role, the role of a *monster*," Ada snapped, her voice cold and hard although her hands shook. "You destroyed my life, and now you want me to forgive you?"

"I never meant for any of that to happen!" Arwen pleaded, "Ada, please believe me! I don't want to kill you, and I don't believe that you want to kill me either!"

Magic mirror on the wall, who is the fairest one of all?

The chanting stopped suddenly, and a floating face appeared in each of the girls' mirrors. Its features were simple, but the eyes ...

They were soulless, a fathomless abyss ...

Suddenly, Ada was falling again, her spirit wrenched from her body and through the glass.

Look at you, a voice crooned. Ada whirled about, searching frantically for an exit, a doorway, anything. She was trapped within her mirror, her body frozen on the other side. Ada pounded her fists against the glass, shouting for Arwen, for anyone.

Hmm. You have such interesting eyes. I suppose you're pretty, but the other one is much better to look at.

Ada shuddered but said nothing.

Let's have a look at the fun stuff, shall we?

You're certainly ambitious, if not a bit delusional. Its adorable that you thought some training, a bit of control, could change what you are.

The voice paused, the silence begging Ada to ask. She conceded, the words almost jumping out of her mouth without her consent. "And what am I, exactly?"

The voice laughed humorlessly. *I think you already know the answer to that.*

The room faded, and suddenly Ada was watching her twelve-year-old self laugh and twirl, fire dancing around her body. The crowd gazed in awe as Ada bent the flames to her will, her eyes gleaming. This was the twins' first public appearance, a demonstration of their gifts. Arwen stood off to the side next to the Queen, both scowling. The crowd had not been near as impressed with her display.

But as young Ada's emotions rose, so did her fire. It grew, swelling with her elation and pride, spreading towards the edges of the platform. And as Ada spun, eyes full of joy, no one noticed Arwen wrap her arms in vines and reach into the flames. Not until she started screaming. Ada panicked, her fire shooting out in the crowd. The arena filled with screams.

Monster.

"No," Ada pleaded. "That wasn't my fault."

But wasn't it? the mirror said. *You lost control, and she took advantage of it.*

"But I can control it now!" Ada pleaded. "I won't hurt anyone!"

Do you really believe that?

Ada opened her mouth to respond, her body shaking, "I—"

Inevitably, you will lose control again. You are the embodiment of your power. Destructive. Uncontrollable.

Each word cut into Ada's skin like a knife, tearing through the barriers she had built to contain her emotions, pierced through fears she had tried so hard to bury.

You are broken. And the most dangerous part of it is that you do not realize that you are.

Ada tumbled back through her mirror and onto the stage. She whirled, searching for her sister, but Arwen was gone, and so was her mirror.

I am sorry, Ada. You have not been chosen.

"No!" Ada screamed. Sparks flew from her hands as she trembled with fear and fury. "You can't do this!" Her fists pounded against her mirror, flames engulfing her hands as her strikes grew more desperate, more erratic. Ada sank to her knees as a fiery storm erupted all around her, her power spiraling out of control, rising with her emotions. "You can't leave me here to die!"

Your mind will be here. You will not register the pain. The Mirror nearly sounded sympathetic.

But Ada wasn't listening. She screamed, a pure, primal sound of rage, and bright cobalt flames erupted from her mouth, spewing across the stage and charring the edges of her mirror.

Ada blinked, her panic ceasing eerily as she assessed the damage. Her flames receded suddenly, and the only remaining sign of the firestorm was the smoke painting the edges of her mirror. She cocked her head, her lips twitching into a slight smile. "Got you," she murmured. Then Ada raised her hands and unleashed herself.

With her fear and restraint gone, Ada's power felt endless, a bottomless pool of destruction responsive to her every whim. Fire erupted from her outstretched hands, enveloping the stage in a wave of blues and reds.

Stop this at once. The Mirror nearly sounded alarmed. But Ada was determined, unleashing the full brunt of her power without fear for the first time in her life. And it felt liberating.

Suddenly the scene shifted, and Ada was falling again, tumbling into another memory.

Crack. Her mother's hand slammed into her younger self's cheek. She reeled back, tears in her eyes as her little hand came up to brush her face in shock. An angry red burn in the shape of a handprint marred her mother's wrist. Little fires flickered across the room as Ada's younger self pleaded and begged.

"I-I didn't mean to! I didn't mean to!"

Ada watched the scene, her anger growing with each strike her mother dealt. She reached deep down, dragging up more magic, and threw her hands out, her fire incinerating the vision.

The memory shifted yet again, but this time Ada didn't wait. She simply rained flames from one scene to the next, tearing through each with ease until a glimpse of pale yellow flashed in the edges of her vision. Ada paused, and the memory enveloped her senses.

She was nine, and Arwen stood in front of her, her hands full of yellow roses.

"I made you these," Arwen whispered, shuffling her feet nervously, "because I want us to be friends. Yellow roses are for friendship. And we'll always be friends, right?"

Young Ada looked at her sister, her eyes filled with hope as she accepted the roses with a small nod.

Something cracked inside Ada as she watched. It had all been a lie. The only love she's ever known was a lie.

Ada screamed, and her power screamed with her. Flames erupted, burning the memory to ash.

When the smoke cleared, Ada found herself in front of her mirror yet again. Its glass was nearly shattered, its frame smoking and crumbling.

Wreathed in flames, Ada prepared to deliver the final blow.

I wouldn't do that.

Ada ignored the Mirror and raised her arms.

If you tear through the fabric of this enchantment and back to your world, you will tear through your psyche. Your mind will be destroyed.

Ada inhaled deeply. She felt hollow, empty of anything but cool, unfeeling fury. "It already is."

Fire streamed from Ada's palms. Her mirror cracked and splintered, then shattered, pieces flying across the stage. For a moment, everything was still.

Then Ada screamed, gripping her head, clawing at her hair as invisible shards wedged their way into her mind, tearing and shredding. Blood trickled out of her eyes and ears as she was yanked from the Mirror, soaring up,

up,

up ...

Ada gasped, her eyes flying open. She was back in the great hall, free of the enchantment, and bound to the throne, her arms and legs wrapped in chains. A pretty girl with green eyes stood above her, the dagger in her hand shaking slightly. Ada's mind stumbled about, trying to remember, but there was only raging fire. Then their gazes locked for a moment.

And Ada remembered.

"Hello, sister," Ada crooned. Then she sucked in a breath and blew a plume of flame into Arwen's face.

Her twin screamed and stumbled back, dropping the dagger. The crowd erupted into panic, shouts echoing around the room. Ada cocked her head slightly, eyeing her chains. She inhaled, forcing the heat of her magic into her arms and legs. The nobles looked on in horror as Ada melted the metal, its burning ore dripping down her body. The scent of cooked flesh filled the throne room, and all Ada could do was laugh as she rose from the throne. Her head was filled with splitting pain, her vision red with the blood that still dripped down her face, staining her teeth a shocking crimson.

"Arrrwennnn," she called, drawing out the syllables with a giggle. "You lied to me." Her sister looked up just in time to dive to the side as a burst of fire shot from Ada's hand. Someone in the crowd screamed, and Ada turned, her attention fixed upon them. She grinned and waved.

And they all went up in flames. The hall had gone eerily silent when Ada turned back to Arwen.

"What happened to you?" Arwen gasped, still clutching at her face.

Ada stalked forwards. "I thought you would be pleased! I only became exactly what you wanted me to be!" She wrenched Arwen's arms away from her face. Her twin sister's skin was an angry red, blisters already lining her cheeks. "A monster." Ada clicked her tongue, shaking her head as her sister trembled. "Poor little princess. You always did have such a pretty face. Such a pretty little face that told such pretty little lies. You know, at least no one else tried to hide their hate. But *you*, you actually had me fooled! I thought you cared for me! I thought you wanted to be *friends!* I thought there might have been one person in my life who didn't hate me simply for existing, for being more powerful, but of course I was wrong!" She laughed again, relishing the fear in her sister's gaze.

"Oh, I'm going to enjoy killing you."

"Y-you can't," Arwen stuttered. "The Mirror—"

"The Mirror is gone! I destroyed it." Ada giggled, gesturing to where the Mirror had hung on the wall. In its place was a smoking crater and a few shards of burnt glass. "And now, I'm going to destroy you."

Arwen stumbled back, flowers and vines streaming from her hands towards Ada, who incinerated them with a wave of her hand.

"Magic mirror, on the wall," she sang.

Arwen's heels hit the back of the throne, and she glanced desperately from side to side, eyes searching for help that wasn't coming.

The burnt corpses of the nobles littered the floor. The Queen had fled the moment Ada's eyes had flown open.

"Who is the fairest of them all?"

"Ada, please. I wouldn't have done it. I wouldn't have killed you. We're sisters. *Friends.*"

"Stop lying!" Ada shrieked. "You're still lying to me!" She clenched her fists, and fire roared to life around her sister. Tears streamed down Arwen's face as she screamed, Ada's fire consuming her.

"One for the throne, one for the blade. One for the throne, one for the blade," Ada sang happily as she heaved her sister's body off of the throne and sat, her legs crossed primly as she surveyed the carnage she had wrought. She snapped her fingers, and a crown of blue flames encircled her head, flickering menacingly in the light of the hall, and sparking off of a gleaming shard near Ada's feet. A small smile played at her lips as she eyed the remnant of the Mirror.

"It was a valiant effort, really. You tried, just like so many others, to let me burn within the flames of my pain. But you never anticipated what would emerge from the ashes." Ada grinned. "I'll give you one more chance. Magic mirror, on the wall, who *now* is the fairest one of all?"

Ada smashed her foot down, crushing the shard to dust.

The Girl Who Fell in Love with Stories

Once upon a time, in a land not far from anything but near to nothing, there lived a girl who loved stories. Words on a page, pictures on a screen, she adored it all, devoured it all. And although she had friends at school and at home, her best friends were the characters she had grown to love, brought to life in bright, vibrant shades of imagination.

The girl was always reading new stories or revisiting old ones, and when she wasn't doing that she was thinking about them. Her head was full of stories, full of daydreams and nightmares, her hands always itching to turn to the next page, to leap into the next world. The teachers would frown and scowl and take away her books when she tried to read during class, but she didn't care, because by then the stories had become a part of her. Her head was filled with dragons and daydreams and glittering ballrooms full of enchanting secrets.

To her, the stories were not just a source of wonder and magic in a monotonous world full of prying eyes and expectations, but they were a comfort and light in the bleak boring gray of her life. She turned to stories, traveled to those faraway lands, to drown the shouts and screams of her parents' fighting with words of whimsy and wonder. She journeyed to galaxies far, far away when her small-town world began to feel much too small (it nearly always did). When the expectant voices all around her were too loud, when she was sinking, losing the sparkle of her eyes, she would open a book, get lost in its pages, and everything else would quiet. The stories became a reprieve, and maybe some would call it escapism, and maybe it was, but she didn't believe that. Because those stories shaped her, molded her, crafted her, held her up when her own legs couldn't, calmed her shaking hands, silenced the endless cruel torrent of her own thoughts. She drew her courage, her ideals, and most importantly, her dreaming, from stories, because if those characters could get up every morning and rattle the stars, then so could she.

And so a dreamer was born.

People would laugh at her vacant, faraway stares, her lofty aspirations that longed to whisk her away, far away, outside the realm contained within their small-town small mindedness. They laughed at her excitement and passion when she talked about the stories that meant so much to her. And when she told them her plan for her future they laughed at that too. And little by little, it began to wear her down. Her sparkle began to fade, her voice began to quiet, lost within the cacophony, striving to be just like everyone else. And striving to be like everyone else, in a small town full of small minds, is a dangerous thing. The tangled mess of threads and ink and love and words that consorts to create individuality is repressed, pushed down and strangled by the desire to be liked, embraced, included. And so, for a while, she was ashamed of her stories. She would write and write, and a feeling of immense pride would emerge from those patterns of words she had constructed, and yet, when the teacher asked her to share, she lowered her eyes and shook her head. She hid her wild mind brimming with big ideas, she purposely answered incorrectly or lied about her test scores, all because of some ridiculous, innate desire to fit in. She got her wish.

And she was miserable.

She had never hated herself more. As the days passed, she grew more quiet, more reserved, drew inwards, drew within herself more and more. And her inner self, her mind, was no longer a wondrous place of whimsy and magic. It was a wasteland, leaching every shred of self-love or even respect from its landscape. It was a monster, growing with every negative, derogatory thought, feeding off of every minute spent staring at the girl in the mirror, poking and prodding and wishing for anything but what she had been given. It fed off of her self-hatred, but also off of her success. The monster adored adoration, compliments, validation of any kind ... but not truly *any* kind. The validation had to be derived from the popular mainstream activities. So she quit the things she was truly talented at and threw herself into everything else. Her stories lay forgotten, gathering dust at the bottom of a drawer along with everything else her mind truly yearned for. And as she became someone she was not, the spiral continued, delving down and down into a place of darkness. She tried and tried to satiate the monster, but no matter how hard she worked, it was never enough. She was never good enough, not for those around her, and not for herself. So the monster turned inwards once again, eating away at her very being, devouring the walls she had built, the personas she had erected, all constructed to hide the girl she used to be, the girl she still was when no one was watching. And for a few weeks that seemed to last an eternity, she was empty. Her mind was quiet, the worlds of whimsy and wonder banished to far corners, all of her ambitions and perfectionism forgotten, shoved aside in favor of simply going through the motions. It was at this point, this terrible, lonely point, when she had nothing left to hide behind, that the monster starved.

And the dreamer reemerged from the ashes, a phoenix, brighter and full of fiery conviction. She used a chain of words crafted from her beloved stories to pull herself out of the pit she had dug, all her favorite characters cheering her on from the recesses of her imagination as she climbed.

However, things were still not easy. She did not erupt from the shadows of her old self full of confidence and conviction. Instead, she rose on shaky legs, a newborn foal rising to its feet, unsure of itself and the world around it.

She was not the wide-eyed girl she had been before, but her mind was still full of dragons and daydreams and glittering ballrooms, and this time she was not ashamed of it. She was loud and vibrant and opinionated. She was passionate, excited, and ambitious. And although her small-town world still felt much too small, she had dozens of other worlds to turn to, some old, some new, and some completely and utterly her own. It wasn't perfect, it wasn't full of enchantments and princes and glistening castles and sweeping ballgowns, but it was still magical and wonderful because it was her life, her very own story, and she loved herself for it. She loved her daydreams and vacant stares and her mind full of words and stories. She loved her passions and her goals, loved both who she was and who she wanted to be. And although there were still days when her hands would shake and everything was too loud and too small, she knew she would be fine. Because she'd find a story, get lost in its pages, or even write a few of her own. Some might call it escapism, but to her, the stories meant so much more. They saved her, made her someone she loves, and, for the first time in a long while, that is enough.

She is enough.

Neverland

Rain gushed out of the clouds, cascading down from the sky and pooling around Freya's boots as she dragged them down the road, mumbling under her breath as she attempted to tug her old jacket tighter around her cold, trembling body. The sights and sounds of the city streets faded behind her, replaced by the steady patter of rain and the sad, wet crumple of the rejected manuscript clutched in Freya's hand. The ink, once neatly handwritten in thoughtful penmanship by candlelight, now bled through the paper, staining Freya's hand, dripping down her wrist, the darkened tears the only remnant of her shattered dreams.

The trees rustled in the wind, the cold breeze whipping Freya's curls out of her chignon. She only plowed onward, her heart empty, her eyes dead, already imagining the sad, hollow look on her father's ailing face as she told him she had failed him again. That she had failed herself again. They had no money, all of Freya's meager earnings from shifts at the pub spent on medicine that did nothing to slow her father's worsening health. This book had been Freya's last chance to scrape together enough money to make rent. They would be evicted, thrown to the streets, where her father would surely die.

Freya tilted her face up to the sky, blinking as the rain mixed with her tears, sliding down her cheeks and pooling against her skin. In that moment, time stood still. There was only the empty street and the rain and Freya, standing in the middle of it, looking to the sky as if it could save her, whisk her away to a world full of fantasy and never look back. In that moment, she wished to be anyone else, anywhere else. She wished she had never grown up.

A single chilling, melancholy note broke the silence, echoing against the pavement of the vacant street, ricocheting off the old stone buildings, dancing with the rain as it grew and swelled, layers of harmonies flowing together as the melody soared, full of longing and promise, beckoning Freya closer, closer. She took one step forward, then the next, curiously making her way towards the small alley the music seemed to emerge from. Stairs led down the alleyway, presumably pouring out onto another street, but Freya couldn't quite make out the end through the shadows. They seemed to go on and on, winding away into the darkness. Freya took a step back, suddenly bewildered. What was she doing? But then the song lifted into a crescendo, its waves rolling off of her, carrying her with it. She was adrift, lost at sea, and the music was a compass, leading her home.

Her feet padded down the stairs, slowly at first, but with each new note, each change in tempo, her pace increased until she was dashing down, down, down her feet barely skimming the ground. She felt like she was flying. Freya tore off her coat, laughing as she let it fall behind her.

The stairs slowly shifted from stone to soft, smooth dirt the further Freya descended. Small plants sprouted along the way, their leaves emitting a strange glow. As the source of the music grew nearer, Freya felt her body begin to shift. Her shoulders straightened, the weight of the previous years lifted in one swift note. The worry lines in her face smoothed out, giving way to a youthful glow. She laughed, twirling in circles and admiring her strong, shining body when a soft, tinkling laugh joined hers.

Freya turned and saw a beautiful stranger with delicate features and a head of auburn curls grinning at her while twirling a reed pipe between his fingertips. He was clad entirely in varying shades of green, his clothing appearing as if each item had been pulled from a different century. She blinked, realizing the music had stopped. But the stranger's sparkling eyes, his wicked grin seeping with wicked promises, had cast another spell on her. Her eyes traveled across his features until she reached his ears, which ended in strange, sharp points.

Freya frowned, her eyebrows drawing together. "Are you a faerie?" she asked.

The stranger laughed again, although it didn't reach his eyes. "I am whatever you want me to be."

He offered her his arm and turned toward an elaborate golden door that had suddenly appeared in the stairwell. Freya peeked behind it, noticing it was not attached to anything. There was nothing but shadows on the other side. "Do you trust me?" the stranger asked, eyes simmering with an emotion she couldn't place.

"No," Freya responded, but she took his arm anyways and let him lead her through the door and into paradise. The world on the other side was nothing short of a miracle, a fantasy pulled from the furthest reaches of her mind.

An array of colors so vivid it was nearly blinding rushed in from every side, every corner, dousing Freya in its vibrant beauty. Music flowed out of every pore, flowing around her body and into her soul.

Below them was a valley filled with bright emerald grass and a forest of wildflowers where dozens of youthful, beautiful humans danced, their feet flying across the ground, propelled by the wild sweetness of the music. Freya laughed and twirled, careening from side to side as the sun gleamed down, its golden rays kissing her skin. All around her, revelers, both human and faerie, danced and sang. Everything seemed to glow, teeming with life. Tables laden with exotic food and drink were arranged haphazardly around glittering ponds teeming with gorgeous mermaids and other aquatic delights.

Why had she been so upset? Nothing in this magnificent, shining world could possibly be anything short of perfect. Her bare feet pressed into the soft dirt as the light, flowing skirts of her sky-blue dress floated around her legs. Flowers bloomed in between the folds of fabric, their fragrant scents wafting around her, pulling her further into the embrace of this wondrous place.

Tick, tock. Tick, tock.

The sound came from nowhere in particular, and yet it was everywhere, its cadence in tune to the beat of her heart. Freya glimpsed a flash of gold, a flicker of green, and then—

"You seem to be enjoying yourself."

Freya turned and saw the boy from before grinning at her with a strange glint in his eyes. His auburn curls spilled over his ears, nearly covering the elfish points at the tips. Freya took her skirts in hand and curtseyed, looking up at him from under her eyelashes.

"Want to dance?" she asked, suddenly feeling very bold. Freya had never had much time for boys before, but now, in this place, with her new radiance and the way this stranger's eyes devoured her every move ...

He gently took her hand and lightly pressed a kiss to it, sending a bout of shivers through her body.

"Of course, love," he replied, then looped his other hand around her waist and pulled her into a dance. The music shifted, swelling and slowing to match their steps as they spun around and around. Freya's heart sputtered in her chest, her skirts flowing around them. She looked up at him as he guided her through the dance, his steps sure and confident.

"What's your name?" she asked.

"Peter."

"Really?" Freya laughed, and he raised an eyebrow.

"What's wrong with Peter?" he teased, voice dripping with false hurt, his lips pursed into a slight pout.

"Nothing," Freya replied, giggling. "I was just expecting something whimsical or unique, certainly not *Peter*. My name is Frey—"

"Freya. I know."

Now it was her turn to raise an eyebrow as she looked up at him, a smile playing at her lips—

Her laughter died in her throat as her eyes met his. The warm vibrancy from before was gone. His features remained similar, but there was something not quite right about them. They were too pale, too sharp, too perfect. His hands felt cold and hard against her waist. The only thing that remained the same were his eyes, glinting with hunger.

Tick, tock.

The sound was back, its rhythmic echo seeming to draw nearer with each beat.

She stumbled, and his grip tightened, righting her before she could fall.

"Careful love," he murmured, and as soon as it had appeared, the vision and the sound were gone and the beautiful boy was back, his features warm and inviting. Freya blinked, sure that she had imagined it, but his eyes, his eyes still had a strange gleam, so at odds with the rest of his expression. Her blood grew cold, and she began to pull away—

His hands gripped her arm, pulling her towards him roughly. All it took was that touch, that single act of aggression, to shatter the illusion. The beautiful dreamscape was gone, and in its place was a nightmare.

The land was gray and barren, as if all the life had been sucked from it in the same manner as had been done to the human corpses lying on the ground, their bodies disfigured and folded inwards as if every drop of youth and vitality had been ripped brutally from their veins. The tables that had been laden with all varieties of delicious delicacies instead were covered in an array of rotten foods and the mangled body parts of humans and strange-looking animals. But most horrifying of all were the faeries who took it all in, eyes glittering with wicked amusement as the enchanted mortals danced blissfully over ground littered with the bones of those who came before them. They laughed gleefully as the humans devoured the revolting arrangements lining the tables. Others prowled the fields searching for their next victim, someone teeming with bliss, someone so entranced they wouldn't discover the danger until it was too late.

Tick, tock.

These faeries were still beautiful, but not in the cheerful, inviting way the illusion had portrayed. Their beauty was still breathtaking, but painfully so, and there was a certain wrongness about it, an unnatural perfection that stroked Freya's spine with unease even as she stared, entranced. Because while the scene in front of her eyes was absolutely terrifying, there was something poetic about it, all of these humans seeking escape, youthfulness, and vitality only for it to consume them, swallow them whole, and leave them even more drained than they had been in their previous state. Their greatest fantasy was their ultimate undoing.

Freya gasped in terror, stumbling back. Peter pulled a golden pocket watch from his pocket and assessed it, eyebrows raised. His lips pulled into a slight frown.

"It would appear we've been interrupted."

Tick, tock. Tick, tock.

Freya started. The disembodied sound was much closer than before. Peter eyed her curiously, as if he was taking in every detail, from her lips to the skirts of her dress.

"I would run, if I was you," he said with a wicked, knowing gleam in his eyes.

Freya backed away for a few steps before turning to run, her heart pounding in her chest. She did not have a clue who or what she was running from. There was only an irrational fear pumping through her veins and fueling her terror as she increased her speed to a sprint.

She looked over her shoulder and saw Peter staring at her, eyes narrowed as his lips twitched into a smile. He stooped into a brief bow, eyes glittering, then turned away.

Freya felt remaining whispers of his glance on her as she ran and ran. The scenery flickered around her, shifting from nightmare to dream and back again so quickly it caused her to stumble. She had no idea where she was trying to go. The entryway she had come through had vanished, and there was no other escape route in sight. How had she even arrived here? What kind of hellscape was this place?

How would she ever get back home?

Hopelessness sank into Freya's bones, curling around her and coating her soul in exhaustion. Her surroundings continued to change, flashing back and forth as the illusion wrestled for control. Freya could feel her conviction beginning to slip, her mind and body urging her to just give in, to let the illusion sweep her away into a blissful nothing.

Then, suddenly a flash of blue in the shifting scenery caught her eye. The sea. Its waters glinted through the trees in the distance, beckoning. Freya locked onto it, that flicker of hope, and ran like hell. Over hills and through groves of trees, Freya ran and ran, holding onto the small hope that she could possibly escape this nightmare she had so readily thrown herself into.

Tick, tock.

Freya emerged over the final hill, sliding as her bare feet sunk into cold, wet sand. The small cove was eerily quiet, its water so dark it was nearly black, its waves beating into the rocks, the cool spray splashing across Freya's skin. Something glinted and flashed below the surface, and Freya could have sworn she caught a glimpse of scales, rough and serrated like a crocodile.

Despair tore through Freya like a blade. She would never survive the swim, if there even was an escape beyond the waves. She sank to her knees, her body shaking.

Despite the rough waters, Freya's reflection in the water was clear. She gazed down, and a tired soul gazed back at her, eyes dead and defeated. Freya had made it to the sea, but there was no hope of escape. Death awaited her in these waters just as certainly as it awaited her back in the valley. It was over.

Tick, tock.

But then she saw it. There, on the horizon, a silhouette appeared, bobbing up and down in the waves like a ship. A small spark of hope burned in Freya. Maybe, just maybe, she could make the swim. If she was strong enough, she could do it.

Freya stepped into the water, and, ignoring the shiver the icy waves sent down her spine, dove in headfirst. She had always been a strong swimmer, and her desperation only added to the strength behind her strokes as she propelled her body through the water, fighting the current, fighting the desire to give in, fighting her fate.

As Freya slowly made her way into the deeper waters of the lagoon, she started to hear it again. It was slight, nearly imperceptible, and yet somehow so much closer than it had ever been before.

Tick, tock, tick, tock.

Freya spun, treading water, as she scanned the waves. Nothing. Shaking her head, she continued her swim, her arms feeling heavier and heavier with each stroke. The icy water lapped against her body as she swam, and Freya could feel the energy and warmth seeping out of her bones.

Tick, tock, tick, tock.

It was much closer this time. A splash rippled not far to her left. Fear licked down Freya's spine, but she could do nothing but swim. Except she was no longer making any headway. Even now, she was barely able to keep her head above the waves. She gasped, inhaling a mouthful of water. *I tried,* Freya thought. *I tried so, so hard.*

And it was not enough. It never is.

Tick, tock.

I'm so tired.

A tail, covered in the scales of a crocodile, surfaced directly next to Freya, and vanished again. Then a pair of eyes appeared. Wicked, cunning eyes, followed by a slender neck that bore a golden pocket watch hung on a simple chain.

Tick, tock.

The mermaid grinned, sharp teeth flashing, and tapped the watch with long nails as if to say *time's up.* Freya found herself nodding in understanding. It was time. Her cold, aching body could take no more, and neither could she.

She didn't scream, didn't flinch, as the mermaid lunged, dragging Freya beneath the waves. As she sank down, down into the depths, she kept her gaze on the surface, on the few rays of light that had escaped the gloom, even as her world went dark.

Part of Their World

The fading glow of the evening sun filtered through the water, flickering across the waves in little tongues of fire. I darted through the coral, careful to keep out of sight of the ships bobbing high above me. All I wanted was a single glance, just one look at what life was like up there. Then all the longing, the years of wondering and questioning, would be satisfied. I could go back home, back to our deep-sea dwelling, far below the reach of humans, and I could be content. Even as the thought crossed my mind, I knew it was a lie. I would never be truly happy down there, not when I could swim through the shallows, see the gleam of the sun against the scales on my tail and the breathtaking array of colors splashed across the reef. Not when I could see the humans and their magnificent creations and curious lives. My people had always warned me away from humans, calling them monstrous, greedy creatures. *It's dangerous, Nori. You must let go of this foolishness, Nori,* they would say. But not one of them had ever actually seen a human. They were all paranoid fools, clinging to tradition. But I believed there was more to life than hiding, more to humans than selfish destruction. There had to be.

I took a deep breath, then pushed off from the coral I was hiding behind, my tail propelling me through the water as I climbed towards the surface. *Just one look*, I promised myself again. *Just one look.* My excitement grew as I swam higher and higher, and my entire body felt light. Everything I had dreamed and wondered about for years drew closer and closer and—

I hesitated, coming to a halt just before my head broke the surface. A flicker of doubt coursed through my mind, and I paused. What if I was wrong? What if this truly was dangerous? But I shoved it down and peeked above the waves. A small human ship floated a few feet in front of me. My eyes widened, and I was unable to stop the giddy smile that spread across my lips as I took it in. It was fairly small, its build sleek and streamlined. Humans stood on its deck, holding glasses in their hands, talking and laughing in words that I could not understand. They seemed happy and peaceful, their eyes trained on the sun as it slowly made its way below the horizon, splashing the sky in gorgeous hues of orange and pink.

I slowly treaded water, careful not to make a sound as I watched. A large man with a beard stood in front of the others, gesturing wildly as he talked in a loud, booming voice. The others laughed, occasionally chiming in with words of their own. They all had an easy companionship, the comfort of friendship that I had always longed for among my own people but had never found. I had been a dreamer, eyes full of stars I had never seen, among a people who never looked far beyond the reach of their own arms, a people bound by fear of what they did not understand.

There, in the water, watching the humans laugh and talk, I longed to understand them, to know what they were saying, to ask them about all the amazing things they had seen, to beg them to take me with them.

Then I spotted the boy. He was younger than all the rest, probably near my age, and leaning against the rail. His eyes were fixed on the horizon, his shoulders hunched as he stood in silence. I tilted my head, gazing at him curiously. He had dark hair that curled loosely around his ears and soft brown eyes that spoke of kindness and gentle whispers, yet they had a slight darkness, a glint of loneliness I knew all too well. The feeling that came from being somewhere you did not belong.

I drew closer, entranced by this stranger and his longing gaze that reminded me of myself. Why was he so sad, so lonely, when he was among these joyful creatures? He could go anywhere he wanted, see everything, and yet his eyes remained on the horizon as if he still wanted more.

He's beautiful, I realized. I flicked my tail, wanting to be closer to where he leaned out over the rail.

Splash.

I froze, realizing my mistake, but it was too late. The boy's head snapped up, his gaze locking with mine. His eyes widened, and he tilted his head, confused. I tilted my own, mirroring him. He held my gaze for a few more seconds, and my heart felt as if it would burst. I had been right. Here, right in front of me, was a human. And he wasn't monstrous, he was beautiful.

I saw the boy reach into his pocket and pull out a strange object. He pointed it at me, and a beam of light flooded from it, straight into my eyes. I hissed, raising my arms to cover my face. The boy's gaze locked onto the faint scales embedded in my arms, the gills on my neck, all markings of a siren. He gaped, then began to shout, and soon more voices joined his. The other humans leaned out over the railing, gawking and pointing. The large, bearded man was holding a strange pile of what appeared to be ropes in his hands.

Every bone in my body screamed at me to dive, to hide. Something was very wrong. The gleam in that man's eyes, in the eyes of the other humans, sent shivers down my spine. But I remembered their easy smiles, their booming, joyful laughs. They had seemed so kind, so happy. I hesitated, just for a moment.

It was a moment I would regret forever.

The bearded man threw his pile of ropes into the water, and several of the others did the same. I spun, puzzled, as the ropes began to enclose around me. Too late, I realized what was happening. Too late, I tried to swim away, but the ropes were everywhere. No matter which way I turned, they were there, snaking towards me, caging me in. I dove, my hands tearing at the ropes, trying to find a gap, but they just drew closer and closer, brushing against the scales of my tail, slithering across my arms. I struggled and fought, but it was too late. The ropes wrapped around me and pulled. Suddenly I was rocketing towards the surface, out of the water and onto the boat.

I struck the deck with a force that knocked my breath away. As I lay there panting, struggling against the tangle of ropes encircling my body, the humans shouted and gawked at me. They held strange small rectangular objects that flashed, illuminating the deck and the way my body flopped, trying to swim despite the lack of water. They laughed at me, and I could not believe I had ever thought the sound to be joyful. It was cruel and ugly, their smiles wicked as they leered at me. I tried to claw my way across the deck, arms scrabbling desperately, reaching for the edge, for the ocean, for the home I never should have left, but arms wrapped around me, hauling me back. Hands, so many hands, grabbed and pulled at me, some lingering far too long.

I flailed my arms, swung my tail, lashing out blindly at my attackers. Yet it was not enough, they had me pinned down, and they tightened the ropes until I could barely breathe. They pointed those strange objects at me again, and this time they posed for the lights, grabbing and touching me in ways that made the others laugh. They poured the strange smelling liquid from the glasses they held all over my body, their eyes alight with cruel mirth. The boy stood apart from the others, his brown eyes wary and almost wistful. I met his gaze, my eyes pleading. *Please don't make me do this*, I begged. *I don't want to hurt you.*

Even though you have hurt me.

He dropped my gaze and turned away. Something in me, something pure and innocent, cracked. But I drew in a breath, opened my mouth, and began to sing.

An unearthly, eerie melody poured from my lips, winding around the humans, wrapping them in my song, my will. Their eyes glazed over, and they dropped the ropes and began to walk towards the edges of the ship. *That's it. Just a little more ...*

I sang, my voice growing and building. Several of the humans leaped from the ship, drawn to the water by my siren song. But then I saw him. The boy walked right by me, his gait steady, his eyes fixed on the sea. And again, I hesitated, my song pausing. I couldn't kill him. I wouldn't do it. His eyes cleared as he stood over me.

He did not hesitate. His fist crashed into my skull, snapping my head back against the deck so hard that stars wheeled across my vision, chasing the splotches of darkness as I fought to remain conscious. I looked up at the boy. His lips were moving, mouthing something directed at me, and despite his menacing stance, his eyes were mournful. I tried to fight, to free myself from the ropes, but the darkness grew nearer, its arms reaching forward, pulling me into its cold embrace.

I awoke to a world awash in white. I blinked rapidly, my eyes slowly adjusting to the strange new world around me. I was strapped to a table, lights shining into my eyes from all directions as humans dressed in white robes leaned over me, poking and prodding at me with odd instruments and conversing in hushed tones. One noticed I was conscious and grabbed a long needle, stabbing it into my arm. I thrashed and screamed, attempting to call to my song, but the darkness was too fast, and my movements grew slow and tired as it pulled me back under.

When I awoke again, I was back underwater. For a moment, I believed it had all just been one terrible nightmare. The boat, the boy, none of it had been real.

But something felt wrong. This water didn't feel right, and neither did my body. A dull, throbbing pain pounded in my throat, and I reached my hands up, panic building in me as I felt long ridges of scars and stitching lining my skin. I opened my mouth, calling to my song in desperation.

No sound emerged.

Panicked, I tried again and again, my body shaking with the effort to produce some kind of sound. My hands scrabbled at my throat, and I sobbed soundlessly, the motion producing a sad stream of bubbles. *They took my song.*

I spun around, eyes finally taking in my surroundings. I gasped, panic completely enveloping my senses. I had spent my entire life in the depths of the open ocean, sometimes swimming several miles in one day as I roamed, searching for anything and everything. But now, I could swim from one end of the glass cage I was in to the other in a matter of seconds. My breaths came in short gasps, the strange water flooding in and out of my gills much too quickly.

I was trapped. I pressed my hands to the glass, pounding at it with my fists until I heard a sickening crack. I drew my hand to my chest, clutching the broken digits, screaming in silent pain as I slid down the glass to the bottom of my cage. This could not be real. In a few minutes I would wake up back in the ocean, my voice still intact. I would never wander close to the surface, never succumb to my curiosity again. I would be content with what I had, I would never dream again, if I could just go back, if I could wake up and know it had all been just one horrible dream.

Wake up, wake up, wake up. I clawed at my arms, yanked at my hair and ripped scales from my tail, screamed silently until my throat felt raw, but when I opened my eyes I was still trapped.

As the sun began to rise I was able to make out more of my surroundings outside the cage. Strange metal objects stretched towards the sky in twists and turns and loops all around me. A few other glass tanks were near mine, but it was still too dark for me to make out the inhabitants. Soon, the humans arrived, walking on platforms above my cage carrying buckets full of fish. I eyed the buckets hungrily, realizing how starved I was. I lunged towards them, teeth snapping angrily. The humans only laughed at me from above, and one waved a fish at me mockingly. Then they began to wave strange poles through the air, blowing whistles. It was a piercing, awful noise, and I covered my ears and dove back underwater to escape it. The humans shook their heads and left.

As the sun rose higher in the sky, more humans arrived. But these ones were different. They rode on the strange metal loops and twists, screaming as they flew by. They pressed and poked at the glass of my tank, gazing at me with wide, innocent eyes. For the first few days, I would lunge at them, teeth bared, relishing the way they jumped back, faces startled. However, as the days passed, I became too exhausted to do anything but lay on the bottom of my tank listlessly, longing for food, for freedom, even for death. The humans didn't like that. Although they still brought food with them every morning, they refused to give me any, and simply continued to wave their strange poles in the air and blow their whistles angrily.

On the fourth morning I lunged from the water, arms reaching for the pole, the whistles, anything to make it stop. But the humans only smiled and tossed me a single fish. I grabbed it and devoured it instantly, fearing they would take it from me, but they only watched with calculating eyes. Then, the whistles were blowing, and the pole was in the air again. Soon, I learned the pattern. Over and over, I threw my starved body out of the water for a single fish. It was unnatural and humiliating. I hated the way the other humans watched and clapped, eyes wide like I was some shiny new toy.

Days turned into weeks that turned into months. I performed their tricks, played their game, and every time I did, a new part of me died a little. I was no longer living, but simply going through the motions, wishing I would die but unwilling to let myself. One day, I turned to see a familiar set of eyes gazing at me through the glass. I cocked my head, puzzled. He tilted his back at me, and I remembered. It was the boy from the boat. He was much cleaner than before, his clothing much nicer. I wanted to rush at him, to snarl and bare my teeth, but I couldn't find it within myself. I simply stared, eyes dead, tail dull, skin sallow and sick. I watched emotions flicker in his eyes, warring back and forth before they settled on sorrow.

I drifted to the edge of the tank, somehow still drawn to him, despite everything. And when I pressed my hand to the glass, he did the same. A single tear rolled down his cheek, so small I almost believed I had imagined it. He mouthed something, and somehow I knew it was an apology. My heart hurt, aching to go back to the moment I had first seen him, when I had still believed there was good in this world, good in humans. When my eyes had been full of innocent wonder, my mind bursting with unending dreams.

We stayed like that for a few more seconds, eyes locked, hands pressed against the barrier dividing them. One free, one caged forever.

Then he turned and walked away.

Down the Rabbit Hole

I awoke in a straitjacket. My head lolled to the side as I slowly regained feeling in my limbs. Rows and rows of closed doors flashed by, illuminated by overhead lights. Everything was so bright, so clean and white and shiny. It made my head hurt even more than it already did.

"I'm late, oh no, no, no ..."

I strained my neck as much as I could to fix my gaze on the woman pushing my wheelchair. She was consulting an antique pocket watch, her eyes big and frantic behind her pink glasses. She increased her pace to a near run, and suddenly we were pushing through a set of double doors and into an office.

My eyes were immediately accosted by a flood of color. Nearly every surface was covered in some shade of red. Crimson, ruby, maroon, all bleeding together into a horrendous display of unfortunate interior design. Behind the desk sat a woman. She had delicate features and a heart-shaped face. Her dark gaze locked on my nurse, who whimpered.

"You're late. *Again.*"

"I'm sorry ma'am, I—"

"Leave us, please," the woman behind the desk ordered. She had the petulant air of someone used to giving orders. The door shut quietly behind me, and I fidgeted, trying to free my arms.

"Oh, I wouldn't bother with that, Miss Alice," the woman said pleasantly, "I do apologize for using such primeval means of constraint, but your previous fits didn't leave us much option. My name is Dr. Heart. I am your new therapist. I shall be overseeing your recovery and the pending investigation for now." She flipped through a series of notes on her desk before looking back up at me.

"Alice, do you know why you are here?"

I stared at her. "Dr. Harper said I killed people." Dr. Harper had been my previous therapist. I found, to my surprise, that I missed him. I missed the tea he often served during our sessions when we talked about ... talked about what? My memories were a haze, a dense fog of dreams and reality, blended together into an undecipherable mush. "What happened to him?" I asked.

"Dr. Harper has been let go," Dr. Heart answered primly.

"Why?"

"We employ only the best here at Wonderland House. Unfortunately, that no longer includes Dr. Harper. He worked with you for months and made no progress. In fact, he contributed to your current state by encouraging your ... fantasies."

I blinked again, trying to unravel her meaning.

"Now, Alice, you mentioned that you killed people. Do you recall this?"

I paused, my teeth worrying at my lip as I pondered her question. Had I killed people? I didn't remember. There was something, a type of darkness, guarding my memories, and I much preferred my "current state" to whatever was in the darkness. So I didn't remember anything outside of this place, this prison, with its endless hallways and locked doors. A house, they called it, not an asylum. A beautiful fairytale world for broken minds to heal.

"No, I don't."

Dr. Heart sighed, "You know, Alice, people can repress their traumatizing memories, create their own realities of what happened, all to protect themselves from the truth. Can you tell me anything about your life before Wonderland House?"

I stared at her.

"Alice, please. I am trying to help you, but for this to work I need your full cooperation. Harper's notes claim that you have created a fantasy world in your mind, a warped reality of the Wonderland House, to cope with your trauma. Is this true?"

Fantasy? No, it wasn't fantasy. It was the most real thing I knew.

"Alice!" Dr. Heart snapped, her voice stern. I whipped my head up, eyes locking with hers.

"Wonderland is real. It's just right down the rabbit hole." I giggled. "You can be anything you want in wonderland, anything at all. Nobody cares who you were, what you did, because they're all mad, all completely mad!" I was laughing now, uncontrollable, vicious laughter that caused my whole body to shake.

Dr. Heart looked at me, unperturbed and disappointed. She stood up, grabbing something from her desk, and strode towards me. I thrashed and laughed hysterically as she stabbed the needle into my neck. "We'll try again tomorrow."

The last thing I saw was her heart-shaped face above me as the world faded into nothing.

⋄⋄⋄⋄⋄⋄⋄⋄⋄⋄

I was in a field of poppies. Poppies of every size and color, some as large as skyscrapers, their vibrant petals reaching for the sky, which was a splash of spinning stars and suns and moons, wheeling across space in a perfect whirlwind of chaos. I inhaled, letting the beautiful scent of this place wash over me. My very own wonderland. But someone was missing.

"Chesh!" I called out. This was strange. He was always waiting for me, like a figment of my imagination, always there when I needed him. "Chesh, where are you?"

"He's not heeerreee," a voice sang. I whirled, my face already twisting into a smile despite his words.

"Harper!" I cried, my eyes shining as I looked him up and down. He had changed since I had last seen him. He had forgone his typical dress shirt and slacks for a striped-green suit paired with a gleaming metallic cravat and a magnificent top hat. I launched towards him, wrapping him in a hug, which he returned enthusiastically.

"Harper, do you know where Chesh is?" I asked.

He stared at me, his teeth worrying at his lip and he swayed back and forth on his feet. Suddenly his eyes lit up. "Do you want some tea?" He pulled an old, cracked teapot from his jacket and waved it in my face.

I pushed it away gently. "Harper, please."

"I never liked that boy. Pretty faces tell pretty lies." He sighed. "He's with *her*. At the castle. I wouldn't go looking for him if I was you."

"Why?"

"He discovered the truth of things at that castle. And the truth is never pretty."

"What castle? I don't understand—" He shoved his hand over my mouth, silencing me.

"They're coming. You need to wake up, Alice." That's when I heard the voice, emerging from the poppies.

"I'm late! Oh no, oh, no ..."

◇◇◇◇◇◇◇◇◇◇◇◇◇◇◇◇

The nurse was panicking again, this time running at a full sprint as she wheeled me into Dr. Heart's office.

"Alice! So good of you to join us." The doctor's eyes cut angrily towards the nurse, who squeaked and rushed from the room. "Alice, I know we ended our previous session on a rough note. I apologize for that." Her eyes gleamed in a way that made me shiver. "Today, we're going to try a different tactic. What is your name?"

"Alice," I responded, pleased to finally be able to answer a question, but the doctor frowned.

"Your full name, please."

"Alice."

She sighed. "Your full name is Alice Marie Carroll. Born to James and Eliza Carroll, both deceased. You are 21 years old, and you were living with your boyfriend, Chesh Mayfeld, in an apartment in Chicago. Seven weeks ago, Chesh and another girl were found de—"

But I didn't hear what she said next. My blood was rushing to my head, my heart was pounding, someone was screaming, *I* was screaming, blocking out her voice, thrashing and writhing and trying to escape what I knew was coming. I felt a sharp pain in my neck.

"I will uncover the truth, Alice. I always do …"

Everything faded to black.

◇◇◇◇◇◇◇◇◇◇◇◇◇◇◇

This time I wasn't in the poppy forest. I was in a garden full of roses that dripped blood. Sticky, bright red, oozing blood, dripping from the petals in a steady rhythm. The walls of a castle I had never seen before towered all around me, its walls the same color as the bleeding flowers. "Chesh?" I called out, my voice barely louder than a whisper.

"Late, late, late!" A white rabbit with pink glasses and a pocket watch bounded into the garden. "You're late, we're late, come on!"

"Late for what?" I asked.

"To meet *her*, of course!" I stood there, staring. The rabbit rolled her eyes, then grabbed my hand and tugged me forwards. "Well, come on then!"

She pulled me through the garden, along eerily silent hallways and up and down magnificently winding staircases. Everywhere I looked, there were hearts. On the walls, the floors, the stair rails, everywhere. A strange sense of familiarity and foreboding filled me, but I continued, following the rabbit until we reached a courtyard and I stumbled to a halt, my entire body stiff with shock.

A single head was staked to the wall. A familiar head, with a kind face and a wonderfully strange hat. Harper.

I began to shake, tears streaming down my face as I bit my lip so hard I drew blood. No, no, no, no, this wasn't supposed to happen here. This was *my* wonderland, my escape, my reality. I spun around, my eyes searching for answers that weren't there.

"What's happening?" I screamed.

The rabbit looked up at me with large, sad eyes. "Oh dear," she mumbled. "You're starting to remember."

"Remember what?" I demanded.

"The truth," she answered, eyes wide and solemn. Then her ears pricked up, and she consulted her pocket watch. "Come on, we're late!"

She led me into another courtyard. More bleeding roses lined the cobblestone pathway that led to a throne. A single figure in a massive red ball gown perched on it, a heart-shaped crown resting upon her head. She had delicate features, dark hair, and even darker eyes. A sense of wrongness, of foreboding, filled me as I looked at her.

"Dr. Heart?"

She laughed, a soft, high sound that seemed both fake and real. "Doctor? Do I look like a doctor?"

Rage burned through me, blurring my vision with shades of red. "You're not supposed to be here."

"This is my castle." The woman smiled, but it didn't quite match Dr. Heart's face. "Where else am I supposed to be?"

"Not here." Everything felt wrong. My mind was spiraling, things that weren't supposed to mix were blending together, creating a special brand of madness. "Where's Chesh?" I demanded.

"Chesh? Your boyfriend?" The strange woman laughed again. "He's certainly not here. You killed him, don't you remember?"

"What—no, I didn't, I couldn't have."

"Oh, but you did." She laughed again, her eyes gleaming. "Do you know what our punishment is for murderers here?" She waved to her guards, and they began to march towards me.

"No, I'm not a murderer!" I screamed as they grabbed my arms and dragged me backwards. "Please! I'd never hurt anyone!"

The woman who was and wasn't Dr. Heart stared at me, her lips pulling into a smirk. "Off with her head."

I screamed and kicked as the guards took me away, out of the courtyard and down a winding staircase into a dungeon. Everything was dark and cold, with cells lining each side of the corridor. Most appeared to be empty, but I still heard muttering and giggles emerge from the shadows. A dark block of stone stood on a raised platform at the end of the corridor. A massive scythe leaned against it, its blade gleaming in the torchlight.

The familiar body of a young man was slumped against the stone. My heart stopped, and I dug my heels into the ground, refusing to go any further, somehow knowing exactly who I would see. "Please!" I yelled. "I didn't do this!"

"Oh, but you did."

The voice came from behind me. It was soft and deep, nearly a purr. I knew that voice. I turned, the first brushes of a smile beginning to paint my face, only to be swallowed by a scream of terror.

Chesh stood in front of me, but he was also not-Chesh. He had the same tousled brown hair, the same tall, gangly build, but his face was all wrong. Despite the fact that it was bashed in and bleeding on one side in a way one definitely didn't recover from, his eyes were also manic, glowing nearly yellow with pupils that danced from side to side. His smile stretched too wide across his face, forming a perfect crescent that pulled at his lips until they bled.

I glanced back to the body slumped against the stone that was also Chesh, then back towards the thing in front of me.

"Hello, Alice," he crooned.

"Chesh?" I whispered, reaching my hands towards him tentatively, as if the slightest movement could scare him away. The guards immediately shot forwards, yanking my arms behind my back so roughly I cried out. Not-Chesh only smiled his unnatural smile, even as they began to drag me towards the stone and bind my arms with chains. I stared in horror at the dead body that was also Chesh, the wound on his head perfectly matching the one Not-Chesh had.

"Look familiar?" Not-Chesh asked. "It should. After all, you did that to me."

"No," I sobbed. "I would never hurt you."

"But you did. You did and you don't even remember." Not-Chesh's hands wrapped around the handle of the scythe. His unnatural smile stretched even wider as he hefted it into the air, lining it up with my neck. "You don't remember why you did it. But all the answers are here, in your head." His eyes gleamed.

"Wake up, Alice."

The scythe whistled through the air, easily cleaving flesh and bone.

I gasped, snapping awake, my eyes wide, my heart pounding. I was no longer in a straight jacket, but my arms were zip-tied to the chair I currently sat in.

"Excellent, you're awake." I looked up to see Dr. Heart looking at me from her desk. "Let's pick up where we left off, shall we?"

I felt as if I was spinning, my head, my memories, floating above my body, mixing and stirring together into the beginnings of a storm. I knew I was on the edge of knowing. All I had to do was make the jump.

"Alice, do you remember anything from what happened that night? Anything at all?"

I looked down at my hands and my eyes widened. They were covered in blood. I blinked, and it was all gone.

"Nothing? What about this girl? Do you remember her?" Dr. Heart held up a picture of a girl about my age with wide eyes and a sweet smile. "This is Charlotte Thatcher. Her body was also found at the scene. Can you tell me …"

Her voice faded as I stared at the picture of the girl. As I looked at her, I could feel the memory of that night pounding against its confines, fighting and clawing its way forward out of my wonderland. The truth had been hidden there, in the creations of my mind, the entire time. And now it was there, at the mouth of the rabbit hole. All I had to do was let it out.

"Alice, I'm not accusing you of anything, we just want to know what happened. No charges have been pressed yet, and ..."

I took a deep breath. *I can face this.*

I let the memories in. It came back in a wave, all of it, years of my life, flashes of smiles and sunlight and green trees and rolling waves. It all flooded through me, past me, around me, minutes and hours and days, all leading up to that night. *It was late, nearly midnight, and I was just getting back from a shift at the theater. We'd been showing some old movie that day, a movie full of sense and nonsense and cats with impossibly wide smiles and rabbit holes, and my mind was full of it, its strange scenes playing across my thoughts as I unlocked the door, shoving it open with my shoulder as I tossed my bag onto the floor. That was when I heard the screaming. It was soft and muffled, but the terror in it was unmistakable. I grabbed the old metal bat we kept near the door in shaking hands and crept around the corner into the kitchen.*

When I saw what was happening, I didn't hesitate. I just reacted. I swung the bat into Chesh's skull, barely noticing the way he crumpled as I shoved him away from the girl. She was young, probably my age. And she wasn't breathing. Her neck was red from where Chesh's hands had been just moments ago, choking the life from her. I had no idea who she was, or what she meant to Chesh, but—

Chesh. Reality came flooding back, and the bat in my hands clattered to the floor. Chesh lay there on the ground, blood seeping from his head. I swayed on my feet, not quite registering what I was seeing. One side of his head, the side I had hit, was caved, crumpled in a way that I hadn't known was possible. He wasn't breathing. And the blood ... there was so much, too much. I swayed again, my mind running too fast, everything was going too fast, and I fell to my knees, screaming and sobbing, crying for the girl, for

Chesh, for the boy I thought I knew. It was all too much. And now his blood was all over my hands, my legs, and I scrabbled back, trying to get away, trying to go back, back to before ...

"Alice?" Dr. Heart's hand was on my shoulder, breaking me from the confines of my memories.

"I was trying to save her," I gasped, head spinning.

Dr. Heart's eyes widened, and she stepped back, reaching for the phone on her desk. "Alice, are you all right? You're not making any sense."

"I killed him." I was laughing and crying now, feeling everything and nothing all at once. "I did it."

It was a dooming confession, but I had never felt so free.

The Mistwood

Greta stood at the edge of the woods, looking out into the trees swathed in mist, their branches towering over the small rows of cottages that formed her village. Her entire body shook with fear and a strange combination of barely controlled anger and devastation.

The people of her village looked on, their eyes watching hungrily, waiting for her to step into those trees and never return. *Witch*, they whispered, expressions harsh and hateful. *Unnatural.*

There was only one pair of eyes in that crowd that looked at her with anything other than unbridled disgust and fear. That pair of eyes, a sweet, beautiful blue that Greta had always teased him for, now looked at her pleadingly, begging her not to go. Greta inhaled shakily, trying to communicate everything she felt with a single look, trying to tell her younger brother everything she had not been able to say. Henry's little hand reached towards her, and Greta's heart broke. *I have no choice*, she thought. *They will hang me if I stay.* She took a deep breath, steeling herself, and entered the Mistwood.

Stepping into the Mistwood was like entering an entirely new world. Gone were the thatched cottages and cobblestone roads of the village, the accusing eyes and pointing fingers. As Greta entered the forest, it all faded into nothing. Her past life, the struggles of raising her younger brother with no parents and no money, the difficulty of hiding her magic from her people, it was all gone, swallowed by the swirling fog.

Everything was silent. There was nothing but Greta and the trees and the fog, nothing but gloom and shadows. Greta shivered, her eyes scanning the darkness. She hugged her arms around her body, trying to somehow calm the ache inside of her. *Henry.* What would he do without her? Who would care for him, who would make sure he put his shoes on the right feet and make him laugh and smile and tell him his favorite stories before he fell asleep? She shook her head, trying to banish the thoughts. *Worrying for him will not help you here.*

Greta walked further into the forest, marveling at the massive trees stretching towards the sky she could no longer see, their branches blocking out all but the slightest rays of sun. Her magic felt different here, she noticed. Before, back in the village, it had been nothing more than a slight pulse in her blood, capable of nothing more than growing or enlarging plants. But here, it was a song, crashing into her heart, pounding through her body. It was strange how Greta had been warned away from these woods for her entire life, and yet, here among its trees, she felt a strange call. This place seemed to recognize her, recognize the magic she had been born with that she had tried so hard to keep hidden. Despite the darkness, Greta somehow knew the forest would not hurt her.

The Mistwood required sacrifice. Every child in Greta's village had been raised on this knowledge, because every year her village elders selected a child to be sacrificed to the forest. No one knew what happened to those children, but they were never seen again. The elders believed that the forest consumed them, drawing on their life to feed its dark magic. Greta had never understood the way they spoke of the Mistwood as if it were a sentient being, never truly believed that the wood would devour them all if they did not feed it. But now, surrounded by its silent trees and creeping vines and swirling shadows, Greta could feel the life of the forest. She could feel its magic like a beating heart in her blood. But it wasn't evil, nor was it good, it simply was.

Greta breathed it all in, letting its earthy scent wash over her, calming and soothing, and felt the forest breathe with her. She extended her hand, calling her magic forward, and a small smile crept to her face as the plants of the forest responded and long, thick vines crept forward, growing and swelling and twisting to her will.

Witch, they had called her. *Unnatural.* That was what they had seen when they looked at her. They had not seen the orphan girl with nothing using the only advantage she had to survive. It was amazing, really, how long she had managed to hide her magic even as she sold the products of it every day at the market, the villagers constantly complementing her gift with plants, thanking her for keeping them all fed. Yet their appreciation had turned to hatred and apprehension so quickly, and they had not hesitated to banish her, just another child to feed to the Mistwood.

A monster to feed to the monster.

But now, surrounded by nothing but trees and silence and magic that called to her own, Greta wasn't afraid. This forest was just another victim of humans' fear of that which they could not understand.

"Greta! Wait for me!" a small voice called. Greta whirled, shock and fear building and building inside her.

"Henry? What are you doing here?"

Her little brother skidded to a halt, panting, and looked up at her with bright eyes. "We stick together, remember? I didn't want you to be alone."

Greta's heart melted as she looked at his earnest expression, and she pulled him into a quick, tight hug. "Henry, you have to go home."

He looked up at her with big eyes. "Why?"

"Just trust me." Greta eyed the trees warily. She could hear their whispers, feel the forest's magic reaching out towards Henry. "Please." She grabbed his hand and walked him back to the edge of the Mistwood, then knelt down so her gaze was level with his. "I love you so, so much," she whispered, her voice cracking. "Please remember that." Then she gave him a little push towards the edge.

But as Henry reached the border, the forest groaned, an awful, menacing sound. The trees and vines shifted and swelled, weaving together into a wall of thorns. More vines snaked forwards, reaching for him.

"Greta?" Henry called, eyes wide. "What's happening?" Greta raced towards her brother as the forest shuddered, the mist rising and swirling agitatedly. She grabbed his hand.

"Run!" she yelled.

They raced through the trees, rushing deeper and deeper into the forest. The vines lining the ground began to creep forwards, slithering towards Henry, reaching for him, moving far faster than his little legs could run. Greta tugged him forwards again, but a vine wrapped around his ankle and pulled him down, dragging him back towards the roots of the trees as more vines wrapped around his arms, his torso.

Greta could feel the forest's desire, its instinct, its need to absorb. She screamed, scrambling towards Henry, trying to pull him back towards her, but the vines were too strong, the magic of the forest too overwhelming.

Magic. Greta called to hers, using it to pull at the vines, to yank them towards her. Sweat dripped down her face as she attempted to bend the vines to her will, to drag Henry back to her. She was locked in an invisible game of tug of war with the Mistwood, her will and desperation pitted against its base instinct. And the forest was winning. She could feel her hold slipping, could see Henry beginning to slide back towards the trees, the vines enveloping more and more of his body, even as Greta used every last ounce of magic within her to fight it. She screamed, her insides on fire as she drew up all that she had. Her vision was clouding over, darkness and stars pinwheeling in front of her eyes, and she was losing her grip. It was slipping, fading as her consciousness did the same. Greta sank to her knees, then fell forward into the cool dirt.

She heard footsteps, soft against the undergrowth, and maybe the vines were receding, the forest's magic held back, or maybe this was a dream, a fantasy born from her mind as her body succumbed to exhaustion, the darkness pulling her under.

✧✧✧✧✧✧✧✧✧✧✧✧

Greta awoke to the smell of cinnamon. It wafted across her nose, drawing her out of her sleep. She blinked slowly, taking in the cozy one-room cabin with a brightly burning fireplace and small windows. A pan of cinnamon rolls lay on the table, and Henry sat in one of the wooden chairs, happily munching on one as he talked happily to a woman. She was timelessly beautiful, with strong features and smooth white hair that made it difficult to determine her age.

Greta sat up and swung her legs out of the bed, trying to stand, but everything started spinning, and she fell back with a gasp. Both Henry and the woman turned towards her. Henry smiled, his face radiant and relieved.

"You're awake!" He rushed over and wrapped Greta in a hug. She held her brother tightly, not quite able to believe that he was still there, still safe and breathing and smiling at her. Greta looked over his head of soft curls to the woman. Her eyes narrowed.

"Who are you?" she asked. "And why did you save us?"

The woman smiled. "My name is Vera." She fixed her gaze on Greta, her light eyes unnervingly clear and sharp. "I saved you because I am growing old, and the Mistwood will soon need a new caretaker, and the forest has chosen you. We're the same, you and I. The same magic that lives in the Mistwood has also taken root in us. It feeds us, nurtures us."

Greta stared at the woman in shock. "You're like me?"

"Yes, child. Now come, you have much to learn." Greta rose on shaking legs and followed the woman out of the cabin door, her head still slightly spinning. "Draw your strength from the forest, girl." Vera turned her keen eyes on Greta, noticing her unsteady walk. "Let its magic rejuvenate you, flow through you."

Greta dug her bare feet into the soft earth and inhaled. She could feel the life of the Mistwood, feel its magic flowing around her, begging to be let in. The magic inside her was nothing compared to the power that resided in the forest. But power like that had to be maintained, fed. Greta could feel its hunger gnawing on her insides as if it were her own.

"Do you feel that?" Vera asked. "The Mistwood requires sacrifice to maintain its magic. It is our job to ensure that it receives it. If the Mistwood starves, so do we. We are tied to it."

Greta felt the forest shift, offering her its magic in vine-like tendrils. She tentatively reached out to one, drawing it towards her, letting in run through her body before pushing it back out, using it to call to the vines and ferns surrounding her. *Come to me,* she called, and the plants answered, slithering over the rocks and dirt, growing and swelling at her command. Greta smiled. She had never felt so right, so powerful. She inhaled deeply, reaching for more power. It answered her call, and soon she was twisting and spinning, laughing, truly laughing as her magic flourished.

She turned towards Henry, who had emerged from the cabin holding another cinnamon roll and was gazing at her with an expression of complete awe. There was no fear, no accusation on his face, only sweet child-like wonder and trust. Greta waved, and the plants waved with her, causing Henry's eyes to widen to a comical size.

Greta laughed softly before turning her attention back to the old woman, who was also watching Henry.

Vera's gaze was coldly calculating. "Now for the next lesson," she said. "You must learn how to feed the Mistwood. Often the villagers will take care of it, sending in a new child every year or so. It was very thoughtful of them to send two this time." Her hands twitched, and Greta felt the magic of the forest rising behind Vera, like a snake raising its head to strike. Her breath caught as she realized what was happening.

"Henry, get inside!" she screamed before throwing herself at Vera, tackling the woman to the ground. Vines curled around Greta's limbs and tore her off of Vera, yanking her into the air where she hung suspended, unable to move, unable to do anything but watch as Vera sent more vines to wrap around her little brother, holding him in place just inches from the door. Vera stepped forward, her hands clenched. "The Mistwood must be fed, Greta, or we will die with it!"

"Please, anyone but him," Greta begged. "Take any of the villagers, I don't care, just not him. Please. He's all I have."

"Who are you to decide who lives and who dies, Greta? The forest has brought this boy to us, and it will not allow him to leave. It has marked him, and it will hunt him for the rest of his life." She raised her fist. "Don't you see? His fate is sealed."

Time slowed to a near stop as Vera clenched her fist and twisted it. Greta felt the release of the magic, felt its power burst forward, rushing into the vines holding her brother, flowing into the one wrapped around his neck.

Crack.

Greta screamed as his little body went limp, his neck angled unnaturally. She kept screaming and thrashing as his still form was dragged towards the trees, where it was absorbed into the ground beneath the roots so quickly she almost believed she had imagined it. Seconds ago, she'd had a brother, a living, breathing little brother, so full of life and love and silly smiles that were just for her. They'd been a family, needing only each other to survive. And now she had no one, nothing, not even a body to bury.

The worst part was she could feel the power his death gave to the Mistwood. She could feel it, because it fueled her too, and she would have been lying if she said it didn't feel good. The magic was like nothing she had ever felt before, immense and wonderful and terrifying. Greta could feel it pounding in time with her heart, she could feel it flowing through her blood and through her body in a vengeful rhythm. She leveled her stare at Vera, and although there were tears streaming down her face and she was restrained and there was no reason she should pose any kind of threat to the other woman, Greta saw fear in Vera's eyes. Fear that only increased as Greta gained control of the vines holding her and shredded them to pieces.

Vera backed up, calling more vines to her command, but the forest was behind Greta now. It fed off of her pain, her rage, and it loved it, it shared in it. Greta's will was that of the Mistwood, and the forest responded to her every whim within moments. Vera's vines went limp, shriveling into nothing. Everything she tried, everything she called forth, was easily squandered beneath Greta's vengeful rage.

Vera stumbled back, then turned and sprinted for the cabin, desperate to get away from the forest that had turned on her. Greta only laughed and called on the trees, willing their branches forwards. The first pierced Vera through the leg, the second through her arm, holding her in place as the third buried into her back.

Greta stalked forwards, the forest rising menacingly behind her as she grabbed Vera's chin and forced the woman to meet her gaze. "Let's feed the forest a little extra today, shall we?"

Vera tried to speak, but all that emerged was a strangled gasp. Blood bubbled from her lips, its color a stark crimson against her pale skin. Greta flicked her fingers, and the branch in Vera's back thrust forwards, straight through the women's chest. There was something red and bloody speared on its end. Greta reached forward and plucked the heart from the branch, turning it over in her hands twice before she threw it to the ground and watched the forest devour it. She stood there, panting, her blood rushing with power for a few seconds, before her mind caught up with her body.

Greta scrambled over to the tree where Henry's body had disappeared. Tears streaming down her face, she dug into the dirt with her hands, clawing wildly, desperately trying to find something, anything, just a single piece of him to carry with her. But there was nothing.

He was gone.

Greta sat back against the tree and cried, her body shaking with sobs. She was alone, completely alone in the world. She sniffled and wiped at her eyes, and suddenly she saw a flash of color, its hue so out of place amidst the dreary Mistwood.

It was a flower, small and dainty, with delicate petals colored the same blue as Henry's eyes. Greta covered her mouth to stifle another sob as she stared at it. She felt the power of the forest still coursing through her, and she knew what to do.

Greta threw out her arms and drew on the Mistwood, her own power, anything she could grasp. Never again would a child be lost to these woods. Never again would another know the same pain she felt. Greta pulled at the forest, tore at every tree, every vine, letting all her pain and rage envelop it, tugging it all towards her. Greta let out a scream as the entire Mistwood folded inwards on itself, trees and dirt and plants and fog all crashing together in a massive release of magic.

When the dust settled, the forest was gone, and so was the girl whose life had been linked to it. All that remained were the crumbled ruins of a log cabin and the faint smell of cinnamon.

Hastings College
NEBRASKA'S PREMIER PRIVATE COLLEGE

1. AFFORDABLE
A strong endowment means every admitted student receives generous institutional scholarships — rewarding academic performance and talent.

2. BOOKS INCLUDED
We provide every student with all required textbooks and an iPad and Apple Pencil. This saves families money every year and ensures all students have the tools they need for success.

3. BLOCK SCHEDULE
A block-style semester schedule allows professors and students to focus on just one or two classes at a time — increasing student-professor interaction and academic performance.

4. STUDY AWAY
Every student takes a travel course, which is available at no additional cost. This transformational experience helps students grow and change their perspective.

5. SUCCESS AFTER COLLEGE
The transition from college to a career begins the first semester! Every class, internship, research study and extracurricular activity adds to the experience and employability of our students — 97% are employed or in grad school after graduation.

- facebook.com/hastings.edu
- @HastingsCollege
- instagram.com/HastingsCollege
- HastingsCollege

HASTINGS.EDU

HASTINGS COLLEGE

CPSIA information can be obtained
at www.ICGtesting.com
Printed in the USA
JSHW022304170223
37802JS00004B/21